J.D. SALINGER

GARLAND REFERENCE LIBRARY
OF THE HUMANITIES
(VOL. 436)

J.D. SALINGER
An Annotated Bibliography, 1938–1981

Jack R. Sublette

GARLAND PUBLISHING, INC. • NEW YORK & LONDON
1984

Library of Congress Cataloging in Publication Data

Sublette, Jack R.
J.D. Salinger : an annotated bibliography, 1938–1981.

(Garland reference library of the humanities ;
vol. 436)
Includes indexes.
1. Salinger, J. D. (Jerome David), 1919–   —Biblio-
graphy.   I. Title.   II. Title: JD Salinger.
III. Series: Garland reference library of the humanities ;
v. 436.
Z8779.66.S8   1984   016.813′54   83-48268
[PS3537.A426]
ISBN 0-8240-9077-2 (alk. paper)

Cover design by Laurence Walczak

Printed on acid-free, 250-year-life paper
Manufactured in the United States of America

To the memory of my mother
Hollice E. Sublette
(1908–1983)

CONTENTS

ACKNOWLEDGMENTS

Many individuals and the personnel at several libraries helped me as I located and acquired copies of material. Appreciation for their help goes to the library staffs at Ohio University, Kent State University, Emory University, University of Texas at Austin, University of Pennsylvania, Loyola University, Georgia State University, Auburn University, and the Library of Congress and to the following individual personnel—Ik-Sam Kim, Head of the Oriental Library, University of California at Los Angeles; Jean F. Preston, Curator of Manuscripts, Princeton University Library; Bernard F. Pasqualini, Head of Microforms and Newspaper Department, Free Library of Philadelphia; Steven Lebergott, Head of Interlibrary Loan, Wesleyan University; Delinda Stephens Buie, Assistant Curator of Rare Books, University of Louisville; Jens Holley, Assistant Reference Librarian, University of South Carolina; and, Carol Winchell, Reference Librarian, Ohio State University. The librarians at my own institution have been most cooperative in assisting me, particularly, Nell Bassett at Troy State University—Troy; Sonja Woodham, Troy State University—Fort Rucker; and, Laurette Long, Troy State University—Dothan.

Editors of journals and the editorial personnel at various publishing companies have been generous in furnishing photocopies of materials and in printing my inquiries for help, and I am grateful to them: Roger Machell, Hamish Hamilton; Ceridwen Jenkins, New English Library; Peter Z. Smith, Rights and Permissions, Playboy Publications; Valari Barocas, Subsidiary Rights Manager, St. Martin's Press; Donna Agnello, Assistant to the Editor-in-Chief, *Glamour*; Seiichiro Uyeno, Secretary, Kyushu American Literature Society; Tibor Frank, Editor, *Studies in English and American*; Robert C. Conard, Editor, *University of Dayton Review*; Patricia R. Sullivan, Editor, *California English*; Fr. Maximo Marina, O.P., Editor, *Unitas*; Leslie Keenan, Assistant to the Editor, Book-of-the-Month

Club; R. Neil Beshers, Editorial Assistant, *PMLA; The Chronicle of Higher Education*; Editor, *Literary Half-Yearly*; Sundance, Publishers and Distributors of Educational Materials; Evelyn Strauss, Assistant to the Director of Publications, National Association of Independent Schools; and, Geraldine DeLuca, Editor, *The Lion and the Unicorn*.

My research has been made more enjoyable by the gracious assistance of my colleagues throughout the United States and around the world. Professors Eberhard Alsen, Brooke Workman, David Kirby, George Held, Jean Meral, Sandor Rot, Elizabeth Pribic, Mary Gray Porter, and George Mitrevski have provided valuable help. Professor Donald M. Fiene, the first extensive bibliographer of Salinger material, has been especially helpful. Professor Fiene has kindly and graciously given me permission to use his two Salinger bibliographies: "A Bibliographical Study of J.D. Salinger: Life, Work and Reputation," his master's thesis at the University of Louisville (1962), and "J.D. Salinger: A Bibliography" (*Wisconsin Studies in Contemporary Literature*, 4 [Winter 1963], 109–149).

A special word of thanks is due to the Faculty and Staff Professional Development Committee at Troy State University and to the administration at Troy State University—Dothan/Fort Rucker for granting me a sabbatical leave, which allowed me time to gather and annotate materials, and to Robert M. Paul, Vice President for Troy State University—Dothan/Fort Rucker, who supported my research project.

Those most deserving of my loving appreciation are the members of my family who have unselfishly permitted me to spend extensive time in libraries and at my desk and typewriter. I sincerely thank two fine girls, Susanne and Elizabeth, and a supporting and encouraging wife, Beverly, who has been my constant helper for several years. Without their help and encouragement, I could not have completed this project.

INTRODUCTION

My bibliographical study of J.D. Salinger began about fourteen years ago when I assigned a class of college freshmen the task of writing a research paper on Salinger's *The Catcher in the Rye*. After some brief preliminary research, many of the students complained that sufficient secondary materials were not available. From my previous research, I knew that their complaints were unjustified; in order to guide them in their study, I rather quickly compiled a bibliography of approximately three hundred items of Salinger criticism and made it available to my students. As the years passed, my interest in Salinger's works and my collection of bibliographical data continued and grew, but work on the bibliography was interrupted by my pursuit of an advanced degree, other research interests, and numerous teaching duties.

The idea for this Salinger bibliography came from my use of a similar annotated bibliography for another author and my realization that no comprehensive annotated bibliography of Salinger material exists even though many critics have called Salinger one of the major American authors for the period after World War II and even though the "Salinger industry" continues to flourish. The critical interest in Salinger is great despite the fact that he has not published a large number of literary works—one novel and thirty-five stories, thirteen of which Salinger has republished in three separate book-length volumes. Although Salinger has not published any fiction since 1965 (one piece of non-fiction was printed in 1975 but probably written in 1964 or 1965 [see item 106]), the critical materials and biographical references continue to appear. Much of the biographical interest is probably due to Salinger's reclusive life style. He steadfastly refuses to talk or correspond with his readers and grants almost no interviews. With little literary output in quantity and with nothing recently, Salinger and his works, many of which have been translated into several languages, persist as subjects for study, examination, and enjoyment.

The beginning and ending dates, 1938 and 1981, for this bibliography are derived from realistic and practical considerations. Salinger's first known publication occurred in 1938 in the form of a column he wrote for the Ursinus College newspaper, and 1981 is the last full year for which the bibliographical data are readily available in standard indices and reference works. However, numerous references to Salinger and studies of his works have appeared in both popular and learned periodicals since 1981. One book-length study of Salinger (Eberhard Alsen's *Salinger's Glass Stories as a Composite Novel.* New York: Whitson Publishing Company, 1983) and a book which examines Salinger's works along with those of several other writers (David Kirby's *The Sun Rises in the Evening: Monism and Quietism in Western Culture.* Metuchen, New Jersey: Scarecrow Press, 1982) have recently appeared.

The bibliographical data in my bibliography have been gathered from multiple sources: standard indices and reference works, previous Salinger bibliographies, monographs about Salinger, critical collections, colleagues, friends, students, and my own discoveries. Except for a few reviews and for foreign criticism, I have annotated the entries throughout the bibliography. Often the annotations include quotations from the critics in order to give the reader a sample of the attitude, content, and quality of the writing. As much as possible, I have tried to keep the length of the annotations consistent with the significance of the criticism. However, sometimes when the entry refers to a brief reference to Salinger, the entry is longer than I would prefer in order to explain that reference, but I have tried to make a marked distinction, for example, between brief references and book-length studies. I have attempted to be objective by indicating what the sources say and suggest and not what I think of their statements and suggestions.

Preceding the bibliography is a chronological listing of the significant events of Salinger's personal as well as his literary life.

The items in this bibliography are divided into four major parts: "Primary Sources," "Secondary Sources," "Translations," and "Foreign Criticism." The first of these four parts contains references to works by Salinger in English, including those published in English in foreign countries, as well as to all other known writing by Salinger, both published and unpublished. Under "Books," Salinger's four books are listed in chronological order according to the date of publication. The various editions of each of the four books originally published in the United States are listed under each of the first American editions. Unique foreign English-language editions are listed in the appropriate chronological order. The section "Short Studies" has a subsection for uncollected stories and one for collected stories. Salinger's twenty-two uncollected short stories are listed chronologically by the date of original publication; two of these stories, "I'm Crazy" and "Slight Rebellion off Madison," are used in altered forms in *The Catcher in the Rye*. For those stories that have been reprinted, the bibliographical data are provided for the reprints in the chronological order of reprinting. Even though Salinger has not collected any of these stories, a pirated edition of Salinger's uncollected short stories appeared in two volumes in 1974; that publication appears in the last entry of this subsection.

For the stories included in *Nine Stories*, *Franny and Zooey*, and *Raise High the Roof Beam, Carpenters and Seymour: An Introduction*, I list each story in the order of original publication; for each of these stories, I cite the locations of reprintings in chronological order.

The items in "Miscellaneous Published Material" include a column Salinger wrote for the college newspaper at Ursinus College, various autobiographical statements by Salinger, a letter from Salinger to the editor of the *New York Post Magazine*, and a tribute to Whit Burnett. These entries appear in chronological order of publication.

The section "Unpublished Material" contains four types of items: short stories with accessible manuscripts, stories which are unavailable, letters from Salinger to the personnel of *Story* magazine, and a non-fiction essay.

Included in the materials from *Story* magazine, deposited in the Archives at the Princeton University Library, are the typed manuscripts of five unpublished stories by Salinger. Two of the stories, told by Vincent Caulfield, concern the Caulfield family, including Mary Moriarity (the mother), Holden, Phoebe, and Kenneth (a dead brother). Two more of the stories focus directly on the war, and one has the war in the background. In the subsection "Short Stories" under "Unpublished Material," the two Caulfield stories are listed first and then the war stories with a brief comment on the content of each story.

In Salinger's letters (see items 124–159) to Whit Burnett, editor of *Story* magazine, Salinger mentions the titles of nine other stories that he has written. Those titles are listed in the subsection of "Unavailable Manuscripts" in the order that they are mentioned in Salinger's letters. Because the manuscripts are unavailable and because Salinger does not comment on the stories, it is not possible to determine if these titles refer to stories that have been published with different titles. In addition, Burnett, in his letters to Salinger (see items 315–335), requests permission in 1959 to publish two stories that Salinger originally submitted to *Story* in 1945 or 1946. These two stories are listed last under "Unavailable Manuscripts." In his two bibliographies (see items 341 and 342), Donald Fiene refers to one story sold to *Stag* magazine but never published; that story is listed first in this section.

The materials from *Story* magazine deposited in the Archives at Princeton University Library include thirty-six letters from Salinger to the personnel of *Story*, most to the editor, Whit Burnett. The letters cover a thirty-year period (15 January 1939–18 January 1969). Several of the letters are not dated, but I have been able to assign at least an approximate date to those on the basis of the content of the letters, notes made by Burnett on the letters, and/or letters that Burnett wrote to Salinger (see items 315–335). The letters are listed in approximate chronological order; each citation includes a listing of the date or an approximation, the return address, the salutation, length, and whether typed or handwritten.

Donald Fiene lists one Salinger manuscript of nonfiction that has not been published. That item is included in the subsection "Miscellaneous" under "Unpublished Material."

The entries for "Secondary Sources" are separated into five sections: miscellany, *The Catcher in the Rye*, *Nine Stories*, *Franny and Zooey*, and *Raise High the Roof Beam, Carpenters and Seymour: An Introduction*. Within each of these sections, the items are listed alphabetically; for multiple entries by the same author, items are listed alphabetically by title.

The "Miscellany" contains seven subsections. The first of these subsections, "Biography," lists items of factual biographical information as well as those that focus on Salinger's reputation as a writer and on such topics as Salinger's influence, the influences on his writing, characteristics of his writing, his audience, his place in the tradition of American literature, comparisons and contrasts with other authors, his relationship with publishers and his reactions to his own publications, his ability as a writer, and the significance of his works to book collectors.

Included in the materials from *Story* magazine at Princeton University Library are twenty-one letters from Whit Burnett to Salinger. These letters, which cover the period from 17 January 1940 to 17 April 1965, are listed in chronological order in the second subsection of the "Miscellany."

The subsection "Reference Works" is divided into two categories: previous Salinger bibliographies and other reference works like handbooks, histories, and encyclopedias.

The list of bibliographies is a comprehensive but not necessarily exhaustive catalog of bibliographies of Salinger's own works and reviews and criticism of his works. I include in alphabetical order bibliographies published both individually and as parts of longer works.

In the category "Handbooks, Histories, and Encyclopedias," I cite references to Salinger in these genres which usually provide brief biographical material, a survey and summary of Salinger's works, and sometimes a brief bibliography. Two reference works included in this category—*A Library of Literary Criticism: Modern American Literature* and *Contemporary Literature Criticism: Excerpts from Criticism of Works of Today's Novelists, Poets, Playwrights, and Other Creative Writers*—contain short excerpts of previously published criticism. Each of the excerpts is listed alphabetically by author with the title and the page numbers on which the excerpts appear in the reference works and with a cross-reference to the entry elsewhere in the bibliography where the annotation occurs.

Several book-length studies of Salinger's fiction have appeared: five collections of criticism, six monographs, and two issues of scholarly journals. Each of these works is listed alphabetically in the subsection "Book-length Works." The entries for the collections of criticism and for the two journals contain cross-references to the entries elsewhere in the bibliography where the annotations of individual articles appear. The collections of criticism and the monographs have cross-references to the appropriate reviews, which are included in this same subsection.

The subsection "References, Articles, and Chapters" contains entries for criticism of Salinger's fiction in general, for studies of more than one of Salinger's works, and for brief summarizing comments about Salinger's fiction. Several of the entries refer to studies of Salinger's Glass family. Some of the material in this subsection overlaps with that in later entries. For example, several critical studies concentrate on *The Catcher in the Rye* and its relationship to other works by Salinger. If the critical work emphasizes more than one piece of fiction by Salinger, it is listed in this subsection rather than in a subsection for any one particular Salinger work.

A few pieces of Salinger criticism focus on one of the twenty-two uncollected short stories. These are listed under "Uncollected Stories." Master's theses and doctoral dissertations that concentrate exclusively on Salinger's work and those that include a discussion of work by Salinger and other writers are listed and annotated in the last subsection of the "Miscellany."

Following the "Miscellany" under "Secondary Sources" is a section for each of Salinger's four books. Each of the sections for Salinger's four book-length publications contains at least two subsections: reviews and later references, articles, and chapters. For *The Catcher in the Rye* and *Nine Stories*, there are additional subsections. Under *The Catcher in the Rye*, the work by Salinger most often studied, I include entries for study and pedagogical aids and further subdivide the critical material under "References, Articles, Chapters" into three categories based on the content of the studies: "General Studies," "Censorship, Controversy, Problems in the Classroom," and "Relationship with Other Literary Works and Authors." Under *Nine Stories*, I include a subsection listing unannotated reviews of the movie *My Foolish Heart*, based on Salinger's story "Uncle Wiggily in Connecticut."

The third major part of the bibliography lists translations of Salinger's works. The translations are arranged alphabetically by the name of the country in which they are published. Within each listing for each country, the entries for Salinger's books occur in the chronological order in which they were published originally in the United States: *The Catcher in the Rye*, *Nine Stories* (British title, *For Esmé—with Love and Squalor*), *Franny and Zooey*, and *Raise High the Roof Beam, Carpenters and Seymour: An Introduction*. Translations of unique collections and of individual stories follow the above four titles; the entries occur in the order of publication in the respective countries. The sources of information for the translations are *Index Translationum* and Donald Fiene's two bibliographies (see items 341 and 342).

Following the bibliography are two indices with references to entry numbers. The "Author Index" alphabetically lists the names of the authors, editors, and translators referred to in the bibliography. Salinger's name has been omitted. The "Title Index" alphabetically lists the titles of all of Salinger's writings and the titles of all literary works mentioned in the bibliography.

J.D. Salinger

I. CHRONOLOGY

1919   Birth of Jerome David Salinger, January 1, in
        New York City; second child of Sol and Miriam
        Jillich

1932   Student at McBurney School, Manhattan

1934   Student at Valley Forge Military Academy, Penn-
        sylvania

1935   Literary editor of Valley Forge Military Academy
        yearbook, *Crossed Sabres*

1936   Graduate of Valley Forge Military Academy

1937   Student at New York University in summer; trav-
        eler in Europe

1938   Student at Ursinus College, Pennsylvania; author
        of "The Skipped Diploma" for *Ursinus Weekly*

1939   Student in Whit Burnett's short story class at
        Columbia University; beginning of a long series
        of letters to Whit Burnett

1940   First publication of Salinger's fiction: "The
        Young Folks" in *Story* and "Go See Eddie" in *Uni-
        versity of Kansas City Review*; attendance at
        Writers Club dinner in New York City with Whit
        Burnett; trip to Canada

1941   Publication of "The Hang of It" in *Collier's* and
        "The Heart of a Broken Story" in *Esquire*; sale of
        "Slight Rebellion off Madison" to *New Yorker*--
        actual publication in 1946; Salinger's classifi-
        cation as 1-B for the military draft

1941-   Romance with Eugene O'Neill's daughter Oona
1943

1942   Publication of "The Long Debut of Lois Taggett"
        in *Story* and "Personal Notes on an Infantryman"

3

in *Collier's*; military service in United States
Signal Corps and the Army Aviation Cadets

1943   Publication of "The Varioni Brothers" in *Saturday
Evening Post*; military service, stationed in Bain-
bridge, Georgia, and Nashville, Tennessee

1944   Publication of "Both Parties Concerned," "Soft-
Boiled Sergeant," and "Last Day of the Last Fur-
lough" in *Saturday Evening Post* and "Once a Week
Won't Kill You" in *Story*; military service in Eng-
land and France; meeting between Salinger and
Ernest Hemingway

1945   Publication of "Elaine" in *Story*, "A Boy in France"
in *Saturday Evening Post*, "This Sandwich Has No
Mayonnaise" in *Esquire*, "The Stranger" and "I'm
Crazy" in *Collier's*; discharge from army

1946   Publication of "Slight Rebellion off Madison" in
New Yorker

1947   Publication of "A Young Girl in 1941 with No
Waist at All" in *Mademoiselle* and "The Inverted
Forest" in *Cosmopolitan*

1948   Publication of "A Perfect Day for Bananafish,"
"Uncle Wiggily in Connecticut," and "Just Before
the War with the Eskimos" in *New Yorker*, "A Girl
I Knew" in *Good Housekeeping*, and "Blue Melody"
in *Cosmopolitan*

1949   Publication of "The Laughing Man" in *New Yorker*
and "Down at the Dinghy" in *Harper's*

1950   Publication of "For Esmé--with Love and Squalor"
in *New Yorker*; première of the movie *My Foolish
Heart*, based on "Uncle Wiggily in Connecticut"

1951   Publication of "Pretty Mouth and Green My Eyes"
in *New Yorker* and *The Catcher in the Rye* by
Little, Brown

1952   Publication of "De Daumier-Smith's Blue Period"
in *World Review* (London); selection of Salinger
as one of three Distinguished Alumni of the Year
by Valley Forge Military Academy; trip to Mexico

1953   Publication of "Teddy" in *New Yorker* and *Nine
Stories* by Little, Brown; Shirley Blaney's inter-
view with Salinger in the Claremont, New Hampshire
Eagle; residence in Cornish, New Hampshire

1955   Publication of "Franny" and "Raise High the Roof
Beam, Carpenters" in *New Yorker*; marriage to

Claire Douglas; birth of Salinger's first child,
a daughter Margaret Ann

1957   Publication of "Zooey" in *New Yorker*

1959   Publication of "Seymour: An Introduction" in *New Yorker*

1960   Birth of Salinger's son Matthew

1961   Publication of *Franny and Zooey* by Little, Brown;
Salinger's picture on covers of *Time* and *Life*
with feature articles about him

1963   Publication of *Raise High the Roof Beam, Carpenters
and Seymour: An Introduction* by Little, Brown

1965   Publication of "Hapworth 16, 1924" in *New Yorker*;
Warren French's discovery of Salinger's story "Go
See Eddie" in the December 1940 issue of the *University of Kansas City Review*

1967   Salinger's divorce from his wife Claire

1973   Rumor of Salinger's romance with writer Joyce
Maynard

1974   Notice of Salinger's suit for $250,000 for the
sale of an unauthorized collection of his early
fiction; telephone interview with *New York Times*
reporter Lacey Fosburgh about the unauthorized
publication and sale of his uncollected short
stories; brief interview with Salinger by Bill
Roeder of *Newsweek* at Salinger's doorstep

1975   Abortive attempt by Marcus Eliason to interview
Salinger; latest publication of previously unpublished work by Salinger: "Epilogue: A Salute to
Whit Burnett 1899-1972" in Hallie and Whit Burnett's *Fiction Writer's Handbook*, but Salinger's
piece was written probably in 1965 for the Burnetts' *Story Jubilee: 33 Years of Story*

1977   Appearance of an unsigned story entitled "For
Rupert--With No Promises" in *Esquire*, thought to
be by Salinger but actually written by Gordon
Lish, fiction editor of *Esquire*

1978   Report in *New York Times* of settlement of Salinger's suit about the unauthorized sale of his
uncollected early stories; interview with Salinger on his driveway by Greg Herriges, a high
school teacher

1978-   Report of two brief encounters between Salinger

1979   and Michael Clarkson, a reporter for the *Niagara
        Falls Review*; report in *Newsweek* that "a college-
        age couple waylaid Salinger outside the Windsor
        post office ... [and] engaged him in a fifteen-
        minute conversation"

1980   Interview of Salinger by Betty Eppes, reporter for
        the Baton Rouge *Advocate*; claim by Mark Chapman,
        killer of John Lennon, that *The Catcher in the Rye*
        is his statement

1981   Picture of Salinger's son Matthew in "Newsmakers"
        section of *Newsweek*; rumor reported in *New York
        Times* that Salinger is publishing under the name
        of William Wharton, but denied by all concerned

1982   Report in *People* magazine that Salinger is bring-
        ing suit against Steven Kunes for a fake inter-
        view, which Salinger called "'entirely fantasy, a
        crude concoction'"; Salinger's appearance in Jack-
        sonville, Florida, to see the actress Elaine Joyce
        in *6 RMS Riv Vu*

II. BIBLIOGRAPHY

A. *PRIMARY SOURCES*

The first of the four major parts of the bibliography is divided into four sections: books, short stories, miscellaneous published material, and unpublished material. These sections contain entries for all of Salinger's known published writing in original editions, reprints, and English-language foreign publications and for all known unpublished materials by Salinger.

1. *Books*

This section contains entries for each of Salinger's four books in the order of publication, including English-language foreign editions.

1. *The Catcher in the Rye*. Boston: Little, Brown, 1951.

   Hereafter, for the sake of brevity, Salinger's novel will be referred to as *The Catcher* except when it appears in a title or in a quotation.

2. London: Hamish Hamilton, 1951.

3. New York: Grosset and Dunlap, 1952.

4. New York: New American Library of World Literature, 1953.

5. New York: Modern Library, 1958.

6. Harmondsworth, Middlesex: Penguin Books, 1958.

7. New York: Bantam Books, 1964.

8. New York: Franklin Watts, 1967.

   Large type edition.

9.   Moscow: Progress Publishers, 1968.

        English text with introduction and notes in
        Russian.

10.   *Nine Stories*. Boston: Little, Brown, 1953.

        Included in this first collection of Salinger's
        short stories are the following: "A Perfect Day
        for Bananafish," "Uncle Wiggily in Connecticut,"
        "Just Before the War with the Eskimos," "The Laugh-
        ing Man," "Down at the Dinghy," "For Esmé--with
        Love and Squalor," "Pretty Mouth and Green My
        Eyes," "De Daumier-Smith's Blue Period," and "Ted-
        dy." For the original publications and reprints of
        these stories, see items 60-84.

11.   *For Esmé--with Love and Squalor, and Other Sto-
        ries*. London: Hamish Hamilton, 1953.

        This British edition has a title different from
        that of the American editions.

12.   New York: New American Library of World Litera-
        ture, 1954.

13.   New York: Modern Library, 1959.

14.   *For Esmé--with Love and Squalor*. London: Har-
        borough Publishing, 1959.

        The title of this edition is shortened from the
        earlier British edition.

15.   London: New English Library, 1962.

16.   New York: Bantam Books, 1964.

17.   *Uncle Wiggily in Connecticut*. Eds. Saburo Yamaya
        and Hisashi Shigeo. Tokyo: Shohakusha, 1953,
        1962.

18.   *A Perfect Day for Bananafish*. Ed. Hisashi Shigeo.
        Tokyo: Shohakusha, 1961.

        This collection contains four stories: "A Per-
        fect Day for Bananafish," "Just Before the War
        with the Eskimos," "Down at the Dinghy," and "Ted-
        dy." Donald Fiene (see items 341 and 342) notes
        that this collection, a "college text for study of
        English," is "edited with notes by Hisashi Shigeo."

19.   *Franny and Zooey*. Boston: Little, Brown, 1961.

        Included in Salinger's second collection of

stories are two stories: "Franny" and "Zooey."
For the original publications and reprints of these
stories, see items 85 and 88.

20.   London: William Heinemann, 1962.

21.   Harmondsworth, Middlesex: Penguin, 1963.

22.   New York: Bantam Books, 1964.

23.   *Raise High the Roof Beam, Carpenters and Seymour:
       An Introduction.* Boston: Little, Brown, 1963.

       Included in Salinger's third collection of sto-
       ries are the two stories "Raise High the Roof Beam,
       Carpenters" and "Seymour: An Introduction." For
       the original publications and reprints of these sto-
       ries, see items 86-87, 89.

24.   London: William Heinemann, 1963.

25.   Harmondsworth, Middlesex: Penguin, 1964.

26.   New York: Bantam Books, 1965.

2. *Short Stories*

     This section is subdivided into uncollected stories
and collected stories. The list of uncollected stories
contains twenty-two stories that Salinger has not included in any of his three volumes of collected stories; the
thirteen collected stories are those that Salinger has included in *Nine Stories*, *Franny and Zooey*, and *Raise High
the Roof Beam, Carpenters and Seymour: An Introduction.*

a. Uncollected Short Stories

     This subsection lists in order of publication Salin-
ger's twenty-two published stories that Salinger has not
included in any of his three book-length collections of
stories. Under each story that has been reprinted, the
reprints are listed. A two-volume, pirated edition of
Salinger's uncollected stories appears as the last item
in this subsection.

27.   "The Young Folks." *Story*, 16 (March-April 1940),
       26-30.

28.   "Go See Eddie." *University of Kansas City Review*,
       7 (December 1940), 121-124.

       This story was not listed in Salinger check-
       lists prior to 1965, at which time it was discov-
       ered by Warren French (see item 211).

29.   Rpt. *Fiction: Form and Experience*. Ed. William
        M. Jones. Lexington, Massachusetts: D.C. Heath,
        1969, pp. 161-165.

        Included with five other stories in a section
        entitled "Thematic Meaning."

30.   Rpt. *New Letters*, 45 (Fall 1978), 5-11.

31.   "The Hang of It." *Collier's*, 12 July 1941, p. 22.

32.   Rpt. *The Kit Book for Soldiers, Sailors, and
        Marines. Favorite Stories, Verses, and Cartoons
        for the Entertainment of Servicemen Everywhere*.
        Comp. R.M[arjorie]. Barrows. Chicago: Consoli-
        dated Book Publishers, 1942, 1943.

        This is the first appearance of Salinger's work
        in a book.

33.   "The Heart of a Broken Story." *Esquire*, 16 (Septem-
        ber 1941), 32, 131-133.

34.   "The Long Debut of Lois Taggett." *Story*, 21 (Sep-
        tember-October 1942), 28-34.

35.   Rpt. *Story: The Fiction of the Forties*. Eds.
        Whit and Hallie Burnett. New York: E.P. Dutton,
        1949, pp. 153-162.

36.   Rpt. *Fiction of a Generation*. Eds. Whit and
        Hallie S. Burnett. London: MacGibbon and Kee,
        1960, pp. 159-168.

        This is a reprint of item 35.

37.   "Personal Notes on an Infantryman." *Collier's*, 12
        December 1942, p. 96.

38.   "The Varioni Brothers." *Saturday Evening Post*, 17
        July 1943, pp. 12-13, 76-77.

39.   "Both Parties Concerned." *Saturday Evening Post*,
        26 February 1944, pp. 14, 47-48.

        Originally entitled "Wake Me When It Thunders"
        (see item 154).

40.   "Soft-Boiled Sergeant." *Saturday Evening Post*, 15
        April 1944, pp. 18, 82, 84-85.

        Originally entitled "Death of a Dogface" (see
        item 154).

41.   "Last Day of the Last Furlough." *Saturday Evening
        Post*, 15 July 1944, pp. 26-27, 61-62, 64.

42. "Once a Week Won't Kill You." *Story*, 25 (November-December 1944), 23-27.

43. "Elaine." *Story*, 26 (March-April 1945), 38-47.

44. "A Boy in France." *Saturday Evening Post*, 31 March 1945, pp. 21, 92.

45. Rpt. *The Saturday Evening Post Stories, 1942-1945*. Ed. Ben Hibbs. New York: Random House, 1945, pp. 314-320.

46. "This Sandwich Has No Mayonnaise." *Esquire*, 24 (October 1945), 54-56, 147-149.

47. Rpt. *The Armchair Esquire*. Eds. Arnold Gingrich and L. Rust Hills. New York: G.P. Putnam's Sons, 1958, pp. 187-197.

48. Rpt. *The Armchair Esquire*. Eds. Arnold Gingrich and L. Rust Hills. New York: Popular Library, 1960, pp. 155-164.

49. "The Stranger." *Collier's*, 1 December 1945, pp. 18, 77.

50. "I'm Crazy." *Collier's*, 22 December 1945, pp. 36, 48, 51.

51. "Slight Rebellion off Madison." *New Yorker*, 21 December 1946, pp. 76-79.

52. "A Young Girl in 1941 with No Waist at All." *Mademoiselle*, 25 (May 1947), 222-223, 292-302.

53. "The Inverted Forest." *Cosmopolitan*, 123 (December 1947), 73-80, 85-86, 88, 90, 92, 95-96, 98, 100, 102, 107, 109.

54. Rpt. *Cosmopolitan*, 150 (March 1961), 111-132.

55. "A Girl I Knew." *Good Housekeeping*, 126 (February 1948), 37, 186, 188, 191-196.

56. Rpt. *The Best American Short Stories of 1949; and the Yearbook of the American Short Story*. Ed. Martha J. Foley. Boston: Houghton Mifflin, 1949, pp. 248-260.

57. "Blue Melody." *Cosmopolitan*, 125 (September 1948), 51, 112-119.

58. "Hapworth 16, 1924." *New Yorker*, 19 June 1965, pp. 32-113.

59. *The Complete Uncollected Short Stories of J.D. Sal-
     inger*. 2 vols. n.p.: n.p. [1974].

     This pirated edition of Salinger's uncollected
     short stories appeared in two editions. For a de-
     tailed contrast of the two editions, see George
     Bixby (item 338); for Salinger's reaction to the
     unauthorized publication, see items 206, 207, 229,
     278, 284, 303.

          b. Collected Short Stories

     This subsection lists in the order of original publi-
cation the thirteen stories included in *Nine Stories*,
Franny and Zooey, and *Raise High the Roof Beam, Carpenters
and Seymour: An Introduction*. The reprints of each story
are listed under each story in chronological order.

60. "A Perfect Day for Bananafish." *New Yorker*, 31 Jan-
     uary 1948, pp. 21-25.

61.   Rpt. *55 Short Stories from "The New Yorker"*:
          1940-1950. Eds. *The New Yorker* Editors. New
          York: Simon and Schuster, 1949, pp. 144-155.

*   Rpt. *Nine Stories*, pp. 3-26. Cited above as item
          10.

*   Rpt. *For Esmé--with Love and Squalor, and Other
          Stories*, pp. 7-23. Cited above as item 11.

*   Rpt. *Nine Stories*, pp. 7-17. Cited above as
          item 12.

*   Rpt. *Nine Stories*, pp. 3-26. Cited above as
          item 13.

*   Rpt. *For Esmé--with Love and Squalor*, pp. 7-21.
          Cited above as item 14.

*   Rpt. *For Esmé--with Love and Squalor*, pp. 7-21.
          Cited above as item 15.

*   Rpt. *Nine Stories*, pp. 3-18. Cited above as
          item 16.

62. "Uncle Wiggily in Connecticut." *New Yorker*, 20
     March 1948, pp. 30-36.

*   Rpt. *Nine Stories*, pp. 27-56. Cited above as
          item 10.

*   Rpt. *For Esmé--with Love and Squalor, and Other*

Stories, pp. 25-44. Cited above as item 11.

* Rpt. *Nine Stories*, pp. 18-31. Cited above as item 12.

63. Rpt. *Short Story Masterpieces*. Eds. Robert Penn Warren and Albert Erskine. New York: Dell Books, 1954, pp. 408-423.

64. Rpt. *Short Story Masterpieces*. Eds. Robert Penn Warren and Albert Erskine. 2nd ed. New York: Dell Books, 1958, pp. 408-423.

* Rpt. *Nine Stories*, pp. 27-56. Cited above as item 13.

* Rpt. *For Esmé--with Love and Squalor*, pp. 22-39. Cited above as item 14.

* Rpt. *For Esmé--with Love and Squalor*, pp. 22-39. Cited above as item 15.

* Rpt. *Nine Stories*, pp. 19-38. Cited above as item 16.

65. "Just Before the War with the Eskimos." *New Yorker*, 5 June 1948, pp. 37-40, 42, 44, 46.

66. Rpt. *Prize Stories of 1949*. Ed. Herschel Brickell. Garden City, New York: Doubleday, 1949, pp. 249-261.

* Rpt. *Nine Stories*, pp. 57-82. Cited above as item 10.

* Rpt. *For Esmé--with Love and Squalor, and Other Stories*, pp. 79-96. Cited above as item 11.

* Rpt. *Nine Stories*, pp. 32-43. Cited above as item 12.

67. Rpt. *Manhattan: Stories from the Heart of a Great City*. Ed. Seymour Krim. New York: Bantam, 1954, pp. 22-35.

* Rpt. *Nine Stories*, pp. 57-82. Cited above as item 13.

* Rpt. *For Esmé--with Love and Squalor*, pp. 69-84. Cited above as item 14.

* Rpt. *For Esmé--with Love and Squalor*, pp. 69-84. Cited above as item 15.

* Rpt. *Nine Stories*, pp. 39-55. Cited above as item 16.

68.   "The Laughing Man." *New Yorker*, 19 March 1949, pp.
       27-32.

69.   Foley, Martha, ed. *Best American Short Stories
       of 1950*. Boston: Houghton Mifflin, 1950, p. 449.

       "The Laughing Man" is listed as "one of the most
       distinguished short stories published in American
       magazines in 1949."

*   Rpt. *Nine Stories*, pp. 83-110. Cited above as
       item 10.

*   Rpt. *For Esmé--with Love and Squalor, and Other
       Stories*, pp. 45-63. Cited above as item 11.

*   Rpt. *Nine Stories*, pp. 44-56. Cited above as
       item 12.

*   Rpt. *Nine Stories*, pp. 83-110. Cited above as
       item 13.

*   Rpt. *For Esmé--with Love and Squalor*, pp. 40-56.
       Cited above as item 14.

*   Rpt. *For Esmé--with Love and Squalor*, pp. 40-56.
       Cited above as item 15.

*   Rpt. *Nine Stories*, pp. 56-73. Cited above as
       item 16.

70.   "Down at the Dinghy." *Harper's*, 198 (April 1949),
       87-91.

*   Rpt. *Nine Stories*, pp. 111-130. Cited above as
       item 10.

*   Rpt. *For Esmé--with Love and Squalor, and Other
       Stories*, pp. 65-78. Cited above as item 11.

*   Rpt. *Nine Stories*, pp. 57-65. Cited above as
       item 12.

*   Rpt. *Nine Stories*, pp. 111-130. Cited above as
       item 13.

*   Rpt. *For Esmé--with Love and Squalor*, pp. 57-68.
       Cited above as item 14.

*   Rpt. *For Esmé--with Love and Squalor*, pp. 57-68.
       Cited above as item 15.

*   Rpt. *Nine Stories*, pp. 74-86. Cited above as
       item 16.

71. "For Esmé--with Love and Squalor." *New Yorker*, 8
     April 1950, pp. 28-36.

72. Rpt. *World Review*, No. 18, n.s. (August 1950),
     44-59.

73. Rpt. *Prize Stories of 1950: The O. Henry Awards*.
     Ed. Herschel Brickell. Garden City, New York:
     Doubleday, 1950, pp. 244-264.

74. Rpt. *50 Great Short Stories*. Ed. Milton Crane.
     New York: Bantam, 1952, pp. 252-275.

*   Rpt. *Nine Stories*, pp. 131-173. Cited above as
     item 11.

*   Rpt. *For Esmé--with Love and Squalor, and Other
     Stories*, pp. 97-126. Cited above as item 11.

75. Rpt. *Better Reading Two: Literature*. Eds. Walter
     Blair and John C. Gerber. Rev. ed. Chicago:
     Scott, Foresman, 1954, pp. 436-453.

*   Rpt. *Nine Stories*, pp. 66-84. Cited above as
     item 12.

76. Rpt. *Interpreting Literature*. Ed. K.L. Knicker-
     bocker and H. Willard Reninger. New York: Henry
     Holt, 1955, pp. 274-285.

*   Rpt. *Nine Stories*, pp. 131-173. Cited above as
     item 13.

77. Rpt. *Better Reading Two: Literature*. Eds. Walter
     Blair and John C. Gerber. 3rd ed. Chicago: Scott
     Foresman, 1959, pp. 429-444.

*   Rpt. *For Esmé--with Love and Squalor*, pp. 85-
     110. Cited above as item 14.

78. Rpt. *50 Great Short Stories*. Ed. Milton Crane.
     2nd ed. New York: Bantam, 1959, pp. 188-206.

79. Rpt. *Interpreting Literature*. Ed. K.L. Knicker-
     bocker and H. Willard Reninger. Rev. ed. New
     York: Henry Holt, 1960, pp. 222-233.

80. Rpt. *Reportory*. Eds. Walter Blair and John C.
     Gerber. Chicago: Scott, Foresman, 1960, pp. 663-
     679.

*   Rpt. *For Esmé--with Love and Squalor*, pp. 85-
     110. Cited above as item 15.

*   Rpt. *Nine Stories*, pp. 87-114. Cited above as
     item 16.

81.   "Pretty Mouth and Green My Eyes." *New Yorker*, 14
      July 1951, pp. 20-24.

82.   Rpt. *Anthology of Famous American Short Stories*.
           Eds. J.A. Burrell and B.A. Cerf. New York: Mod-
           ern Library, 1953, pp. 1297-1306.

*   Rpt. *Nine Stories*, pp. 174-197. Cited above as
           item 10.

*   Rpt. *For Esmé--with Love and Squalor, and Other
           Stories*, pp. 127-142. Cited above as item 11.

*   Rpt. *Nine Stories*, pp. 85-95. Cited above as
           item 12.

*   Rpt. *Nine Stories*, pp. 174-197. Cited above as
           item 13.

*   Rpt. *For Esmé--with Love and Squalor*, pp. 111-
           124. Cited above as item 14.

*   Rpt. *For Esmé--with Love and Squalor*, pp. 111-
           124. Cited above as item 15.

83.   Rpt. *Tampa Tribune*, 25 August 1962, p. 11a.

           Donald Fiene (see items 341 and 342) notes that
      most of the story is reprinted from the New Ameri-
      can Library edition.

*   Rpt. *Nine Stories*, pp. 115-129. Cited above as
           item 16.

84.   "De Daumier-Smith's Blue Period." *World Review*,
      No. 39, n.s. (May 1952), 33-48.

*   Rpt. *Nine Stories*, pp. 198-252. Cited above as
           item 10.

*   Rpt. *For Esmé--with Love and Squalor, and Other
           Stories*, pp. 143-179. Cited above as item 11.

*   Rpt. *Nine Stories*, pp. 96-121. Cited above as
           item 12.

*   Rpt. *Nine Stories*, pp. 198-252. Cited above as
           item 13.

*   Rpt. *For Esmé--with Love and Squalor*, pp. 125-
           157. Cited above as item 14.

*   Rpt. *For Esmé--with Love and Squalor*, pp. 125-
           157. Cited above as item 15.

*   Rpt. *Nine Stories*, pp. 130-165. Cited above as item 16.

85. "Teddy." *New Yorker*, 31 January 1953, pp. 26-36, 38.

*   Rpt. *Nine Stories*, pp. 253-302. Cited above as item 10.

*   Rpt. *For Esmé--with Love and Squalor, and Other Stories*, pp. 181-215. Cited above as item 11.

*   Rpt. *Nine Stories*, pp. 122-144. Cited above as item 12.

*   Rpt. *Nine Stories*, pp. 253-302. Cited above as item 13.

*   Rpt. *For Esmé--with Love and Squalor*, pp. 158-188. Cited above as item 14.

*   Rpt. *For Esmé--with Love and Squalor*, pp. 158-188. Cited above as item 15.

*   Rpt. *Nine Stories*, pp. 166-198. Cited above as item 16.

86. "Franny." *New Yorker*, 29 January 1955, pp. 24-32, 35-43.

       As Donald Fiene (see items 341 and 342) notes, the page numbers in the *New Yorker* for this story and for the following three stories "vary from city to out-of-town edition."

*   Rpt. *Franny and Zooey*, pp. 3-43. Cited above as item 19.

*   Rpt. *Franny and Zooey*, pp. 3-43. Cited above as item 20.

*   Rpt. *Franny and Zooey*, pp. 3-43. Cited above as item 21.

*   Rpt. *Franny and Zooey*, pp. 3-44. Cited above as item 22.

87. "Raise High the Roof Beam, Carpenters." *New Yorker*, 19 November 1955, pp. 51-58, 60-116.

88. Rpt. *Stories from "The New Yorker," 1950-1960*. New York: Simon and Schuster, 1960, pp. 46-95.

*   Rpt. *Raise High the Roof Beam, Carpenters and Seymour: An Introduction*, pp. 1-107. Cited above as item 23.

*   Rpt. *Raise High the Roof Beam, Carpenters and
         Seymour: An Introduction*, pp. 1-107. Cited
         above as item 24.

*   Rpt. *Raise High the Roof Beam, Carpenters and
         Seymour: An Introduction*, pp. 7-71. Cited above
         as item 25.

*   Rpt. *Raise High the Roof Beam, Carpenters and
         Seymour: An Introduction*, pp. 3-92. Cited above
         as item 26.

89.   "Zooey." *New Yorker*, 4 May 1957, pp. 32-42, 44-139.

*   Rpt. *Franny and Zooey*, pp. 47-201. Cited above
         as item 19.

*   Rpt. *Franny and Zooey*, pp. 47-201. Cited above
         as item 20.

*   Rpt. *Franny and Zooey*, pp. 47-201. Cited above
         as item 21.

*   Rpt. *Franny and Zooey*, pp. 47-202. Cited above
         as item 22.

90.   "Seymour: An Introduction." *New Yorker*, 6 June
         1959, pp. 42-52, 54-111.

*   Rpt. *Raise High the Roof Beam, Carpenters and
         Seymour: An Introduction*, pp. 109-248. Cited
         above as item 23.

*   Rpt. *Raise High the Roof Beam, Carpenters and
         Seymour: An Introduction*, pp. 109-248. Cited
         above as item 24.

*   Rpt. *Raise High the Roof Beam, Carpenters and
         Seymour: An Introduction*, pp. 73-157. Cited
         above as item 25.

*   Rpt. *Raise High the Roof Beam, Carpenters and
         Seymour: An Introduction*, pp. 95-213. Cited
         above as item 26.

3.   *Miscellaneous Published Material*

        Salinger's miscellaneous publications include a col-
umn for the Ursinus College newspaper, various autobiographical statements, a letter to the editor of the *New
York Post Magazine*, and a tribute to Whit Burnett, editor
of *Story* magazine and Salinger's short story instructor
at Columbia University. The entries are listed chronologically.

91. "Musings of a Social Soph: The Skipped Diploma."
     Ursinus Weekly, 10 October 1938, p. 2.

     For nine weeks, Salinger wrote a column for the
     college newspaper. The title for the last eight
     columns varies slightly from that for the first
     one. A copy of each of these columns is included
     in Donald Fiene's thesis (see item 341).

92. "J.D.S.'s The Skipped Diploma." *Ursinus Weekly*, 17
     October 1938, p. 2.

93. "J.D.S.'s The Skipped Diploma." *Ursinus Weekly*, 24
     October 1938, p. 2.

94. "J.D.S.'s The Skipped Diploma." *Ursinus Weekly*, 31
     October 1938, p. 2.

95. "J.D.S.'s The Skipped Diploma." *Ursinus Weekly*, 7
     November 1938, p. 2.

96. "J.D.S.'s The Skipped Diploma." *Ursinus Weekly*, 14
     November 1938, p. 2.

97. "J.D.S.'s The Skipped Diploma." *Ursinus Weekly*, 21
     November 1938, p. 2.

98. "J.D.S.'s The Skipped Diploma." *Ursinus Weekly*, 5
     December 1938, p. 2.

99. "J.D.S.'s The Skipped Diploma." *Ursinus Weekly*, 12
     December 1938, p. 2.

*   "Contributors." *Story*, 21 (September-October 1942),
     2. Cited below as item 186.

100. "Biographical Notes." *Story*, 25 (November-December
     1944), 1.

     Statement contributed to accompany the publica-
     tion of "Once a Week Won't Kill You."

101. [Autobiographical statement on dust jacket.] *The
     Catcher in the Rye*. Boston: Little, Brown, 1951.

102. "Man-Forsaken Men." *New York Post Magazine*, 9 De-
     cember 1955, p. 49.

     Salinger laments the condition of men sentenced
     for life to prison: "Surely, it must concern him
     [governor of New York] that the New York State lifer
     is one of the most crossed-off, man-forsaken men on
     earth." A copy of this letter is included in Don-
     ald Fiene's thesis (see item 341) and is partly re-
     printed in the *Realist* (see item 253).

103. "J.D. Salinger--Biographical." *Harper's*, 218 (Feb-
      ruary 1959), 87.

      Harper's prints what Salinger submitted in 1949
      when "Down at the Dinghy" appeared. Salinger ex-
      plains that he opposes providing biographical in-
      formation.

104. [Autobiographical statement on dust jacket.] *Franny
      and Zooey*. Boston: Little, Brown, 1961.

105. [Autobiographical statement on dust jacket.] *Raise
      High the Roof Beam, Carpenters and Seymour: An
      Introduction*. Boston: Little, Brown, 1963.

106. "Epilogue: A Salute to Whit Burnett 1899-1972." In
      Fiction Writer's Handbook. Hallie and Whit Bur-
      nett. New York: Harper and Row, 1975, pp. 187-
      188; rpt. Barnes and Noble, 1979.

      The Burnetts print a piece in which Salinger
      praises Burnett and his short story class at Colum-
      bia. Salinger focuses on a time when Burnett read
      Faulkner's "That Evening Sun" without once coming
      "between the author and his beloved reader." Sal-
      inger originally sent this essay to Burnett about
      1964 or 1965 as a "foreword" for the Burnetts' *Sto-
      ry Jubilee: 33 Years of Story* (1966), but it was
      not included (see item 335). The entire piece, in-
      cluded in the *Story* materials in the Archives at
      Princeton University Library, contains an introduc-
      tory paragraph, not printed here. (See item 291.)

              4. Unpublished Material

      The unpublished material listed in this section in-
cludes manuscripts of five stories, references to titles
of twelve stories, letters to the editor and other personnel of *Story* magazine, and an essay rejected by *Saturday
Review*.

              a. Short Stories

      Salinger's known unpublished short stories are those
typed manuscripts included in the materials from *Story*
magazine deposited in the Archives at Princeton University
Library (see item 295). Because it is currently impossible
to date the stories, they are listed below by subject matter: the two stories about the Caulfield family appear
first followed by three war stories.

107. "The Last and Best of the Peter Pans." (12 pp. of
      double-spaced typescript with the by-line J.D.

Salinger)

Written from the point of view of Vincent (Caulfield), older brother of Holden and Phoebe, and
with references to a dead brother named Kenneth,
the story focuses on a conversation between Vincent
and his mother--Mary Moriarity, an actress. Their
talk occurs because Vincent found his questionnaire
from the draft board that his mother had hidden.
The conversation, which involves Mary's concern for
Vincent and Vincent's concern for his family, ends
with a reference to her "want[ing] to save a child
from crawling off a cliff" and Vincent's feeling
sorry for various people just as Holden misses various people at the end of *The Catcher*.

108. "The Ocean Full of Bowling Balls." (18 pp. of
      double-spaced typescript with the by-line J.S.
      Salinger)

Like the narrators in Sherwood Anderson's stories
"I'm a Fool" and "I Want to Know Why" who tell their
tales because they want "to get everything straight
and be O.K.," Vincent Caulfield writes of his relationship with one of his younger brothers, Kenneth,
and of Kenneth's death because "maybe setting all
this down will get him [Kenneth] out of here." Included in the story are Kenneth's expression of
love for Holden and Phoebe, Kenneth's anger at an
adult for calling Holden "the crazy little one,"
and a letter to Kenneth from Holden at "Camp Good-
crest for slobs," in which Holden complains about
life and people at camp. Even though he does not
call them phonies, Holden cites the hypocrisy of
the adults at camp: Mr. Grover, who "smiles at you
but is all the time very mean when he gets the
chance," and Mrs. Grover, who "trys [sic] to be like
your mother and smiles all the time but she is mean."

Donald Fiene (see items 341 and 342) comments as
follows on this story: "Sold to *Woman's Home Companion* in 1947 or 1948. [According to Knox Burger,
editor of Gold Medal Books, former fiction editor
of *Collier's* ... the publisher objected to the story as too 'downbeat'--after the fiction editor of
WHC had bought it. Later, 1950 or 1951, the same
man rejected it for *Collier's* too. But at about
this time Salinger withdrew the story which is an
early experiment with the Glass family and concerns
the death of one of the younger children. Mr. Burger says: 'It contains the greatest letter home
from camp ever composed by man or boy.']" The version of this story that I have seen concerns the
Caulfield family, not the Glass family.

109. "The Magic Foxhole." (21 pp. of double-spaced type-
      script with the by-line J.D. Salinger)

          Told in first person by a compulsive-talking
      soldier, identified only as Garrity, to another
      hitch-hiking soldier called Mac, whom Garrity has
      picked up in a jeep near "the Beach" soon after D-
      Day, this story recounts Garrity's association with
      a soldier named Lewis Gardner, who suffers severe
      battle fatigue ("when you get to look like you're
      dead, or when you start telling everybody real loud,
      that you wish you was a civilian and not in no god-
      damn Army"). Gardner now stands on the beach in
      his "G.I. pyjamas ... holding on to some pole they
      got stuck in the sand ... like as if he's at Coney
      Island on one of them rides where if you don't hold
      on tight you'll go flying off and get your head
      cracked open" and waits to be evacuated. As the
      story ends, Garrity, presumably eager to tell this
      story again or perhaps another one "about this
      broad at the Hospital," yells to another hitch-
      hiker. The dramatic monologue-like story suggests
      that Garrity suffers from battle fatigue, but to a
      lesser degree than Gardner.

110. "Two Lonely Men." (27 pp. of double-spaced type-
      script with the by-line Jerry Salinger)

          An unnamed narrator, who "worked at Ground School
      ... as Morse Code instructor" at a United States
      Army base in the South, tells the story of a devel-
      oping friendship between Master Sergeant Charles
      Maydee and Captain Huggins. Their friendship grows
      with nightly games of gin rummy until Captain Hug-
      gins sets his wife up in a nearby hotel and moves
      in with her. Maydee and Huggins do not see much of
      each other then until Huggins' wife reveals to her
      husband that she has been having an affair three
      times a week with Bernie Farr. Maydee promises to
      intercede with Huggins' wife, but Maydee apparently
      begins having an affair with her (a situation simi-
      lar to that of Arthur, Lee, and Joanie in "Pretty
      Mouth and Green My Eyes"). As the story ends, May-
      dee tells the narrator that he has "put in for over-
      seas" because he "can't stand that old fool's [Hug-
      gins'] sweaty, inefficient ... damn face."

111. "The Children's Echelon." (26 pp. of double-spaced
      typescript with the by-line J.D. Salinger)

          A two-part story in the form of eleven diary en-
      tries by Bernice Herndon with the first entry on
      January 12, her "eighteenth birthday--so what," and
      the last on March 25 of the same but unspecified
      year. With the war in the background, Bernice

changes her opinion about almost everything she men-
tions--her friends, family, and the war. In one entry, Bernice, like Holden Caulfield, mentions that
she "stayed at the merry-go-round for ages, watching
the children go round and round ... [where] one darling little boy in a navy blue suit and beanie ...
nearly fell off the horse once and I nearly
screamed."

b. Unavailable Manuscripts

Salinger has written a number of short stories for
which the manuscripts are not available and which have not
been published. Donald Fiene lists one of these stories
in his two bibliographies (see items 341 and 342), Salinger
mentions nine more titles in his letters to Whit Burnett,
editor of *Story* (see items 124-159), and Burnett mentions
two more titles in his letters to Salinger (see items 315-
335). These titles are listed below in the order that they
are mentioned by Fiene, Salinger, and Burnett, respectively.
Each title has a cross-reference to the entry in which it
is mentioned by Fiene, Salinger, or Burnett.

112. "Paula."

Donald Fiene (see items 341 and 342) notes that
this story was sold to *Stag* magazine in 1942, but
that it is "no longer in the files."

113. "The Survivors."

See items 129, 137.

114. "The Kissless Life of Reilly."

See item 139.

115. "The Broken Children."

See item 145.

116. "Rex Passard on the Planet Mars."

See item 147.

117. "Bitsey."

See item 150.

118. "Are You Banging Your Head Against the Wall?"

See item 150.

119.   "Total War Diary."

      See item 155.

120.   "Boy Standing in Tennessee."

      See item 158.

121.   "What Babe Saw, *or* 'Ooh-La-La!'"

      See item 158.

122.   "A Young Man in a Stuffed Shirt."

      See items 331-332.

123.   "The Daughter of the Late, Great Man."

      See items 331-332.

c. Letters

Included in the materials from *Story* magazine deposited in the Archives at Princeton University Library (see item 295) are thirty-six letters and post cards from Salinger to the personnel at *Story* magazine, most to Whit Burnett, editor. The letters that are dated are listed in chronological order; those that are not dated have been assigned an approximate date on the basis of the content of the letters, notes made by Burnett on the letters, and/or letters that Burnett wrote to Salinger (see items 315-335). Each citation contains a listing of the date or an approximation, the return address, the salutation, length, and an indication of whether typed or handwritten.

124.   15 January 1939 (1 p., typed, 1133 Park Avenue, New York City; Dear STORY)

      Salinger provides autobiographical information for *Story* magazine, perhaps as a classroom assignment in Burnett's short story class at Columbia University, comments on the short story class, on his personality ("alternately cynical and Polyanna-like, happy and morose, affectionate and indifferent"), and on his emotional state ("I can't think. Magnesia-white feathers fluffing around in my stomach.").

125.   21 November 1939 (2 pp., handwritten, 1133 Park Avenue, New York; Dear Mr. Burnett)

      Salinger mentions an unusual story that he has just submitted to *Collier's*, apologizes for not

reading all of the assigned material in Burnett's
class because he has "been too lazy or too bottled
up in my own ego" and for an autobiography that he
had written the previous semester in Burnett's
course, and finally comments on "the good short
story" and "the good reader."

126. 28 January (1 1/2 pp., typed, 1133 Park Avenue,
       New York City; Dear Mr. Burnett)

       Salinger reports that he is not returning to
       "Columbia this semester," that he is pleased about
       the acceptance of his story, presumably "The Young
       Folks," by *Story* (he includes six apparently fic-
       tional comments that have been made about him and
       his publishing), that he has recently seen "a swell
       play" ("Juno and the Paycock") and one by Saroyan,
       whose work Salinger likes while "dopes like Walter
       Winchell and Dorothy Kilgallen" find fault with
       "him for the wrong things"; Salinger ends by criti-
       cizing himself as "Knowitall Salinger."

127. 7 February 1940 (1 p., typed, 1133 Park Avenue, New
       York City; Dear Miss Kean)

       Salinger lists the names and addresses of people
       to whom he would like *Story* to send cards announc-
       ing the publication of his story "The Young Folks."

128. 24 February 1940 (2 pp., handwritten, 1133 Park Av-
       enue, New York; Dear Miss Foley)

       Salinger belatedly thanks Foley for the accep-
       tance of "The Young Folks," comments on his recent
       personal activities, compliments Burnett on the
       short story class at Columbia, and mentions that
       because the current issue of *Story* is late, "Every
       night is Christmas Eve-ish."

129. 1 March 1940 (1 p., typed, 1133 Park Avenue, New
       York; Dear Mr. Burnett)

       In response to a letter from Burnett (see item
       318), Salinger writes that his story "The Young
       Folks" in *Story* "looks swell in the magazine"; Sal-
       inger mentions a "complimentary" letter he has re-
       ceived from a literary agent, "a long story" that
       Salinger is working on entitled "The Survivors,"
       and his willingness to attend "the Writers Club
       dinner in May or any other time."

130. 17 April 1940 (1 p., typed, 1133 Park Avenue, New
       York; Dear Mr. Burnett)

In response to Burnett's letter of 16 April 1940
(see item 319), Salinger writes that even though
Story rejected his story "Go See Eddie," the fact
that Burnett liked the story "pleased" Salinger
("That's satisfaction enough almost"); he has sent
the story to "*Esquire* along with your [Burnett's]
note"; Salinger praises the growth of *Story*.

131.   3 May 1940 (1 p., typed, 1133 Park Avenue, New York
       City; Dear Mr. Burnett)

       Salinger accepts Burnett's invitation to attend
       the Writers Club dinner, mentions that *Esquire* re-
       jected "Go See Eddie," that he has another story at
       Harper's Bazaar, and complains about the way edi-
       tors express their rejection of his work. Most of
       the letter concerns Salinger's desire to write
       plays and to act in them himself.

132.   3 May 1940 (1 p., typed, 1133 Park Avenue, New York
       City; Dear Mr. Burnett)

       Having just seen a play by William Saroyan which
       the critics "panned," Salinger writes to Burnett to
       complain that even though the critics "were right
       ... it's their fault. They shaped his destiny, so
       far anyway, with their own lousy reviews of his
       earlier plays." Salinger writes to Burnett in
       hopes that Burnett will encourage his friend Sa-
       royan.

133.   16 May 1940 (1 p., typed, 1133 Park Avenue, New
       York; Dear Mr. Burnett)

       In this letter, written the day after he attend-
       ed the Writers Club dinner, Salinger thanks Burnett
       for the good time and for "the pleasure of meeting
       Mrs. Burnett," for whom Salinger wants "to write a
       story that she'll like immensely." Apparently Bur-
       nett has asked Salinger to write a "radio script of
       'The Trouble with People,'" which Salinger says he
       would "start right away if I didn't have this other
       radio script to do."

134.   [8 August 1940, postmark] (Picture post card, Manoir
       Richelieu, Canada; Dear Mr. Burnett)

       Salinger writes, "The place is full of stories.
       I'm doing a long one, which is new for me." On the
       picture of Manoir Richelieu, Murray Bay, Salinger
       writes, "This is the hotel where I don't live."

135.   4 September 1940 (1 p., typed, 1133 Park Avenue,
       New York City; Dear Mr. Burnett)

Salinger says that he is "not heartbroken" that
Story has rejected one of his stories, that he has
not yet been paid for "The Young Folks," that he is
thinking about writing an autobiographical novel,
and that his recent time away has helped to make
him "full of ego and confidence again."

136. 6 September 1940 (2 pp., typed, 1133 Park Avenue,
     New York; Dear Mr. Burnett)

Salinger acknowledges receiving his check for
"The Young Folks," mentions some people from the
short story class at Columbia, and says that he
"shipped off the long hotel story" to an agent.
Salinger's plans include beginning "the novel" and
voting "for Roosevelt, the lesser of two evils.
There's something more phoney about Willkie."
Salinger comments briefly on using his initials
"J.D."

137. 19 September 1940 (1 p., typed, 1133 Park Avenue,
     New York City; Dear Mr. Burnett)

This is a note attached to Salinger's story "The
Survivors" (see item 113), which he "picked ... out
of the bottom drawer last night and re-wrote most
of."

138. 11 December 1941 (1 p., typed, 1133 Park Avenue,
     New York; Dear Mr. Burnett)

Salinger writes of three topics: a "largely dialogue piece" which is "coming out in The New Yorker, probably in the next issue" (presumably "Slight
Rebellion off Madison," which Donald Fiene notes
was "bought by *New Yorker* originally in 1941, set
into type, and then delayed because of the War");
"a rich girl," Harriet Ann Willets, who "is in town
trying to peddle a novel"; and, his classification
as "I-B with the other cripples and faggets."

139. 22 January 1942 (1 p., typed, 1133 Park Avenue, New
     York; Dear Mr. Burnett)

Salinger requests that Burnett comment on Harriet
Ann Willets' novel (see item 138), complains that
his story has not yet appeared in the *New Yorker*,
mentions that he has "written a long story called
'The Kissless Life of Reilly' which kills me" and
that his agent "has sent 'The Long Debut of Lois
Taggett' to" Burnett. With references to works he
likes--F. Scott Fitzgerald's, particularly *The Last
Tycoon*, Sherwood Anderson's, and "'McEwin's Affair'
in the last issue" of *Story*--Salinger complains,
"It's almost impossible to write with the Post or

Collier's or Cosmopolitan in mind. Those mags will
let you scratch the surface, but they won't let you
make an incision."

140. [c. February--May 1942] (1 p., handwritten, Company
       "A," 1st Battalion, U.S. Signal Corps, Fort Mon-
       mouth, New Jersey; Dear Mr. Burnett)

       As Salinger awaits "another mental & physical
exam for the Aviation Cadets," he "miss[es] my little typewriter terribly," but feels that he "was
getting a little stale as a writer."

141. 8 June 1942 (1 p., typed, Company I, 1st Sig. Tng.
       Bn., Fort Monmouth, New Jersey; Dear Mr. Bur-
       nett)

       "In the Officers, First Sergeants, and Instruc-
tors Prep School of the Signal Corps," Salinger "at-
tend[s] classes" in the mornings and "drill[s] re-
cruits" in the afternoons. Salinger requests from
Burnett "a letter of character reference" for "Officers' School." Unsure that he has "anything to
say anymore," Salinger has not been writing. He
has fears that he is "going to preach" in his writing, and he is "tired--God, *so* tired--of leaving
them [his characters] all broken on the page with
just 'The End' written underneath."

142. 12 July [1942] (1 p., typed, 1133 Park Avenue, New
       York; Dear Mr. Burnett)

       Writing at home for the weekend, Salinger thanks
Burnett "for letters, acceptances, and burnettery
in general" and mentions that he "finally passed all
the examinations for transfer to the Army Aviation
Cadets" ("Me in Aviation. Me what could never even
put a Tinker-Toy together.").

143. [c. mid-1942] (1 p., typed, 1133 Park Avenue, New
       York [mailing address]; Dear Whit)

       Salinger's major concern in this letter is a book
"about a boy" that he plans to write "as a novel and
not as a series of short stories." He mentions two
stories that he has just completed which contain "no
more tricks"--"Elaine" and "Last Day of the Last Furlough."

144. [ack. 3 September 1942] (1 p., handwritten, 322nd
       Base Hq. and Air Base Squadron, AAF, BFS, Bain-
       bridge, Georgia; Dear Mr. Burnett)

       Without mentioning the title, Salinger says that
he has seen his story ("The Long Debut of Lois

Taggett") in *Story*, and it "bored me to death."
Georgia "is hot, swampy country. Faulkner and Cald-
well could have a literary picnic," but Salinger
prefers to be "a little further North. About a
thousand miles or so."

145. [c. early 1943] (2 pp., typed, 322nd Base Hq. and
     Air Base Squadron, AAF, BFS, Bainbridge, Geor-
     gia; Dear Mr. Burnett)

     Salinger mentions a story called "The Broken
     Children" that his agent has sent to *Story*, some
     writing that he is doing for *Collier's* and the
     New Yorker, that he "want[s] to sell some stuff to
     the movies"; he praises Burnett's anthology, crit-
     icizes Somerset Maugham and William Saroyan, and
     refers to some friends he has made in the army "who
     like the jug and ... Thomas Wolfe."

146. [c. March--April 1943] (1 p., typed, 322nd Base Hq.
     and Air Base Sqdrn., AAF, BFS, Bainbridge, Geor-
     gia; Dear Whit)

     Salinger refers to health problems--arthritis,
     tooth extractions, and being "always one jump ahead
     of the white jacket crowd--mentions some writing he
     is doing and a rejected suggestion from Houghton
     Mifflin that he apply "for Fellowships and stuff,"
     and suggests that Burnett include in *Story* a review
     by Mary H. Colum, "a fine critic and never precious,"
     in contrast to Clifton Fadiman, whom Salinger says
     he "hates."

147. [c. April--May 1943] (1 p., typed, 322nd Base Hq.
     and Air Base Sqdrn., AAF, BFS, Bainbridge, Geor-
     gia; Dear Whit)

     While in New York recently, Salinger wanted to
     visit Burnett but did not because he "felt too damn
     G.I. to do anything but stay pretty tight and pret-
     ty close to the music." He mentions the recently
     sold story "The Varioni Brothers" and a newly writ-
     ten story "Rex Passard on the Planet Mars": "If the
     money keeps rolling in, I plan to get married."
     The library at the military base is "good, solid,
     stinking," but "the notes on the fly-leaves are
     sometimes pretty terrific." Salinger reminisces
     about the people in Burnett's short story class who
     called Salinger "a craftsman! What a helluva thing
     to go around calling people."

148. [ack. 1 July 1943] (1 p., typed, Squadron A-2,
     AAFCC, Nashville, Tenn.; Dear Whit)

     Salinger comments on his military routine, "a
     three-day-pass to a place called Dyersburg, Tenn.,"

his unmarried life, and his writing routine: "I
work on at least four stories at a time; whichever
I finish first gets sent out first. Best system I
ever had; avoids over-writing, going stale on a
piece, draft-happy, etc."

149. [c. 1943] (1 p., handwritten, Dear Mr. Burnett)

Salinger writes that he has "time to write
nights" and praises a novel by William Saroyan and
"a fine old Scott Fitzgerald story."

150. [c. July--October 1943] (2 pp., typed, 85th Depot
      Supply Squadron, Patterson Field, Fairfield,
      Ohio; Dear Whit)

Salinger brags about the publication of "The
Varioni Brothers" in the *Saturday Evening Post* and
mentions a story entitled "Bitsey" that he hopes
to sell to *Saturday Evening Post*. Salinger thinks
that he may be transferred to Public Relations in
the army. "The O'Neill-Chaplin nuptials" depress
Salinger. The letter contains several remarks: his
"own wedding plans are going to hell"; he has "been
re-reading Anna Karenina" and "one of those paper-
book editions of John O'Hara's short stories";
"Edith Kean wrote ... and said she practically published STORY singlehanded"; his mother recently met
a salesgirl at Saks' who was in the short story
class at Columbia; he had recently seen "My Friend
Flicka" ... worst scenario and job of casting I
know of"; and, he has a story at the *New Yorker* entitled "Are You Banging Your Head Against the Wall?"
about "the kid I wanted to do a play about, doing
his part myself."

151. [4 October 1943, postmark] (Post card, handwritten;
      Dear Whit)

Salinger writes that "special orders came through,"
and he will "try to go on working on the book."

152. 14 January 1944 (2 pp., handwritten; Dear Whit)

As he awaits orders to be shipped overseas, Salinger writes that he sold three stories to *Saturday
Evening Post*, including "Last Day of the Last Furlough," which "has mention of young Holden Caul-
field--the kid in the book I want to do for Story
Press." Having "been a short story writer since I
was seventeen," Salinger feels that there is "Something new ... in my work."

153. 19 March [1944] (8 half-pages, handwritten, Div.
      Hqs. Co., APO #4, c/o Postmaster, New York; Dear
      Whit)

Corresponding from England, Salinger comments on
his writing and that of others: his story "Both
Parties Concerned" came out recently in *Saturday
Evening Post*; he wrote a story in London; he "no
longer want[s] to cut ... [his] characters down";
he is "working with nostalgia chiefly because that's
all there seems to be anymore"; he is "the first to
write good short stories for S.E.P. since Lardner
and Fitzgerald"; he has written "about six chapters
on the book"; he asks that Burnett get his story
"Elaine," which he calls "a full-length, all-the-
way story"; Salinger offers to contribute to the
"college short story contest" sponsored by *Story*;
and, he has recently read a book on the short story
by an Englishman Bates, who "knows his Hemingway,
but not Sherwood Anderson."

154.   22 April [1944] (3 half-pages, handwritten; C.I.C.
       Section, 4th Inf. Div., APO #4, c/o PM, New
       York; Dear Whit)

Salinger complains about the "gay, 'charming'
Post illustrations" and about the fact that the
Saturday Evening Post changed the titles of his
story "Death of a Dogface" to "Soft-Boiled Sergeant"
and "Wake Me When It Thunders" to "Both Parties Concerned." Salinger is "through with the slicks"; he
continues "to work on the novel," and he received a
letter of complaint from Edith Kean about his writing "that she was trying to get control of STORY."

155.   2 May [1944] (9 pp., handwritten; Dear Whit)

Salinger responds to Burnett's suggestion (see
item 329) about putting together a collection of
Salinger's stories by saying "many of my stories
are flops in one way or another." He then lists
eight stories that "are the best ones I've done"
and mentions that he has with him "about six Holden
Caulfield stories" for the book, that his agent has
"ten or fifteen other stories, none of which do any
respectable bell-ringing," that he is sending his
agent another one entitled "Total War Diary." He
has quit working on the Holden Caulfield book. Salinger misses the short story class at Columbia, en-
closes a check for *Story*'s contest, comments on the
"Bernard DeVoto--Sinclair Lewis clash in the Sat
Review of Literature," and criticizes "Bennett Cerf's
column."

156.   12 June [1944] (2 pp., post card size, handwritten,
       C.I.C. Detach., 4th Inf. Div., APO #4, c/o PM,
       N.Y.C.; Dear Whit)

Writing from France, Salinger reports that he is
"doing mostly intelligence work" and asks if his
agent has sent "copies of my last stuff."

157. 28 June 1944 (1 p., typed with handwritten note,
        France; Dear Whit)

Salinger writes that he prefers to write "the
novel before turning out a book of stories"; he
"should be able to finish it in six months, maybe
less." Salinger's military activities scare him:
"you never saw six-feet-two of muscle and typewriter
ribbon get out of a jeep and into a ditch as fast as
this baby can. And I don't get out till they start
bulldozing an air field over me." He thanks Burnett for accepting his story "Elaine" and asks about
the check he sent.

158. 9 September 1944 (5 pp., handwritten, CIC Sect, 4th
        Inf. Div. APO #4, c/o Postmaster, NYC; Dear Whit)

Salinger reports on his recent very pleasant experience in Paris: "If we had stood on top of the
jeep and taken a leak, Paris would have said 'Ah,
the darling Americans! What a charming custom!'"
Two paragraphs in the letter concern Salinger's
meeting Ernest Hemingway overseas. Salinger speaks
of Hemingway in completely positive terms. Continuing to consider Burnett's suggestion about a book
of short stories, Salinger reports that he has "written six, and ... working on three more." He mentions "Boy Standing in Tennessee" and "Two Lonely
Men" as "really good." The three are "The Magic
Fox Hole," "What Babe Saw, or Ooh-La-La!" and "another piece untitled."

159. 18 January 1969 (1 p., typed, c/o Harold Ober Asso-
        ciates, 40 East 49th Street, New York, N.Y.
        10017; Dear Whit)

Sending this letter through his agent, Salinger
writes to Burnett that he has "no fiction at hand,
published or unpublished that I care to have an-
thologized."

*   See Donald Fiene's thesis (item 341) for three more
        letters from Salinger--two to Fiene and one to
        an official at Ursinus College.

                    d. Miscellaneous

The one miscellaneous unpublished item refers to an
essay Salinger submitted to *Saturday Review*.

160.   Manuscript about Ross, Shawn, and the *New Yorker*.

According to Donald Fiene (see items 341 and 342), this is "an open-letter essay, 25-30 pp., submitted to the *Saturday Review* in 1960 ... and rejected because of its length and unusual style."

B.   SECONDARY SOURCES

The second of the four major parts of the bibliography is divided into five sections: a miscellany of secondary sources, *The Catcher*, *Nine Stories*, *Franny and Zooey*, and *Raise High the Roof Beam, Carpenters and Seymour: An Introduction*, respectively. These sections, which make up the largest part of the bibliography, contain entries for materials about Salinger and his works. The citations refer to materials that range from short, one-line references to Salinger and his writing to comprehensive, book-length works.

1.   *Miscellany*

The miscellany of secondary sources has seven subsections in the following order: biographical materials; letters from Salinger to Whit Burnett, editor of *Story*; reference works; book-length studies; references, articles, and chapters; studies of uncollected stories; and, dissertations and theses.

a.   Biography

The citations for biographical material are listed alphabetically. The materials listed in this subsection include those that present factual biographical details as well as those that comment on Salinger's personal and literary reputation. Many of the articles comment on Salinger's reclusiveness. The biographical materials cited in this subsection refer to separately published articles on Salinger and also to mention of Salinger in books with predominant subjects other than Salinger. See the subsection on book-length studies (items 398-429) for further biographical materials and for reprints of some of the materials listed here.

161.   Aldridge, John W. *Time to Murder and Create: The Contemporary Novel in Crisis*. New York: David McKay, 1966, passim; rpt. Freeport, New York: Books for Libraries Press, 1972, passim; rpt.

*The Devil in the Fire: Retrospective Essays on
American Literature and Culture 1951-1971*. New
York: Harper's Magazine Press, 1972, passim.

Aldridge makes brief comparisons between Salinger
and other writers like Bellow, Mailer, and Styron.

162.   ————. "What Became of Our Postwar Hopes?" *New York
         Times Book Review*, 29 July 1962, pp. 1, 24; rpt.
         "The War Writers Ten Years Later." In *Contempo-
         rary American Novelists*. Ed. Harry T. Moore.
         Carbondale, Illinois: Southern Illinois Univer-
         sity Press, 1964, pp. 32-40.

         Aldridge includes Salinger in a list of impor-
         tant new novelists.

163.   Angoff, Allan. *American Writing Today*. Freeport,
         New York: Books for Libraries Press, 1971, pp.
         169, 183, 189.

         Brief references to Salinger as a short story
         writer.

164.   "Are There Any Hemingways in the House? ... Report
         on Young Writers." *Newsweek*, 13 January 1958,
         pp. 90-91.

         Salinger is listed as one of the "American nov-
         elists under 40 who have attracted national atten-
         tion."

165.   Auer, Bernhard M. "A Letter from the Publisher."
         Time, 15 September 1961, n.p.

         Introduction to *Time*'s cover story on Salinger:
         Robert Vickery, cover artist; Russell Hoban, story
         illustrator; Jack Skow, cover story writer.

166.   "Backstage with Esquire." *Esquire*, 16 (September
         1941), 24.

         Biographical information to accompany the ap-
         pearance of "The Heart of a Broken Story," called
         here a "satire on formula fiction."

167.   ————. *Esquire* 24 (October 1945), 34.

         Biographical information written by Salinger to
         accompany the appearance of "This Sandwich Has No
         Mayonnaise." Salinger mentions that "it is probable
         that I will never write a novel" and criticizes
         current war novels as having "too much of the
         strength, maturity and craftsmanship critics are
         looking for, and too little of the glorious imper-
         fections which teeter and fall off the best minds."

168. Baker, Carlos. *Ernest Hemingway: A Life Story*. New
     York: Charles Scribner's Sons, 1969, pp. 420, 646.

     Baker claims that Salinger and Hemingway met a-
     bout August 1944 and that Salinger "found Heming-
     way both friendly and generous, not at all impressed
     by his own eminence, and 'soft'--as opposed to the
     hardness and toughness which some of his writing
     suggested"; Baker also mentions a 1946 letter from
     Salinger to Hemingway, in which Salinger claims to
     be writing a play about Holden Caulfield, a part
     Salinger himself hopes to play.

169. Baker, Carlos, et al. "The Careful Young Men: To-
     morrow's Leaders Analyzed by Today's Teachers."
     Nation, 9 March 1957, pp. 200-214.

     Stanley Kunitz mentions that Salinger is "praised
     vociferously ... for his discovery of childhood."

170. Berman, Ronald. "Myth or Criticism." *Kenyon Review*,
     31, No. 3 (1969), 378-383.

     Comments that "both Salinger and Steinbeck rein-
     vigorate our sense of the present failing the past,
     and cast Hegelian shadows upon our ways of sustain-
     ing modern life."

171. Blaney, Shirley. "Twin State Telescope." [Claremont,
     New Hampshire] *Daily Eagle*, 13 November 1953;
     rpt. Kosner, Edward. "The Private World of J.D.
     Salinger." *New York Post: Week-End Magazine*, 30
     April 1961, p. 5; rpt. "The Last Published Inter-
     view with J.D. Salinger." *Crawdaddy*, March 1975,
     p. 39.

     Based on an interview with Salinger, Blaney's
     article reports some biographical details about
     Salinger and the publication of *The Catcher* and
     comments on his writing.

172. Brandon, Henry. "A Conversation with Edmund Wilson:
     'We Don't Know Where We Are.'" *New Republic*, 30
     March 1959, pp. 13-15.

     Wilson says that members "of the 'beat' genera-
     tion ... have gone in for Zen Buddhism and things
     like that, which divorce them from social reality."

173. Braudy, Leo. "Realists, Naturalists, and Novelists
     of Manners." In *Harvard Guide to Contemporary
     American Writing*. Ed. Daniel Hoffman. Cambridge,
     Massachusetts: The Belknap Press, 1979, pp. 144-
     145.

In a descriptive summary of Salinger's work, Braudy calls Salinger "as much a cult figure as a literary one" and says that "the celebrity of Salinger's work ... combined with his own reticence to turn him into the vanishing man of American letters."

174. Brickell, Herschel, ed. "Introduction." *Prize Stories of 1950: The O. Henry Awards*. Garden City, New York: Doubleday, 1950, pp. x-xi, 244.

Brief biography to accompany "For Esmé--with Love and Squalor" and a few comments about the story itself.

175. ————. "J.D. Salinger." *Prize Stories of 1949: The O. Henry Awards*. Garden City, New York: Doubleday, 1950, p. 249.

In a brief biographical paragraph, Brickell reports that Salinger "thinks he may start a novel."

176. ————. *Prize Stories of 1949: The O. Henry Awards*. Garden City, New York: Doubleday, 1949, pp. 4, 249.

Brief biography and the following comment: "This year's group [of readers] included a well-read nurse in New York Hospital whose favorite story by J.D. Salinger, 'Down at the Dock,' in May *Harper's* was not included only because the editor liked Mr. Salinger's 'Just Before the War with the Eskimos' a little better."

177. Brown, Robert McAfee. "Salinger, Steinbeck and Company: Assyrians in Modern Dress." *Presbyterian Life*, 1 May 1962, pp. 16-17, 32-33.

God can use the "Modern Writer" in order to stir the believers whose faith is not as strong as it could be.

178. Burnett, Whit, ed. *This Is My Best*. Garden City, New York: Doubleday, 1970, pp. 104 ff.

Salinger is listed as one of the authors voted on as the best.

179. Burnett, Whit, and Hallie Burnett, eds. "Biographical Notes." *Story: The Fiction of the Forties*. New York: E.P. Dutton, 1949, p. 616.

Biographical information to accompany the reprinting of "The Long Debut of Lois Taggett."

180. Burrell, Angus, and Bennett Cerf. "Biographical Notes: J.D. Salinger." In *An Anthology of Famous American Stories*. Eds. Angus Burrell and Bennett Cerf. New York: Random House, 1953, p. 1340.

Biographical information to accompany "Pretty Mouth and Green My Eyes."

181. Carter, Albert Howard. "The New Dickens." *Western Humanities Review*, 16 (Summer 1962), 239-241.

Salinger and Dickens are similar in trying "to teach Us that everybody is an eccentric."

182. "The Catcher on the Hill." *Newsweek*, 18 November 1974, p. 17.

Survey of the "public" Salinger with reference to *Newsweek*'s Bill Roeder's brief interview with Salinger.

183. Chugunov, Konstantin. "Soviet Critics on J.D. Salinger's Novel 'The Catcher in the Rye.'" *Soviet Literature*, No. 5 (1962), 182-184.

Chugunov quotes from some of the Russian comments about *The Catcher* and praises Rita Wright-Kovaleva's translation of it; in general, Chugunov suggests, the Russian readers "are glad to have made the acquaintance of this writer and are ready to welcome new and significant works by him."

184. Clarke, Gerald. "Checking In with Vladimir Nabokov." *Esquire*, 84 (July 1975), 67-69, 131, 133.

In response to the question "'Whom do *you* most admire?'" Nabokov included "J.D. Salinger ... [as] another writer I admire tremendously."

185. "Contributors." *Story*, 16 (March-April 1940), 2.

Biography to accompany "The Young Folks": "J.D. Salinger, who is twenty-one years old, was born in New York. He attended public grammar school, one military academy, and three colleges, and has spent one year in Europe. He is particularly interested in playwriting."

186. ————. *Story*, 21 (September-October 1942), 2.

Biography to accompany "The Long Debut of Lois Taggett."

187. ————. *Story*, 25 (November-December 1944), 1.

Biography to accompany "Once a Week Won't Kill You."

188.   ——. *Story*, 26 (March-April 1945), 4.

Biography to accompany "Elaine": "J.D. Salinger is a young New York writer who is at present in Germany with the U.S. Army. *Story* has published a number of his pieces, including his first published story which appeared in this magazine several years ago."

189.   "Controversial Story Not by J.D. Salinger." *New Orleans Times Picayune*, 27 February 1977, Sec. 1, p. 18, col. 3.

"Gordon Lish, fiction editor of Esquire magazine, says he wrote the unsigned story ["For Rupert--With No Promises"] in the magazine's February issue that generated speculation that J.D. Salinger was the author.

190.   Cooney, Neill L., S.J. "Salinger and Golding." *America*, 23 February 1963, pp. 242, 244.

In a letter to the editor, Cooney takes issue with Francis Kearns' oversimplified conclusion (see item 900) "that Salinger is asserting the innocence of human nature."

191.   Costello, Donald P. "Salinger and his Critics." *Commonweal*, 25 October 1963, pp. 132-135.

Costello comments on the fact that the critics seem to be abandoning Salinger.

192.   *A Directory of American Fiction Writers*. 1976 ed. New York: Poets & Writers, 1976, p. 36.

Lists Salinger's agent and notes that Salinger is "not available for readings."

193.   Ducharme, Edward R. "J.D., D.B., Sonny, Sunny, and Holden." *English Record*, 19 (December 1968), 54-58.

From secondary sources, Ducharme "pieced together a small amount of data relevant to the study of *The Catcher in the Rye* from an autobiographical standpoint."

194.   Dudar, Helen. "In Search of J.D. Salinger, Publishing's Invisible Man." *Chicago Tribune*, 19 June 1979, Sec. 2, pp. 1, 6.

Brief biography and news of the reprinting of "Go See Eddie" (see item 30), including mention of the fact that Salinger uncharacteristically went to Long Island to help an old friend celebrate his retirement from New York City detectives.

195. [Elfin, Mel.] "The Mysterious J.D. Salinger ... His Woodsy, Secluded Life." *Newsweek*, 30 May 1960, pp. 92-94.

Relying on Salinger's works, criticism, and people who know Salinger, Elfin comments on the writer whose "name probably bobs up oftener in current literary conversations than that of any other writer."

196. Eliason, Marcus. "Salinger Fan Respects Author's Desired Privacy." *The Montgomery Advertiser Alabama Journal*, 21 December 1975, p. 11D; "Conspiracy of Silence Guards Private World of J.D. Salinger." *New Orleans Times Picayune*, 21 December 1975, Sec. 3, p. 15, col. 1.

Eliason went to Cornish, New Hampshire, and Windsor, Vermont, in hopes of interviewing Salinger, but saw him only from a distance in a bookstore at Dartmouth.

197. Eppes, Betty. "What I Did Last Summer." *Paris Review*, 23 (Summer 1981), 221-239.

Eppes gives a detailed account of the planning and actual experience of a short interview she had with Salinger, in which he tells her, "I am really writing. I told you. I love to write and I assure you that I write regularly. I'm just not publishing. I write for myself. For my own pleasure. I want to be left alone to do it. So leave me alone. Don't drop in here like this again."

198. Fabre, Michel. "Jack Conroy as Editor." Trans. David Ray. *New Letters*, 39 (Winter 1972), 115-137.

"As the final curtain was falling [c. 1939-40] on *The New Anvil*, Conroy reluctantly sent back with an approving letter a manuscript from a beginning youngster who responded gratefully, 'Thanks so much for your warm note. It took the chill off many a rejection slip.' It was some time before the writer, J.D. Salinger, became famous with The Catcher."

199. Farrell, James T. "Literary Note." *American Book Collector*, OS 17 (May 1967), 6.

Farrell notes that "writers who are in the public eye" find themselves "lifted to genius by teenage empathy with the characters of a minor work,
which is illustrated by Salinger."

200. Feinstein, Herbert. "Contemporary American Fiction:
      Harvey Swados and Leslie Fiedler." *Wisconsin
      Studies in Contemporary Literature*, 2 (Winter
      1961), 79-98.

Salinger and "the best authors of the first half
of the Fifties have been people who have had something to say and who have in some instances said it
quite well"; Salinger is "an accomplished writer
... but in a very small way and in a very narrow
way."

201. Fenton, Charles. "The Lost Years of Twentieth-Cen-
      tury American Literature." *South Atlantic Quar-
      terly*, 59 (Summer 1960), 332-338.

"For every worthwhile essay on Wright Morris or
Mark Harris or Harvey Swados there are eleven on
the love song of J.D. Salinger, so newly trivial
that once again, as with Faulkner and Eliot and
Hemingway, the screen of repetitive homage almost
obscures the meaningful writer."

202. Fiedler, Leslie A. "Master of Dreams." *Partisan Re-
      view*, 34 (Summer 1967), 339-356.

"In our time ... Joseph has once more been hauled
into Pharaoh's court, once more lifted up in the
sight of his enemies and brothers; once more recog-
nized as a true Master of Dreams, under his new
names of J.D. Salinger and Bernard Malamud and
Philip Roth and Saul Bellow."

203. Field, G.W. "Herman Hesse as Critic of English and
      American Literature." *Monatshefte*, 53 (April-
      May 1961), 147-158.

Field mentions that "we can measure Hesse's
deepened understanding of America in a review of
J.D. Salinger's The Catcher at the end of 1953."

204. Foley, Martha. *The Story of "Story" Magazine*. New
      York: W.W. Norton, 1980, pp. 8, 23, 265, 271.

In his "Introduction" to this book, Jay Neugeboren mentions that Salinger is among "an extraor-
dinary number of American writers" who were "published for the first time" in *Story* and that Salinger among others "shaped the taste and hopes of
so much that has come since." In his "Afterword,"

Neugeboren mentions Salinger's contribution of $200 for "*Story*'s college contest."

205. ————. "Salinger, J.D." *The Best American Short Stories of 1949: and the Yearbook of the American Short Story*. Boston: Houghton Mifflin, 1949, p. 319.

Brief biography, which includes a list of the magazines in which Salinger's stories have appeared.

206. Fosburgh, Lacey. "J.D. Salinger Speaks About his Silence." *New York Times*. 3 November 1974, pp. 1, 69.

Fosburgh reports on a telephone interview with Salinger about the unauthorized publication of his early stories. Salinger's complaint is that the illegal publication is an invasion of his privacy. Salinger says, "I'm not trying to hide the gaucheries of my youth. I just don't think they're worthy of publishing."

207. ————. "Salinger Books Stir F.B.I. Search." *New York Times*, 10 November 1974, p. 75.

Report of an investigation by the F.B.I. after "about 30,000 unauthorized editions of J.D. Salinger's early works" were sold.

208. ————. "Why More Top Novelists Don't Go Hollywood." *New York Times*, 21 November 1976, pp. 1, 13-14.

Report that because of his disappointment with the movie version of "Uncle Wiggily in Connecticut" Salinger "made an iron-clad decision never to allow another of his stories to be filmed."

209. French, Warren. "The Age of Salinger." In *The Fifties: Fiction, Poetry, Drama*. Ed. Warren French. Deland, Florida: Everett/Edwards, 1970, pp. 1-39.

Salinger's writing displays "a defeatist attitude" and "works embodying such an attitude were extremely popular during the 50s." Rpt. in 381, 385.

210. ————. "September 11, 1949." In *The Forties: Fiction, Poetry, Drama*. Ed. Warren French. Deland, Florida: Everett/Edwards, 1969, p. 297.

In the introduction to an essay about Nelson Algren, French points out that Algren is similar to the writers of the 1930s and with "his sense of alienation and his concern for style ... to the 50s, to writers like Salinger."

211.   ————. "An Unnoticed Salinger Story." *College Eng-
        lish*, 26 (February 1965), 394-395.

        French makes known a story not listed in any pre-
        vious Salinger checklist: "Go See Eddie." *University
        of Kansas City Review*, 7 (December 1940), 121-124.

212.   Furnas, J.D. "Limey Howlers." *New Statesman*, 6 Sep-
        tember 1958, pp. 314, 316.

        Suggests that "if English writers must put words
        in American mouths, let them study, say, Ring Lard-
        ner, J.D. Salinger, Wolcott Gibbs, perhaps John
        O'Hara."

213.   Gallagher, Michael P. "Human Values in Modern Lit-
        erature." *Studies: An Irish Quarterly Review*,
        57 (Summer 1968), 142-153.

        Salinger, Bellow, Nabokov, Malamud, and Updike
        "search for positive values through comedy."

214.   Gary, Sandra. "Newsmakers." *Newsweek*, 12 October
        1981, p. 113.

        Gary presents a few details about the lives of
        Jan Kerouac, daughter of Jack Kerouac, and Matthew
        Salinger, J.D. Salinger's son, who in 1981 is "a
        full-time undergraduate at Columbia" and "also takes
        three acting classes at the Lee Strasberg Institute
        and one singing class a week." There are photo-
        graphs of both the young Kerouac and Salinger.

215.   Geismar, Maxwell. "Henry James and the Jacobites."
        American Scholar, 31 (Summer 1962), 373-381.

        Compares Henry James to Salinger as "a perfect
        figurehead."

216.   Gelb, Arthur, and Barbara Gelb. *O'Neill*. New York:
        Harper and Brothers, 1962, pp. 843, 850, 851.

        Salinger dated and wrote letters to O'Neill's
        daughter Oona; Carol Grace, a friend of Oona, re-
        ports that "'Oona was receiving a letter almost
        every day from a boy named Jerry [Salinger] in New
        York ... some ... fifteen pages long, and they were
        very witty, with comments about all kinds of things."
        Grace cribbed from Salinger's letters in letters she
        wrote to William Saroyan, her fiancé.

217.   Gill, Brendan. *Here at the New Yorker*. New York:
        Random House, 1975, pp. 228, 247, 276.

        Salinger is listed as "perhaps the most

startling" of John O'Hara, Irwin Shaw, John Cheever,
Shirley Jackson, and John Updike and as "a new and
unexpected talent ... to leap Roman-candle-like
straight off the pages of the magazine"; the publication of Shirley Jackson's "The Lottery" brought
in "hundreds of letters ... from troubled and ex-
cited readers, causing a furor not to be equalled
until the publication of Salinger's 'Franny'"; "Salinger has sold thirteen" stories to the *New Yorker*.

218. Gilman, Richard. "Salinger Considered." *Jubilee*, 9
     (October 1961), 38-41.

     Gilman compares and contrasts Thomas Wolfe, "the
     literary hero of my college generation," and Sal-
     inger, "today the lion of the campus," and con-
     cludes that Wolfe, "for all his roughness, super-
     fluity and indiscriminate embrace of everything the
     world had to offer, [may] outlast J.D. Salinger"
     because "in Wolfe ... there was an acceptance of
     the truth that we are all members of one another."

219. Gold, Herbert. "Fiction of the Sixties." *Atlantic*,
     206 (September 1960), 53-57.

     Brief mention that "Truman Capote and J.D. Sal-
     inger attempted to raise elegant eccentricity and
     child psychology to the level of literature."

220. Gooder, R.D. "'One of Today's Best Little Writers?'"
     Cambridge Quarterly, 1 (Winter 1965/66), 81-90.

     Gooder questions whether, as Martin Green sug-
     gests (see item 479), "Salinger's reputation was
     now established beyond question." Gooder finds
     Salinger's "old skill--the methods, locutions, and
     mannerisms--is intact, but the matter, never abun-
     dant, seems quite to have run out."

221. Graustark, Barbara. "Newsmakers." *Newsweek*, 17 July
     1978, p. 57.

     Graustark reports Salinger's surprise visit at
     a testimonial dinner to honor "ex-chief of detectives
     John L. Keenan, a World War II buddy."

222. Green, Martin Burgess. "Cultural Images in England
     and America." In *A Mirror for Anglo-Saxons*. Ed.
     Martin Burgess Green. New York: Harper and Broth-
     ers, 1960, pp. 85-88.

     Green writes that Salinger is "a phoenix" that
     "create[s] a whole image for Anglo-Saxons, in which
     people of the greatest intelligence and sensitivity
     could recognize themselves, and find themselves
     therein transformed, valuable and beautiful."

223.   ————. *Transatlantic Patterns: Cultural Comparisons
        of England with America*. New York: Basic Books,
        1977, pp. 189-190.

        "The American writers I picked on to admire in
        Re-Appraisals [see item 479], Emerson and Salinger,
        are not in the least Faustian. Salinger's gradual
        dematerialization, his fading from the national
        retina, is a striking demonstration of the hegemony
        gradually established by the Faustian temperament
        over the American imagination since 1945."

224.   Gross, Barry. "'Would 25-Cent Press Keep *Gatsby* in
        the Public Eye--Or is the Book Unpopular?" In
        *Seasoned "Authors" for a New Season: The Search
        for Standards in Popular Writing*. Ed. Louis Fil-
        ler. Bowling Green, Ohio: Bowling Green Univer-
        sity Popular Press, 1980, pp. 51-57.

        Even though Salinger and Holden Caulfield were
        the idols of Gross's generation, these readers "had
        to turn from Salinger and to a future"--to Fitzger-
        ald.

225.   Gross, Theodore L. "Preface," "Introduction" [to
        Part II], and "Introduction" [to Part III]. In
        The Literature of American Jews. Ed. Theodore L.
        Gross. New York: Free Press, 1973, pp. xv-xvii,
        52-54, 172-181.

        Salinger is not as "aware" of himself as a Jew
        as some other writers; "the self-conscious clown
        ... has a central place in the work of ... Salin-
        ger"; although Jews make up a small "percent of the
        American population," they have contributed signif-
        icant "cultural achievement since World War II."

226.   Grunwald, Henry Anatole. "'He Touches Something Deep
        in Us ...'" *Horizon*, 4 (May 1962), 100-107.

        In what will become the introduction to his *Sal-
        inger: A Critical and Personal Portrait* (see item
        404), Grunwald enjoys the fact that Salinger offers
        "delight" and laments that "his output is too small,
        that his Songs of Innocence do not reach us often
        enough."

227.   Gunn, Giles B. "Bernard Malamud and the High Cost
        of Living." In *Adversity and Grace*. Ed. Nathan A.
        Scott, Jr. Chicago: University of Chicago Press,
        1968, pp. 59-85.

        Mentions Salinger in a group of "diverse" but
        similar writers.

228. Hainsworth, J.D. "J.D. Salinger." *Hibbert Journal*, 64 (Winter 1965-1966), 63-64.

In a short article with passing comments on several of Salinger's works, Hainsworth suggests that Salinger's life and his works pose similar questions: "How, if you have any sensitivity or discrimination, do you live in a society, which, to use the recurrent Salinger words, is just so *goddam phoney*?" and "how do you live with the people who are passive victims of phoniness, without knowing it?"

229. Haitch, Richard. "Follow-Up in the News: J.D. Salinger." *New York Times*, 12 February 1978, p. 41.

Report that Salinger has returned to his writing after a court settlement with some bookstores about the sales of the unauthorized *The Complete Uncollected Short Stories of J.D. Salinger*, but that the perpetrator, a John Greenberg, has never been found.

230. Hassan, Ihab. *The Dismemberment of "Orpheus": Toward a Postmodern Literature*. New York: Oxford University Press, 1971, p. 251.

Hassan cites Salinger as an example of "sacramental language of silence ... in contemporary American literature" and asks if the fact that "Salinger ceases to publish" might be "some form of holy refusal." Rpt. in 385.

231. ————. "The Novel of Outrage: A Minority Voice in Postwar American Fiction." *American Scholar*, 34 (Spring 1965), 239-253; rpt. *The American Novel Since World War II*. Ed. Marcus Klein. Greenwich, Connecticut: Fawcett, 1969, pp. 196-209.

Hassan indicates that he has "not mentioned such writers as Saul Bellow and J.D. Salinger, who exert a wide influence on contemporary imagination."

232. Havemann, Ernest. "The Search for the Mysterious J.D. Salinger: The Recluse in the Rye." *Life*, 3 November 1961, pp. 129-130, 132, 135, 137-138, 141-142, 144; rpt. *J.D. Salinger and John Updike. Life* Educational Reprint 8, pp. 6-12.

In an article with several pictures, Havemann calls Salinger "the most influential man of letters in the U.S. today--and also the most inaccessible, mysterious and fascinating recluse in all U.S. literary history."

233. Hayman, Jane. "The White Jew." *Dissent*, 8 Spring 1961), 191-196.

Salinger has "passion for little boys and girls."

234. Herriges, Greg. "Ten Minutes with J.D. Salinger."
     Oui, 8 (January 1979), 86-88, 126-130.

     A high school teacher, Herriges recounts his
     trip during the summer of 1978 to Cornish, New Hamp-
     shire, to interview Salinger. Herriges talks with
     a storekeeper, whose wife received an autographed
     copy of *Franny and Zooey*, personally delivered by
     Salinger, when the woman was in the hospital; Ethel
     Nelson, a clerk in a store and one who had known
     Salinger well when she was younger and who had been
     a baby sitter for Salinger's two children; a man
     named Osworth, who knew Salinger; Bernice Johnson,
     the town clerk, who knew Salinger; and, finally,
     Salinger himself. On his driveway in the rain, Sal-
     inger told Herriges the following: "Contact with the
     public hinders my work"; "Publication is an agoniz-
     ing thing to go through. It takes at least a year
     and a half *after* publication to get back in stride";
     "There will be more [stories]. There is hope for
     more"; and, "Everything I have to say is in my fic-
     tion."

235. Hicks, Granville. "J.D. Salinger: Search for Wisdom."
     Saturday Review, 25 July 1959, pp. 13, 30.

     "Millions of young Americans," Hicks found, are
     "closer to Salinger than to any other writer." The
     fact "that Salinger can make the search for wisdom
     seem important to large numbers of young people" is
     significant. Rpt. in 378, 385, 404, 413, 428.

236. ————. "These Are Their Lives." *Saturday Review*,
     4 November 1961, p. 21.

     Hicks deals with the problem for Salinger of
     privacy in his personal life and his reputation.

237. Hollowell, John. *Fact and Fiction: The New Journal-
     ism and the Nonfiction Novel*. Chapel Hill: Uni-
     versity of North Carolina Press, 1977, p. 17.

     "J.D. Salinger ... ceased to write fiction after
     1963 and retreated to the woods of New England."

238. Hough, Graham. *The Dream and the Task: Literature
     and Morals in the Culture of Today*. New York:
     W.W. Norton, 1964, pp. 21, 23.

     Mentions that "Salinger, Mailer, Ginsberg, and
     Kerouac have converted younger generations."

239. Hutchens, John K. "On an Author." *New York Herald*

Tribune Book Review, 19 August 1951, p. 2.

A brief biography of Salinger which stresses his desire for privacy and mentions that in 1945 he sent a $250 check to *Story* magazine "for the help of other writers."

240. Kazin, Alfred. "The Alone Generation: A Comment on the Fiction of the 'Fifties.'" *Harper's*, 219 (October 1959), 127-131; rpt. *Writing in America*. Eds. John Fischer and Robert B. Silvers. New Brunswick, New Jersey: Rutgers University Press, 1960, pp. 14-26; rpt. *Contemporaries*. Boston: Little, Brown, 1962, pp. 207-217; rpt. *The American Novel Since World War II*. Ed. Marcus Klein. Greenwich, Connecticut: Fawcett, 1969, pp. 114-123.

Salinger, an author lacking "strength but ... competent and interesting," writes what "is rather too obviously touching, and put together on a frame presented to it by *The New Yorker*." Rpt. in 378, 385.

241. ———. "J.D. Salinger: 'Everybody's Favorite.'" *Atlantic*, 208 (August 1961), 27-31.

Kazin explains that Salinger's popularity is based "on the vast numbers who have been released by our society to think of themselves as endlessly sensitive, spiritually alone, gifted, and whose suffering lies in the narrowing of their consciousness to themselves, in the withdrawal of their curiosity from a society which they think they understand all too well, in the drying up of their hope, their trust, and their wonder at the great world itself." Rpt. in 385, 400, 404, 413.

242. "Keeping Posted: A Thin Slice of College." *Saturday Evening Post*, 15 April 1944, p. 4.

Brief biography to accompany the publication of "Soft-Boiled Sergeant."

243. Keerdoja, E., and P.E. Simons. "Dodger in the Rye." *Newsweek*, 30 July 1979, pp. 11, 13.

The authors report some details of Salinger's reclusive life and an incident in which "a college-age couple waylaid Salinger outside the Windsor post office." He reportedly told them "'not to take anybody's advice, including his, and that it's very important to read.'"

244. Kernan, Alvin B. *The Imaginary Library: An Essay on*

Literature and Society. Princeton: Princeton
University Press, 1982, p. 45.

Kernan mentions "the actual willed disappearance
from any public existence of writers like J.D. Sal-
and Thomas Pynchon."

245. Kleban, Barbara. "Young Writer Brings the World a
        Message from J.D. Salinger: 'Go Away.'" *People*,
        25 February 1980, pp. 43-44.

Kleban recounts the somewhat successful attempts
of Michael Clarkson to interview Salinger.

246. Klein, Marcus. *After Alienation: American Novels in
        Mid-Century*. Cleveland: World Publishing, 1964,
        p. 32.

Klein chose not to examine Salinger in this book:
Salinger "has remarkably little to say"; he "dis-
likes ... the moral complications of real, living
experience."

247. Klinkowitz, Jerome. *Literary Disruptions: The Mak-
        ing of a Post-Contemporary American Fiction*.
        Urbana: University of Illinois Press, 1975, p.
        120; 2nd ed., 1980, p. 120.

Ronald Sukenick, the major character in Ronald
Sukenick's novel *Up*, "is a walking casebook on American Fiction since the war, having the intellect of
a Glass child."

248. ————. *The Practice of Fiction in America: Writers
        from Hawthorne to the Present*. Ames: Iowa State
        University Press, 1980, p. 90.

Claims that Henry Bech of John Updike's *Bech: A
Book* is "an amalgamation of many serious writers
of the time," including J.D. Salinger.

*   Kosner, Edward. "The Private World of J.D. Salin-
        ger." *New York Post: Week-End Magazine*, 30 April
        1961, p. 5.

Cited above as item 171.

249. Kostelanetz, Richard. *The End of Intelligent Writ-
        ing: Literary Politics in America*. New York:
        Sheed and Ward, 1973, pp. 1, 72, 94.

Mentions that *Commentary* often criticized writers like Salinger and that Salinger "owe[s] ...
initial fame to the continuing support of *The New
Yorker*."

250. ————. "The Short Story in Search of Status."
     Twentieth Century, 174 (Autumn 1965), 65-69.

     "The American story of the 1940's--particularly
     those by ... J.D. Salinger [and others] ... --de-
     scend directly from the twenties' story."

251. Krassner, Paul. "The Age of Form Letters." *Realist*,
     February 1960, p. 6.

     Krassner quotes the response received from Gov-
     ernor Rockefeller's secretary when Krassner sent
     Rockefeller a copy of the *Realist* containing part
     of "Salinger's letter, which referred to the plight
     of those sentenced to life terms in New York State
     (and other) prisons." See item 253.

252. ————. "Naked Emperor." *Crawdaddy*, March 1975, p.
     12.

     Krassner, the "Editor and Zen Bastard of *The
     Realist*," writes a letter to Salinger in which he
     thanks him for "the notion that an imaginary friend
     could have more influence than a real person."

253. ————. "What Makes Critics Happy?" *Realist*, Decem-
     ber 1959-January 1960, pp. 5-6.

     Krassner quotes part of a letter to the *New York
     Post* by Salinger, in which he suggests "that when a
     man ... is sentenced to life imprisonment the real
     terms of his sentence ... [should be] pronounced in
     full, for all the world to hear" and insists that
     Governor Rockefeller needs to know "that the New
     York State lifer is one of the most crossed-off,
     man-forsaken men on earth." See item 251.

254. Langenbruch, Theodor. "Goethe and Salinger as Models
     for Ulrich Plenzdorf's Novel *Die neuen Leiden des
     jungen W.*" *Perspectives on Contemporary Litera-
     ture*, 2 (November 1976), 60-70.

     Langenbruch identifies and discusses "specific
     parallels between Plenzdorf and his models Goethe
     and Salinger" and shows that "the wide appeal of
     Plenzdorf's work is largely due to the successful
     artistic combination of diverse literary models,
     notably Goethe and Salinger."

255. Larner, Jeremy. "Salinger's Audience: An Explana-
     tion." *Partisan Review*, 29 (Fall 1962), 594-598.

     Larner renders a negative view of both Salinger
     and his audience. Rpt. in 379.

*   "The Last Published Interview with J.D. Salinger."
       Crawdaddy, March 1975, p. 39.

       Cited above as item 171.

256.   Lewis, R.W.B. "American Letters: A Projection."
       Yale Review, 51 (Winter 1961-1962), 211-226.

       Lewis includes Salinger's name with several
       others "for honor in the postwar generation" of
       writers of fiction.

257.   [Lish, Gordon.] "For Rupert--With No Promises."
       Esquire, 87 (February 1977), 83-87.

       An unsigned story that some mistakenly thought
       Salinger wrote.

258.   Lodge, David. *The Modes of Modern Writing: Metaphor,
       Metonymy, and the Typology of Modern Literature*.
       Ithaca, New York: Cornell University Press, 1979,
       pp. 241-242.

       In a few comments about the identification of
       Buddy Glass with Salinger, Lodge comments that "in
       their play with ideas of illusion, authorship and
       literary convention ... Nabokov and Salinger main-
       tain a precarious poise."

259.   Lydenberg, John. "Cozzens and the Critics." *College
       English*, 19 (December 1957), 99-104.

       Refers to Salinger as "a pedigreed romantic in
       the great American tradition."

260.   Madden, David. *American Dreams, American Nightmares*.
       Carbondale, Illinois: Southern Illinois Univer-
       sity Press, 1970, pp. xxxvi, 54.

       Includes Salinger in a "school of writers ...
       who are always leading up to something that never
       happens, and never can happen ... such writers as
       J.D. Salinger, whose ineffable Glass family has
       moved further and further into Zen mysticism, total
       alienation, abstractedness, and pathology."

261.   Mailer, Norman. "Evaluation: Quick and Expensive
       Comments on the Talent in the Room." In *Adver-
       tisements for Myself*. New York: G.P. Putnam's
       Sons, 1959, pp. 467-468.

       Mailer thinks that his criticism of Salinger
       "may come from nothing more graceful than envy."

262.   Margolis, John D. "The Place of Love in Society:

Salinger's Heroes." *Haverford* [College, Pennsylvania] *News*, 9 February 1962, p. 2.

Margolis writes that "Salinger stands in much the same relation to today's undergraduate as F. Scott Fitzgerald stood to his readers in the 20's"; for Salinger, "one can find meaning only in lovingly relating oneself to other people.

263. Maxwell, William. "J.D. Salinger." *Book-of-the-Month Club News*, July 1951, pp. 5-6.

Maxwell provides a brief biography of Salinger.

264. McCarthy, Colman. "The Limelight Industry." *Washington Post*, 25 January 1979, Sec. A, p. 23, col. 1.

In an article about Salinger's privacy and Americans' desire to know about celebrities, McCarthy calls Salinger "the National Carthusian Hermit."

265. McConnell, Frank D. *Four Postwar American Novelists: Bellow, Mailer, Barth, and Pynchon*. Chicago: University of Chicago Press, 1977, pp. xxv, 159.

Salinger and Pynchon are similar in their "obscurity and anonymity."

266. McDowell, Edwin. "Publishing: Visit with J.D. Salinger." *New York Times*, 11 September 1981, Sec. 3, p. 24.

Report of Betty Eppes' conversation with Salinger, the subsequent publication of the interview (see item 197), and George Plimpton's comments.

267. ———. "The Rumor Mill." *New York Times*, 15 February 1981, Sec. 7, p. 39.

Report of the rumor that Salinger is publishing under the name of William Wharton. The agents of both Wharton and Salinger deny the rumor.

268. Mellard, James M. *The Exploded Form: The Modernist Novel in America*. Urbana: University of Illinois Press, 1980, p. 94.

Mellard lists those writers, including Salinger, studied by Ihab Hassan in *Radical Innocence: The Contemporary American Novel* (1961) and indicates that Salinger and others "would now [be] drop[ped] ... as of minor consequence."

269. Merrill, Robert. *Norman Mailer*. Boston: Twayne, 1978, p. 145.

Mention of Mailer's referring to Salinger as "'no more than the greatest mind ever to stay in prep school.'"

270.   "Mlle Passports." *Mademoiselle*, 25 (May 1947), 34.

To accompany "A Young Girl in 1941 with No Waist at All," this brief biographical statement indicates that "Salinger does not believe in contributors' columns."

271.   "The No-Nonsense Kids." *Time*, 18 November 1957, pp. 51-52, 54.

For the college student of 1957, "the one new American author who has something approaching a universal appeal is J.D. Salinger, with his picture of the tortured process of growing up."

272.   "Notes on People: J.D. Salinger Privately Passes a Milestone." *New York Times*, 1 January 1979, p. 22.

Notice of the sixtieth anniversary of Salinger's birth.

273.   "Personal and Otherwise." *Harper's*, 198 (April 1949), 9-10.

Brief introduction of Salinger to accompany the appearance of "Down at the Dinghy."

274.   Petersen, Clarence. *The Bantam Story*. New York: Bantam, 1970, p. 27; 2nd ed., 1975, p. 27.

Besides indicating that Salinger's four books are in print by Bantam, Petersen mentions that "Bantam has enjoyed ... long and rewarding relationships with some of the best known writers of our time" including Salinger.

275.   Phelps, Robert. "Salinger: A Man of Fierce Privacy." *New York Herald Tribune Books*, 17 September 1961, p. 3.

Brief biography to accompany Phelps' review of *Franny and Zooey* (see item 1050).

276.   Pillsbury, Frederick. "Mysterious J.D. Salinger: The Untold Chapter of the Famous Writer's Years as a Valley Forge Cadet." [Philadelphia] *Sunday Bulletin Magazine*, 29 October 1961, pp. 23-24.

Pillsbury writes about Salinger's connection with the Valley Forge Military Academy: his grades, his

behavior and activities, subsequent correspondence
to and from school officials, Salinger's receiving
the Distinguished Alumni Award, and comments by the
personnel of the school about Salinger. Included
is a copy of the school song, originally "a very
sentimental poem," presumably written by Salinger.

277. Proffer, Carl R. "Preface," "Introduction: American
     Literature in the Soviet Union," "Panova on Sal-
     inger," and "Aksyonov on Salinger." In *Soviet
     Criticism of American Literature in the Sixties*.
     Ed. and Trans. Carl R. Proffer. Ann Arbor, Michi-
     gan: Ardis, 1972, pp. ix-xii, xiii-xxxii, 3, 11.

     Proffer introduces the Russian translations of
     Salinger and the Russian commentators on Salinger.

278. Ray, David. "Editorial X-Rated." *New Letters*, 41
     (Winter 1974), 3-5.

     Ray discusses Salinger's objection to "the un-
     authorized reprint in an offset edition of his un-
     collected stories" and broadens his discussion to
     the problem of University Microfilms "routinely ap-
     propriating the contents of little magazines for
     years."

279. Rodgers, Bernard F., Jr. *Philip Roth*. Boston: Twayne,
     1978, pp. 17, 20.

     Salinger was one of "the more immediate models
     for his [Roth's earlier] fictions," but Salinger
     seems "to have retreated ... into mysticism."

280. Ross, Danforth. *The American Short Story*. Minneap-
     olis: University of Minnesota Press, 1961, pp.
     40-41.

     Salinger is included in a long list of authors
     of "superior stories."

281. Ross, Theodore J. "Notes on J.D. Salinger." *Chicago
     Jewish Forum*, 22 (Winter 1963-1964), 149-153.

     Ross proposed "to consider the stories [Salin-
     ger's fiction] chiefly from the point of view of
     their popular ingredients, giving most attention
     to *Catcher in the Rye*." His conclusion is that
     Salinger's work is not as good as the "hilariously
     solemn 'casebooks' and 'portraits' and 'critiques'--
     all the paraphernalia by which an author is sanc-
     tioned as proper school fare--" would make it seem.

282. Rovit, Earl H. "Bernard Malamud and the Jewish Lit-
     erary Tradition." *Critique*, 3 (Winter-Spring
     1960), 3-10.

54

Secondary Sources

Nathanael West and Salinger "ignore almost entirely the Jewish background, choosing rather to work with an individualized or abstracted framework ... [with] the results ... often undeniably effective, gaining as much in emotional cogency as they lose perhaps in their excessively subjective bases."

283.   "Salinger: An Introduction." *Christian Century*, 27 February 1963, p. 287.

Even though the writer hopes that Salinger will move on to other themes, he still comments favorably: "At his worst and most trivial, Salinger still has more character and skill than almost anyone else around. At his best and most significant, he is more probably than anyone else adding to that deposit by which our time's temper will be judged."

284.   "Salinger Says He's 'Upset.'" *Washington Post*, 4 November 1974, Sec. B, p. 2, col. 3.

Salinger is irritated about the unauthorized publication of *The Complete Short Stories of J.D. Salinger*.

285.   Schrader, Allen. "Emerson to Salinger to Parker." *Saturday Review*, 11 April 1959, pp. 52, 58.

Schrader explains how he came to the realization that "the reading of a work of art--whether Shakespeare, Emerson, Salinger, or 'cool' jazz!--is a highly complex experience, an experience that can't be approached with a mind already cluttered with too many *things in the way*." Rpt. in 428.

286.   Scott, Nathan A., Jr. "Black Literature." In *Harvard Guide to Contemporary American Writing*. Ed. Daniel Hoffman. Cambridge, Massachusetts: Belknap Press, 1979, pp. 287-288.

Scott lists Salinger as one of many Jewish novelists.

287.   Scott, Walter. "Personality Parade." *St. Louis Post-Dispatch Parade*, 23 May 1971, p. 4.

A report that Salinger is working "on a novel, purportedly based on his World War II experiences" and that he has divorced "his English wife, Claire."

288.   [Skow, Jack.] "Sonny: An Introduction." *Time*, 15 September 1961, pp. 84-90.

With a drawing of Salinger on the cover, *Time* magazine presents a summary of *Franny and Zooey*, some biographical material, and a summary of Salinger's fiction. Rpt. in 400, 404.

289. Snow, C.P. "Which Side of the Atlantic?" *Harper's*, 219 (October 1959), 163-166.

Mentions Salinger as possible candidate for one "who, under fifty, is really in a literary sense established."

290. S[proul], K[athleen]. "The Author." *Saturday Review*, 14 July 1951, p. 12.

Brief biographical sketch of Salinger to accompany Harrison Smith's review of *The Catcher*.

291. Stoltz, Craig. "J.D. Salinger's Tribute to Whit Burnett." *Twentieth Century Literature*, 27 (Winter 1981), 325-330.

Stoltz calls attention to Salinger's last published work, "a 500-word piece of prose, 'Epilogue: A Salute to Whit Burnett, 1899-1972,' which appears in the final pages of Whit and Hallie Burnett's *Fiction Writer's Handbook*" (see item 106).

292. Swados, Harvey. "Must Writers Be Characters?" *Saturday Review*, 1 October 1960, pp. 12-14, 50.

Swados claims that Salinger's reputation is based, at least partly, on his personal life: "The legend of mysterious private suffering cohabiting with a singularly Christian literary mortality is self-generating and self-perpetuating; it is also conducive to exalted appraisals of a writer's importance based finally on what must be regarded as extraliterary considerations." Rpt. in 413.

293. Swinton, John. "A Case Study of an 'Academic Bum': Salinger Once Stayed at Ursinus." *Ursinus Weekly*, 12 December 1960, pp. 2, 4.

Mentioning the few known biographical details about Salinger, Swinton treats Salinger, unrecognized by Ursinus as a distinguished former student, as a typical example of the "brilliant student," one "who failed to distinguish ... [himself] academically," one "who forsook the satisfaction of good grades and academic recognition for perhaps a greater enjoyment," a "student who refused to study."

294. Thomas, N.L. "Werther in a New Guise: Ulrich Plenzdorf's *Die neuen Leiden des jungen W.*" *Modern Languages*, 57 (December 1976), 178-182.

"The reader will enjoy the conversational language of the novel and the Salinger-like, amusingly
irreverent style of Wibeau's utterances."

295. Thorp, Willard. "Whit Burnett and *Story* Magazine."
      Princeton University Library Chronicle, 27
      (Autumn 1965), 107-112.

      Mentions that in the newly acquired papers of
      Whit Burnett there are some Salinger letters.

296. Trebbe, Ann L. "Personalities." *Washington Post*, 8
      July 1980, Sec. B, p. 2, col. b.

      Brief summary of Betty Eppes' interview (see
      item 197) with Salinger.

297. Trombetta, Jim. "On the Untimely Demise of J.D.
      Salinger." *Crawdaddy*, March 1975, pp. 34-38.

      Trombetta recounts the difficulties and frustra-
      tions involved in trying to meet and interview Sal-
      inger and an interview Trombetta had with Larry
      Taylor and his wife, neighbors of Salinger. To the
      questions "Why all this isolation? What does it
      mean?" Trombetta suggests three answers: Salinger
      "has 'copped out'"; "paralyzing self-consciousness
      and the rejection of egotism and vanity"; "*Salinger
      is dead* ... an act of spiritual transcendence."

298. Turner, Robert. "the catcher in the wry: through
      j.d. salinger with gun and camera." *Playboy*,
      3 (July 1956), 43-44, 71-72.

      This piece is a parody of Salinger and Holden,
      told by Wally about his brother Otto and Wally's
      escapades in New York City.

299. Unger, Craig. "Salinger Speaks; Still Inscrutable."
      New York, 21 July 1980, p. 11.

      Unger provides a brief summary of Eppes' inter-
      view with Salinger. See item 197.

300. Wakefield, Dan. "The Heavy Hand of College Humor:
      Superman, Sex, and Salinger." *Mademoiselle*, 55
      (August 1962), 288-289, 341-343.

      Wakefield cites Salinger as the "only one new
      hero [who has] implanted himself in the conscious-
      ness of youth as firmly as Superman--a later, more
      sensitive champion of justice"; Salinger's style is
      often parodied in college magazines.

301. Waldmeir, Joseph J. "'Accommodation' in the New

Novel." *University College Quarterly*, 11 (November 1965), 26-32.

Waldmeir suggests that Marcus Klein in *After Alienation* (1964) would have found Mailer, Salinger, Styron, Flannery O'Connor, or Updike "more worthy of his effort than Wright Morris."

302. Walter, Eugene. "A Rainy Afternoon with Truman Capote." *Intro Bulletin*, 2 (December 1957), 1-2.

In mentioning authors who had an influence on him, Capote writes that Salinger "makes an immediate electrical contact."

303. *Washington Post*, 15 October 1974, Sec. B, p. 6, col. 2.

Salinger sues for "$250,000 damages against 17 San Francisco area booksellers" and a man "for selling unauthorized collection of Salinger's early stories."

304. Weatherby, W.J. "J.D." [Manchester] *Guardian*, 15 January 1960, p. 8.

Speculating on the reasons for Salinger's privacy and commenting briefly on some of his works, Weatherby concludes that "Salinger's attitude remains so refreshing at a time when writers are behaving like public relations officers or big business men ... that one can only hope that he will manage to retain his privacy, or at least as much of his as a creative writer can."

305. ————. "The Rejection World." *Twentieth Century*, 170 (Spring 1962), 74-75.

Chronicles Salinger's attempts to put off "the pressure to conform as a Commodity."

306. West, Ray B., Jr. *The Short Story in America 1900-1950*. 1952; rpt. Freeport, New York: Books for Libraries Press, 1968, p. 120.

Mentions Salinger as a regular contributor to the *New Yorker*.

307. Whittemore, Reed. "But Seriously." *Carleton Miscellany*, 3 (Spring 1962), 58-76.

Whittemore refers to Salinger as a writer for the *New Yorker*.

308. Willeford, Charles. "Notes on Beat Writing." *Chicago*

Jewish Forum, 19 (Spring 1961), 234-237.

In general the beat writers are "concerned with a search for meanings for the hurtling pace of our modern existence"; in particular, Salinger "attempts, with considerable skill, to extract every nuance of meaning from every vagrant thought he considers germane to contemporary existence."

309. Williams, Cecil B. "The German Picture of American Literature." *Descant*, 5 (Fall 1960), 33-37.

In 1960, Williams reports that "of recent American novelists, probably Truman Capote, J.D. Salinger, and Jack Kerouac were causing the most excitement."

310. Wilson, John F. "The Step Beyond." *Saturday Review*, 15 August 1959, p. 21.

In responding to Granville Hicks (see item 235), Wilson writes of Salinger that "the really important thing ... is ... that he has the courage and depth to want to evolve into something better."

311. Wilson, Robert A. *Modern Book Collecting*. New York: Alfred A. Knopf, 1980, pp. 88-89.

Wilson mentions that of Salinger's works "only *Catcher in the Rye* and *Nine Stories* are salable" for book collectors. Their rates are lower than what they were earlier.

312. Wright, Austin McGiffert. *The American Short Story in the Twenties*. Chicago: University of Chicago Press, 1961, p. 375.

Salinger and others have attempted "to reinstate the narrator's 'personality' in their stories."

313. "Writers' Writers." *New York Times*, 4 December 1977, Sec. 7, pp. 3, 58, 62, 68, 74.

In a series of comments by authors about a "living author they most admire," Richard Yates cites Salinger as "a man who used language as if it were pure energy beautifully controlled, and who knew exactly what he was doing in every silence as well as in every chord."

314. "Young Authors: Twelve Whose First Novels Make Their Appearance This Fall." *Glamour*, 26 (September 1951), 202-205.

Even though *The Catcher* had appeared earlier in

the year, the article includes a picture and biographical statement about Salinger along with Herbert Gold, Stanley Baron, William Case, Calvin Tom-
kins, David Niven, Wirt Williams, Winston Brebner,
Henry Giles, Benn Sowerby, and William Styron.

b. Letters to Salinger

The materials from *Story* magazine deposited in the
Archives at Princeton University Library (see item 295)
contain twenty-one letters from Whit Burnett, former editor of *Story*, to Salinger. These letters, which cover the
period from 17 January 1940 to 17 April 1965, are listed
below in chronological order. For Salinger's letters to
Burnett, see items 124-159.

315. 17 January 1940

"Belated acknowledgment of the acceptance of
your delightful story, 'The Young Folks,'" for
which Salinger is paid $25.

316. 1 February 1940

Acknowledgment of a "little note" from Salinger
and regret that Burnett and Salinger "won't be getting together for a little while."

317. 5 February 1940

Notice that "'The Young Folks' will appear in
the March-April issue of STORY out February 16,"
that Salinger will receive an advance copy, and a
request for names and addresses of people to whom
Salinger wants an announcement of publication sent.

318. 28 February 1940

Acknowledgment of a note from Salinger and expression of Burnett's desire that the published
story "The Young Folks" "meets well your discrimi-
nating eye" and that Salinger will be able to at-
tend the Writers Club dinner in May.

319. 16 April 1940

Note of rejection of an unidentified story by
Salinger, which Burnett suggests that Salinger
send "to Gingrich of *Esquire*, together with this
letter."

320. 5 September 1940

Acknowledgment that Salinger's check for "The

Young Folks" has been sent belatedly, that Burnett
is "definitely interested in [the novel]," and that
Story just "signed up Frances Eisenberg," someone
who might have been in the short story class with
Salinger.

321. 24 October 1940

Rejection of an unidentified story by Salinger.

322. 16 May 1941

Rejection of an unidentified story by Salinger
and expression of joy that Salinger is "hitting
Esquire."

323. 17 December 1941

Congratulations that Salinger "hit the *New Yorker*" and a request to know if Willets (see item 138)
has "a book that might be interesting to The Story
Press."

324. 1 July 1942

Notice of an enclosed "little note of character
reference" and acknowledgment of receipt of Salinger's "The Long Debut of Lois Taggett," which Burnett "like[s] ... very much" and will try to publish.

325. 16 March 1943

Request for information about "any motion picture
idea that is developable into novella length."

326. 11 May 1943

"Congratulations on the POST successes" and re-
grets that Salinger was not "able to drop in for a
schmoos."

327. 27 July 1943

Acknowledgment of a letter from Salinger and an
apology for being "a hell of a poor correspondent,"
mention of getting a copy of Salinger's "The Varioni
Brothers," and a request from the War Department for
Burnett's "opinion of your discretion, integrity and
loyalty."

328. 8 November 1943

Acknowledgment of a letter from Salinger and expression of delight that Salinger plans to write a
novel.

329. 14 April 1944

Acknowledgment of receipt of Salinger's story "Elaine," expression of gratitude for Salinger's "letter of March 19th ... one of the most interesting I have ever received from an author" and for Salinger's offer to contribute to a "fund for the discovery of new talent among college writers," and congratulations on Salinger's publication of "Soft-Boiled Sergeant," and a proposal that Salinger publish a book of short stories, perhaps to "be called THE YOUNG FOLKS": "All of the people in the book would be young, tough, soft, debutante, social, army, etc. Perhaps the first third of the book would be stories of young people on the eve of the war, the middle third in and around the army and then one or two stories at the close of the war."

330. 19 February 1952

Request, through Salinger's agent, for a submission from Salinger for a forthcoming issue of *Story* "devote[d] to the most outstanding writers who have appeared in STORY" even though it probably will not pay much.

331. 7 November 1959

A long letter informing Salinger of the reinstatement of *Story* magazine and the request to buy ($100 each) two stories that Salinger submitted much earlier to *Story*, which "stand up beautifully over the years": "A Young Man in a Stuffed Shirt" ("one," the editors of *Story* think, "of the best things of its kind we have read") and "The Daughter of the Late, Great Man" ("more like 'Elaine' and 'The Long Debut of Lois Taggett'").

332. 18 November 1959

Note of regret, through Salinger's agent, that at Salinger's request the stories "A Young Man in a Stuffed Shirt" and "The Daughter of the Late, Great Man" are being returned and that Salinger did not send "a little note ... personally."

333. 19 November 1963

Note, through Salinger's agent, that the editors of *Story* request permission to reprint "The Long Debut of Lois Taggett" in the "first big book anthology out of STORY"; handwritten note at the bottom that a negative reply was received 21 November 1963.

334.   5 December 1963

        Another request (see item 332), through Salin-
     ger's agent, "to include 'The Long Debut of Lois
     Taggett' in the first and very likely the last an-
     thology from STORY." Burnett expresses his will-
     ingness to include a statement that Salinger is re-
     luctant to have this printed since it was a very
     early work," to state when it was originally pub-
     lished, assures Salinger that it "would do your
     literary reputation no harm," and appeals to Salin-
     ger on the basis that the inclusion of this story
     might "call attention to the magazine and help its
     continuance."

335.   17 April 1965

        Notice to Salinger, through his agent, that Bur-
     nett has sent Salinger "a copy of Story Jubilee,
     for your personal shelves, wherever you are, with
     my fond affection and my kindest thanks for your
     having written a preface for it" (see item 106),
     which Burnett "felt embarrassed to use"; mention
     that *Story* has ceased publication and that "a num-
     ber of some of your letters from the army days have
     turned up, mis-filed," which "might well work in
     either my own autobiography or something else of
     those days"; a closing comment of praise for Salin-
     ger: "You were a very warm and outgiving [sic] guy
     in those days and it has always been a regret that
     I was in such a reorganizing phase of my own life
     I could not then fully appreciate it."

                    c.   Reference Works

        This subsection is further subdivided into bibliog-
   raphies and all other reference works (handbooks, histories, encyclopedias, etc.). Within each of the categories,
   the entries are listed alphabetically.

(1.) Bibliographies

        Previous Salinger bibliographies range from short
   catalogues of Salinger's works and a list of four or five
   critical works to a master's thesis and a book-length, unannotated bibliography. With the entries arranged alphabetically, the bibliographies listed below include those
   published both individually and as parts of longer works.

336.   Adelman, Irving, and Rita Dworkin. "Salinger, (J)
          erome (D)avid, 1919-." *The Contemporary Novel:
          A Checklist of Critical Literature on the British*

and American Novel Since 1945. Metuchen, New Jersey: Scarecrow Press, 1972, pp. 447-458.

This bibliography is divided into three parts: general, *The Catcher*, and bibliographies.

337. Beebe, Maurice, and Jennifer Sperry. "Criticism of J.D. Salinger: A Selected Checklist." *Modern Fiction Studies*, 12 (Autumn 1966), 377-390.

Although it omits "foreign criticism, unpublished theses or dissertations, transient reviews, and routine discussions in encyclopedias, handbooks, and histories of literature," this is an extensive bibliography divided into two parts: "general studies dealing with Salinger's life and writing" and "discussions of his individual works of fiction."

*   Belcher, William F., and James W. Lee. "Bibliography." *J.D. Salinger and the Critics*. Belmont, California: Wadsworth Publishing, 1962, pp. 172-179.

Belcher and Lee list Salinger's fiction through 1961 and seventy-six items of criticism, with those items annotated for material not included in this collection. Cited below as item 400.

338. Bixby, George. "J.D. Salinger: A Bibliographical Checklist." *American Book Collector*, NS 2 (May-June 1981), 29-32.

"Offering bibliographical information sufficient for accurate identification of the first edition of every title listed," Bixby's checklist of Salinger's works in book form contains "primary publications" and "secondary appearances."

339. Bruccoli, Matthew J., et al. *First Printings of American Authors: Contributions Toward Descriptive Checklists*. Detroit: Gale Research Company, 1977, I, 315.

A list of the first editions of Salinger's four books in both American and English editions, the pirated two-volume edition of Salinger's uncollected short stories (including pictures of the cover of each volume), and R.M. Barrows' *The Kit Book for Soldiers, Sailors, and Marines*, which contains "Salinger's first publication in a book."

340. Davis, Tom. "J.D. Salinger: A Checklist." *Papers of the Bibliographical Society of America*, 53 (January-March 1959), 69-71.

Davis lists Salinger's fiction through 1957 and
seventeen unannotated items of criticism.

341.   Fiene, Donald M. "A Bibliographical Study of J.D.
       Salinger: Life, Work and Reputation." Thesis.
       University of Louisville 1962.

       An extensive annotated bibliography divided into
       three parts: "Bibliography of Biography"; "Bibliog-
       raphy of Fiction: Editions, Translations and Re-
       printings," arranged chronologically; "Bibliography
       of Criticism: Chronologically by Country, According
       to Date of First Publication by Salinger: Alphabet-
       ically within Each Country." Fiene includes numer-
       ous appendices with an "Autobiography of J.D. Sal-
       inger (Illustrated with photographs)," "Photostats
       of Letters and Documents," "College Newspaper Col-
       umns by J.D. Salinger," and several letters. See
       item 342.

342.   ————. "J.D. Salinger: A Bibliography." *Wisconsin
       Studies in Contemporary Literature*, 4 (Winter
       1963), 109-149.

       Fiene's extensive bibliography is divided into
       two parts (I. Works by Salinger: Books, Short Sto-
       ries, and Miscellaneous Publications; II. Works A-
       bout Salinger: Books and Articles in English, Book
       Reviews in English, Criticism and Reviews in Other
       Languages). This bibliography, "an abridged and
       condensed version" of Fiene's master's thesis (see
       item 341), is the first Salinger bibliography to
       contain non-English entries.

*   French, Warren. "Selected Bibliography." *J.D. Sal-
       inger*. New York: Twayne, 1963, pp. 179-186; Rev.
       ed. Boston: G.K. Hall, 1976, pp. 179-186.

       The bibliography in each edition contains both
       primary and secondary sources; the entries for sec-
       ondary sources are briefly annotated. Cited below
       as item 403.

*   Gwynn, Frederick L., and Joseph L. Blotner. "Bib-
       liography." *The Fiction of J.D. Salinger*. Pitts-
       burgh: University of Pittsburgh Press, 1958, pp.
       57-62.

       Gwynn and Blotner chronologically list Salinger's
       fiction and forty-four unannotated items of criti-
       cism. Cited below as item 407.

*   Hamilton, Kenneth. "Selected Bibliography." *J.D.
       Salinger: A Critical Essay*. Grand Rapids, Michi-
       gan: William B. Eerdmans, 1967, pp. 46-47.

Hamilton lists Salinger's publications and nine
unannotated items of criticism. Cited below as
item 408.

*   Laser, Marvin, and Norman Fruman. "A Checklist of
J.D. Salinger's Work." *Studies in J.D. Salinger:
Reviews, Essays, and Critiques of "The Catcher
in the Rye" and Other Fiction*. New York: Odyssey
Press, 1963, pp. 265-266.

Laser and Fruman list Salinger's fiction and no
criticism. Cited below as item 413.

343.   Leary, Lewis. "Salinger, J.D." *Articles on American
Literature 1950-1967*. Durham, North Carolina:
Duke University Press, 1970, pp. 473-478.

An unannotated bibliography of Salinger criticism: 158 items, including several foreign entries.

344.   Leary, Lewis, and John Auchard. "Salinger, J.D."
Articles on American Literature 1968-1975. Durham, North Carolina: Duke University Press, 1979,
pp. 450-452.

An unannotated bibliography of Salinger criticism: 65 items, including several foreign entries.

*   Lettis, Richard. "A Salinger Bibliography." *J.D.
Salinger: "The Catcher in the Rye."* Woodbury,
New York: Barron's Educational Series, 1964,
pp. 44-50.

Lettis lists Salinger's publications chronologically through 1963, reviews of *The Catcher*, and
fifty-five unannotated items of criticism. Cited
below as item 646.

*   Light, James F. "Bibliography." *Salinger's "The
Catcher in the Rye": A Critical Commentary*.
New York: Barrister Publishing, 1966, pp. 68-70.

Light lists Salinger's four books and twenty-
eight unannotated items of criticism. Cited below
as item 647.

*   Lundquist, James. "Bibliography." *J.D. Salinger*.
New York: Frederick Ungar, 1979, pp. 163-184.

Lundquist lists Salinger's fiction and 291 unannotated items of criticism. Cited below as item 414.

345.   Magill, Frank N., ed. "J.D. Salinger." *Magill's
Bibliography of Literary Criticism*. Englewood
Cliffs, New Jersey: Salem Press, 1976, III,
1791-1800.

The 153 unannotated items in this bibliography
are arranged around eight of Salinger's works: *The
Catcher*, "De Daumier-Smith's Blue Period," "For Es-
me--with Love and Squalor," "Franny," "A Perfect Day
for Bananafish," "Raise High the Roof Beam, Carpenters," "Seymour: An Introduction," and "Zooey."
Some items appear in more than one section.

*   Marsden, Malcolm. "Bibliography." *If You Really Want
      to Know: A "Catcher" Casebook*. Chicago: Scott,
      Foresman, 1963, pp. 158-160.

      Marsden lists Salinger's publications through
      1963 and fourteen unannotated items of criticism.
      Cited below as item 415.

*   Miller, James E., Jr. "Selected Bibliography." *J.D.
      Salinger*. Minneapolis: University of Minnesota
      Press, 1965, pp. 46-48.

      Miller lists Salinger's fiction and nine unanno-
      tated items of criticism. Cited below as item 416.

346. Nevius, Blake. "Salinger, J.D. (1919--   )." *The
      American Novel: Sinclair Lewis to the Present*.
      Northbrook, Illinois: AHM Publishing Corpora-
      tion, 1970, pp. 83-85.

      In this bibliography, Nevius lists three Salin-
      ger bibliographies, eight biographical and criti-
      cal books, and forty-eight unannotated entries for
      critical essays.

347. Pownall, David E. "Salinger, Jerome David." *Arti-
      cles on Twentieth Century Literature: An Anno-
      tated Bibliography 1954-1970*. New York: Kraus-
      Thomson Organization, 1978, VI, 3622-3658.

      This bibliography, organized around Salinger's
      work in general and around individual works, con-
      tains 267 annotated items.

*   Simonson, Harold P., and Philip E. Hager. "Sugges-
      tions for Library Work." *Salinger's "Catcher in
      the Rye": Clamor vs. Criticism*. Lexington, Massa-
      chusetts: D.C. Heath, 1967, pp. 110-111.

      Simonson and Hager list critical material by
      topics. Cited below as item 428.

348. Starosciark, Kenneth. *J.D. Salinger: A Thirty-Year
      Bibliography 1938-1968*. St. Paul, Minnesota:
      The Croixide Press, 1971.

      The only published book-length bibliography of

Salinger, Starosciark's work lists both Salinger's
works and criticism in chronological order. Each
of the two major parts of the bibliography has three
subsections: Salinger's material is listed as works,
letters, and unpublished manuscripts, and the criticism is divided into books, pamphlets, special issues; articles, and book reviews. In his introduction, Starosciark mentions that he omits "many book
reviews ... certain articles in foreign periodicals
... dissertations ... [and] except when they seemed
significant, brief references to Salinger in books
and articles.

349. Waldmeir, Joseph J. "J.D. Salinger." In *Recent Amer-
      ican Fiction: Some Critical Views*. Ed. Joseph J.
      Waldmeir. Boston: Houghton Mifflin, 1963, pp.
      287-288.

      A twenty-one item unannotated bibliography.

(2.) Handbooks, Histories, Encyclopedias

     This group of reference works cites works which usual-
ly provide brief biographical material, a survey and summary
of Salinger's works, and sometimes a brief bibliography.
Two reference works included here--*A Library of Literary
Criticism: Modern American Literature* and *Contemporary Literary Criticism: Excerpts from Criticism of Works of Today's
Novelists, Poets, Playwrights, and Other Creative Writers*--
contain short excerpts of previously published criticism.
Each of the excerpts is listed alphabetically by author with
the title and the page numbers on which the excerpts appear
in the reference works and with a cross-reference to the entry elsewhere in the bibliography where the annotation occurs. These entries are arranged alphabetically.

350. Ashley, Leonard R.N. "American Short Fiction in the
      Nineteenth and Twentieth Centuries." In *Critical
      Survey of Short Fiction*. Ed. Frank N. Magill.
      Englewood Cliffs, New Jersey: Salem Press, 1981,
      II, 528-562.

      Even though Salinger earned his reputation for
      The Catcher, "his short stories ... have also gained
      him a devoted following, and inclusion of one of his
      pieces is almost compulsory in textbook anthologies."

351. Boyce, Daniel F. "*The Catcher in the Rye*." In *Survey
      of Contemporary Literature*. Ed. Frank N. Magill.
      Rev. ed. Englewood Cliffs, New Jersey: Salem
      Press, 1977, II, 1121-1124.

      Besides listing the essential facts about *The
      Catcher* and identifying the central characters,

Boyce summarizes the plot, comments on it, and lists
five other commentaries and five reviews.

352.   Bradbury, M.S. "Salinger, J.D." In *Webster's New
       World Companion to English and American Litera-
       ture*. Ed. Arthur Pollard. New York: World Pub-
       lishing, 1973, p. 585.

       One-sentence biography, brief commentary conclud-
       ing that Salinger is "one of postwar America's most
       important writers of fiction," and a list of Salin-
       ger's books.

353.   Burgess, Anthony. "Novel." *The New Encyclopedia
       Britannica: Macropaedia*. 15th ed., XIII, 276-
       299.

       In the subsection on novels of "apprenticeship,"
       Burgess cites *The Catcher*, "which concerns the at-
       tempts of an adolescent American to come to terms
       with the adult world in a series of brief encoun-
       ters," as an example of a novel in which "learning
       ... may go beyond what is narrowly regarded as edu-
       cation."

354.   Burke, W.J., and Will D. Howe. *American Authors and
       Books*. 3rd Rev. ed. New York: Crown Publishers,
       1972, p. 554.

       Lists Salinger's four books.

355.   Cunliffe, Marcus. *The Literature of the United States*.
       Rev. ed. Baltimore, Maryland: Penguin Books, 1961,
       pp. 345-346.

       Cunliffe summarizes the concerns of Salinger's
       fiction and concludes "that he produced a modern ver-
       sion of *Huckleberry Finn* in *Catcher in the Rye*, then
       pyrotechnically fizzled out."

356.   Dekle, Bernard. "J.D. Salinger: Voice of Frustrated
       Youth." *Profiles of Modern American Authors*.
       Rutland, Vermont: Charles E. Tuttle, 1969, pp.
       167-172.

       With a brief sketch of Salinger's life and the
       thesis that Salinger's major topic and also his ap-
       peal to readers is the idea of youth, Dekle concludes
       that Salinger's work "can be read, aside from any
       meaning ... [it] may or may not contain, as sheer
       poetry." Rpt. in 385.

357.   "*Franny and Zooey*." In *Survey of Contemporary Lit-
       erature*. Ed. Frank N. Magill. Rev. ed. Englewood
       Cliffs, New Jersey: Salem Press, 1977, IV, 2767-
       2769.

Besides listing the essential facts about *Franny and Zooey* and identifying the central characters, the commentator summarizes the plot, comments on it ("Strongest ... embodiment thus far of Salinger's interest in the individual's quest for spiritual advancement"), and lists three other commentaries and five reviews.

358. French, Warren. "J.D. Salinger." In *American Novelists Since World War II*. Eds. Jeffrey Helterman and Richard Layman. Detroit: Gale, 1978, pp. 434-444.

French provides biographical details about Salinger, a brief analysis of Salinger's fiction, some comments on Salinger criticism, and a bibliography.

359. ———. "Salinger, ... J.D." *Encyclopedia Americana*, 1981, XXIV, 151.

French provides a cursory survey of Salinger's work and concludes that the later fiction has become "increasingly affected."

360. ———. "Salinger, J(erome) D(avid)." *Great Writers of the English Language: Novelists and Prose Writers*. Eds. James Vinson and D.L. Kirkpatrick. New York: St. Martin's Press, 1979, pp. 1060-1062.

In a typical reference book entry, French provides biographical information, a list of Salinger's books, a brief list of secondary material, and commentary on *The Catcher*, *Nine Stories*, and the "Glass saga" stories.

361. ———. "Salinger, J(erome) D(avid)." In *20th-Century American Literature*. New York: St. Martin's Press, 1980, pp. 509-511.

French provides a biographical statement about Salinger, a list of Salinger's books and books about him, and a brief critical commentary on the corpus of Salinger's fiction.

362. Garber, Eugene K. "Salinger, J.D. (1919-)." *The World Book Encyclopedia*, 1981, XVII, 61.

Garber calls *The Catcher* "a minor classic" and thinks that "of the seven Glass children, Seymour ... best represents the desperate search for lost innocence and the mystic bliss that is glimpsed by Salinger's major fictional characters."

363. G[oldman], A[rnold]. "Salinger, J(erome D(avid) (1919-)." In *The Penguin Companion to Literature*. Eds. Eric Mottram, Malcolm Bradbury, and

Jean Franco. Baltimore, Maryland: Penguin Books,
1971, III, 228.

Brief survey of Salinger's fiction. The commentator notes that "in the Glass family, Salinger has
created an object of almost Janeite interest for
some, while others have found the increasingly el-
liptical and qualificatory manner of writing and
the air of total knowledgeability and of familial
mutual appreciation distasteful."

364. Grigson, Geoffrey. "Salinger, J[erome] D[avid]
      (1919-   )." *The Concise Encyclopedia of World
      Literature*. New York: Hawthorn Books, 1963, pp.
      398-399.

      Brief commentary on Salinger's works, particu-
larly *The Catcher*: "Salinger has a quality of concern which is the moralist's and even the Christian's, but seems no more than an involvement in
freshness, a self-congratulation on the precarious
decencies of the world."

365. Hart, James D. "Salinger, J(erome) D(avid)." *The
      Oxford Companion to American Literature*. 3rd ed.
      New York: Oxford University Press, 1965, p. 738.

      Hart presents a brief descriptive discussion of
Salinger's works.

366. Harte, Barbara, and Carolyn Riley, eds. *200 Contem-
      porary Authors*. Detroit: Gale Research, 1969,
      pp. 237-238; *Contemporary Authors: A Bio-Biblio-
      graphical Guide to Current Authors and Their
      Works*. 1st Rev. Detroit: Gale Research, 1969,
      V-VIII, 997-999.

      Besides listing sources of biographical and crit-
ical information, the editors provide commentary on
Salinger's biography, career, and his writings.

367. Hassan, Ihab. *Contemporary American Literature 1945-
      1972: An Introduction*. New York: Frederick Ungar,
      1973, pp. 42-44, 64, 71, 88.

      Hassan provides brief commentaries on a few sto-
ries, *The Catcher*, and the later Glass stories. He
concludes that Salinger, "parodist of suburbia becomes, like his own character, Seymour Glass, a kind
of holy suicide."

368. ————. "Salinger, Jerome." In *Encyclopedia of World
      Literature in the 20th Century*. Ed. Bernard Wolf-
      gang Fleischmann. New York: Frederick Ungar, 1971,
      III, 224-225.

At the end of a short summary of Salinger's work, Hassan writes that "in his evolution from a satirical toward a religious writer, S[alinger]. shows that his main concern is a kind of love that reaches out to mystical experience but usually falls back to redeem the vulgarity of the world below."

369. Hayashi, Tetsumaro, ed. *A Study Guide to Steinbeck: A Handbook to his Major Works*. Metuchen, New Jersey: Scarecrow Press, 1974, pp. 44, 255, 256.

In study questions and paper topics, parallels are mentioned between Salinger and Steinbeck.

370. Heiney, Donald W. "J.D. Salinger." *Recent American Literature*. Woodbury, New York: Barron's Educational Series, 1958, pp. 281-284, 585.

Intended as a guide for "the student, the teacher, the reviewer, and others whose daily business demands a convenient source of information," Heiney provides commentary on Salinger's reputation, life, chief works and stories, and a brief bibliography.

371. Herzberg, Max J. "Salinger, J[erome] D[avid]." *The Reader's Encyclopedia of American Literature*. New York: Thomas Y. Crowell, 1962, pp. 988-989.

Brief biography and commentary on each of Salinger's then published three books. The commentator feels that "perhaps no other author of so few works has been the subject of so many analyses in the scholarly journals."

372. Hoffman, Hester R. *The Reader's Adviser*. 10th ed. New York: R.R. Bowker, 1964, p. 1133.

Hoffman gives a list of Salinger's books, a brief biography with quotations from the commentators, and a list of books about Salinger. Similar information is given in other editions of this work.

373. Ivask, Ivar, and Gero von Wilpert, eds. *World Literature Since 1945: Critical Survey of the Contemporary Literatures of Europe and the Americas*. New York: Frederick Ungar, 1973, pp. 11-12, 18, 21, 164, 175, 186.

The commentator briefly surveys Salinger's output of fiction and finds that in the course of his writing "sentiment and satire gave way to a sacramental view of existence."

374. Kearns, G.A. "Salinger, Jerome David." In *Cassell's Encyclopedia of World Literature*. Ed. J. Buchanan-

Brown. New York: William Morrow, 1973, III, 455.

Ignoring *Nine Stories*, Kearns lists Salinger's
other works and seven book-length studies of Salinger and comments that Salinger's "characters seek
the presence of grace in life even when they know
the quest is an impossible one."

375. Kunitz, Stanley J., and Vineta Colby, eds. "Salinger, Jerome David (1919-)." *Twentieth Century
Authors*. New York: H.W. Wilson, 1955, pp. 859-
860.

Quotes Salinger's own statement about himself,
William Maxwell's comments on Salinger's method of
writing (see item 263), and part of Eudora Welty's
review of *Nine Stories* (see item 967); lists Salinger's then two published books and three articles
about Salinger's works.

376. McNutt, Robert J. "J.D. Salinger." In *Critical Survey of Short Fiction*. Ed. Frank N. Magill. Englewood Cliffs, New Jersey: Salem Press, 1981, VI,
2175-2181.

After short statements about Salinger's biography,
his influence as a short story writer, and the characteristics of his stories, McNutt concentrates on
an analysis of *Nine Stories*.

377. Miller, James E., Jr. "J.D. Salinger 1919--." In
*American Writers: A Collection of Literary Biog-
raphies*. Ed. Leonard Unger. New York: Charles
Scribner's Sons, 1974, III, 551-574.

Miller concludes his survey of Salinger's fiction
with the statement that "no serious history of post-
World War II American fiction can be written without awarding him a place in the first rank, and even,
perhaps, the pre-eminent position. Included are a
checklist of Salinger's works and a bibliography of
secondary sources.

378. Nyren, Dorothy, ed. "Salinger, J.D. (1919-)." *A
Library of Literary Criticism: Modern Literature*.
New York: Ungar, 1960, pp. 414-416.

A collection of excerpts from previously published
criticism. The excerpts are listed below alphabetically by author with the title of the work and the
page number(s) in Nyren.

*   Baro, Gene. [from] "Some Suave and Impressive
Slices of Life," p. 415. Cited below as item
941.

*   Barr, Donald. [from] "Saints, Pilgrims and Art-
          ists," p. 415. Cited below as item 438.

*   Hicks, Granville. [from] "J.D. Salinger: The
          Search for Wisdom," p. 416. Cited above as item
          235.

*   Kazin, Alfred. [from] "The Alone Generation: A
          Comment on the Fiction of the 'Fifties,'" p. 416.
          Cited above as item 240.

*   Krim, Seymour. [from] "Surface and Substance in
          a Major Talent," pp. 414-415. Cited below as
          item 950.

*   Mizener, Arthur. [from] "The Love Song of J.D.
          Salinger," pp. 415-416. Cited below as item 530.

*   Peden, William. [from] "Esthetics of the Story,"
          p. 414. Cited below as item 956.

*   Stevenson, David L. [from] "J.D. Salinger: The
          Mirror of Crisis," p. 415. Cited below as item
          555.

*   Welty, Eudora. [from] "Threads of Innocence,"
          p. 414. Cited below as item 967.

379.   ————. "Salinger, J.D. (1919-   )." *A Library of
          Literary Criticism: Modern American Literature.*
          3rd ed. New York: Ungar, 1964, pp. 414-416; 582-
          584.

          A collection of excerpts from previously pub-
          lished criticism. This edition contains the same
          excerpts included in the 1960 edition (see item 378)
          and four additional excerpts.

*   Adams, Robert M. [from] "Fashions in Fiction,"
          pp. 583-584. Cited below as item 1076.

*   DeMott, Benjamin. [from] "Dirty Words?" pp. 582-
          583. Cited below as item 465.

*   Fiedler, Leslie A. [from] "Up from Adolescence,"
          p. 583. Cited below as item 1023.

*   Larner, Jeremy. [from] "Salinger's Audience: An
          Explanation," p. 583. Cited above as item 255.

380.   Nyren, Dorothy Curley, Maurice Kramer, and Elaine
          Fralke Kramer, eds. "Salinger, J.D. (1919-   )."
          *A Library of Literary Criticism: Modern American
          Literature.* 4th enl. ed. New York: Ungar, 1969,
          III, 119-125.

A collection of excerpts from previously published criticism. This edition contains the same
excerpts included in the 1960 edition (see item 378)
and the four additional excerpts included in the
1964 edition (see item 379) and six additional excerpts.

*   Baskett, Sam S. [from] "The Splendid/Squalid
     World of J.D. Salinger," p. 123. Cited below
     as item 440.

*   Baumbach, Jonathan, Jr. [from] "The Saint as a
     Young Man: A Reappraisal of *The Catcher in the
     Rye*," p. 124. Cited below as item 659.

*   Chester, Alfred. [from] "Salinger: How to Love
     Without Love," p. 123. Cited below as item 457.

*   Goldstein, Bernice, and Sanford Goldstein. [from]
     "Zen and Salinger," pp. 124-125. Cited below as
     item 478.

*   Harper, Howard M., Jr. [from] *Desperate Faith:
     A Study of Bellow, Salinger, Mailer, Baldwin,
     and Updike*, p. 125. Cited below as item 488.

*   Miller, James E., Jr. [from] *J.D. Salinger*,
     p. 124. Cited below as item 416.

381. ———. "Salinger, J.D. (1919-)." *A Library of
     Literary Criticism: Modern American Literature*.
     Supp. to 4th ed. New York: Ungar, 1976, IV, 415-
     417.

     A collection of excerpts from previously pub-
lished criticism.

*   Coles, Robert. [from] "Reconsideration: J.D.
     Salinger," pp. 416-417. Cited below as item 458.

*   French, Warren. [from] "The Age of Salinger,"
     p. 415. Cited above as item 209.

*   Gross, Theodore L. [from] "Suicide and Survival
     in the Modern World," pp. 415-416. Cited below
     as item 482.

*   Kazin, Alfred. [from] *Bright Book of Life: Ameri-
     can Novelists and Storytellers from Hemingway to
     Mailer*, p. 416. Cited below as item 507.

*   Rupp, Richard H. [from] "J.D. Salinger: A Soli-
     tary Liturgy," p. 415. Cited below as item 542.

382. Ousby, Ian. "J.D. Salinger." *Reader's Guide to Fifty*

American Novels. New York: Barnes and Noble, 1979, pp. 322-329.

Ousby's section on Salinger includes a brief introduction to Salinger's fiction, a plot summary of *The Catcher*, and a summary of "critical commentary" on the novel.

383. Prakken, Sarah L., ed. "Salinger, J(erome) D(avid). 1919-." *The Reader's Adviser: A Layman's Guide to Literature*. 12th ed. New York: R.R. Bowker, 1974, I, 618.

A brief biographical collage from early sources and a list of books both by and about Salinger.

384. R[ichardson], S[allyann]. *Twentieth Century Writing: A Reader's Guide to Contemporary Literature*. Levittown, New York: Transatlantic Arts, 1971, pp. 539-540.

In an introduction to Salinger's work, Richardson erroneously says that Salinger is a college English teacher.

385. Riley, Carolyn, et al., eds. *Contemporary Literary Criticism: Excerpts from Criticism of the Works of Today's Novelists, Poets, Playwrights, and Other Creative Writers*. 22 vols. Detroit, Michigan: Gale Research, 1973-1982.

These volumes constitute "an ongoing 'encyclopedia' of current literary criticism," presenting excerpts of previously published criticism for authors "who are either now living or who have died since January 1, 1960." Volumes 1, 3, 8, and 12 contain excerpts of Salinger criticism. The contents of each volume are listed below alphabetically.

Contents of I (1973), 295-300:

*   Allen, Walter. [from] *The Modern Novel*, p. 298. Cited below as item 864.

*   Baumbach, Jonathan. [from] "The Saint as a Young Man: *The Catcher in the Rye* by J.D. Salinger," p. 299. Cited below as item 659.

*   Burgess, Anthony. [from] *The Novel Now: A Guide to Contemporary Fiction*, pp. 299-300. Cited below as item 672.

*   Dekle, Bernard. [from] "J.D. Salinger: Voice of Frustrated Youth," p. 300. Cited above as item 356.

*   French, Warren. [from] *J.D. Salinger*, pp. 297-298. Cited below as item 403.

*   Geismar, Maxwell. [from] "J.D. Salinger: The Wise Child and the *New Yorker* School of Fiction," p. 295. Cited below as item 472.

*   Green, Martin. [from] *Reappraisals: Some Common-sense Readings in American Literature*, p. 298.

*   Gross, Theodore L. [from] "J.D. Salinger: Suicide and Survival in the Modern World," p. 300. Cited below as item 482.

*   Hassan, Ihab. [from] *Radical Innocence: Studies in the Contemporary American Novel*, p. 296. Cited below as item 492.

*   Kazin, Alfred. [from] "The Alone Generation," pp. 295-296. Cited above as item 240.

*   ————. [from] "J.D. Salinger: 'Everybody's Favorite,'" pp. 296-297. Cited above as item 241.

*   Miller, James E., Jr. [from] *J.D. Salinger*, pp. 298-299. Cited below as item 416.

*   Westbrook, Max. [from] *The Modern American Novel: Essays in Criticism*, p. 299. Cited below as item 569.

*   Wiegand, William. [from] "J.D. Salinger's Seventy-eight Bananas," p. 295. Cited below as item 570.

Contents of III (1975), 444-446:

*   Galloway, David D. [from] *The Absurd Hero in American Fiction*, pp. 445-446. Cited below as item 471.

*   Hall, James. [from] "Play, the Fractured Self, and American Angry Comedy: From Faulkner to Salinger," pp. 444-445. Cited below as item 701.

*   Hassan, Ihab. [from] *The Dismemberment of "Orpheus": Toward a Postmodern Literature*, p. 446. Cited above as item 240.

*   Hyman, Stanley Edgar. [from] "J.D. Salinger's House of Glass," p. 444. Cited below as item 503.

*   Kazin, Alfred. [from] *Bright Book of Life: American Novelists and Storytellers from Hemingway to Mailer*, p. 446. Cited below as item 507.

* McCarthy, Mary. [from] "J.D. Salinger's Closed Circuit," p. 444. Cited below as item 525.

Contents of VIII (1978), 463-465:

* Glasser, William. [from] *The Catcher in the Rye*," pp. 464-465. Cited below as item 696.

* Newlove, Donald. [from] *The Village Voice*, pp. 463-464. Cited below as item 575.

* Roth, Philip. [from] *Reading Myself and Others*, p. 464. Cited below as item 541.

Contents of XII (1980), 496-521:

* Browne, Robert M. [from] "In Defense of Esmé," p. 511. Cited below as item 970.

* DeLuca, Geraldine. [from] *The Lion and the Unicorn*, pp. 517-518. Cited below as item 684.

* Didion, Joan. [from] "Finally (Fashionably) Spurious," pp. 511-512. Cited below as item 1020.

* Fiedler, Leslie. [from] "Up from Adolescence," pp. 512-513. Cited below as item 1023.

* French, Warren. [from] "The Age of Salinger," pp. 514-516. Cited above as item 209.

* Heiserman, Arthur, and James E. Miller, Jr. [from] "J.D. Salinger: Some Crazy Cliff," pp. 496-497. Cited below as item 708.

* Hermann, John. [from] "J.D. Salinger: Hello Hello Hello," pp. 510-511. Cited below as item 985.

* Hicks, Granville. [from] "J.D. Salinger: Search for Wisdom," pp. 502-503. Cited above as item 235.

* Kermode, Frank. [from] "Fit Audience," pp. 497-498. Cited below as item 712.

* Levine, Paul. [from] "J.D. Salinger: The Development of the Misfit Hero," pp. 498-500. Cited below as item 515.

* Lundquist, James. [from] *J.D. Salinger*, pp. 518-521. Cited below as item 414.

* Mizener, Arthur. [from] "The Love Song of J.D. Salinger," pp. 501-502. Cited below as item 530.

*   Ohmann, Carol, and Richard Ohmann. [from] "Reviewers, Critics, and *The Catcher in the Rye*," pp. 516-517. Cited below as item 748.

*   Strauch, Carl F. [from] "Kings in the Back Row: Meaning Through Structure--A Reading of Salinger's 'The Catcher in the Rye,'" pp. 505-510. Cited below as item 771.

*   Updike, John. [from] "Anxious Days for the Glass Family," pp. 513-514. Cited below as item 1059.

*   Wakefield, Dan. [from] "Salinger and the Search for Love," pp. 500-501. Cited below as item 564.

*   Walzer, Michael. [from] "In Place of a Hero," pp. 503-505. Cited below as item 565.

386.   Robinson, William R. "*Raise High the Roof Beam, Carpenters and Seymour: An Introduction.*" In *Survey of Contemporary Literature*. Ed. Frank N. Magill. Rev. ed. Englewood Cliffs, New Jersey: Salem Press, 1977, IX, 6238-6241.

Besides listing the essential facts about *Raise High the Roof Beam, Carpenters and Seymour: An Introduction* and identifying the central characters, Robinson summarizes the plot, comments on it, and lists two other commentaries and six reviews.

387.   "Salinger, J.D." *Academic American Encyclopedia*, XVII, 32.

Brief entry which suggests that "Salinger's popularity with the young is thought to rest in part on the strain of Zen Buddhism in his stories of the Glass family."

388.   "Salinger, Jerome David." *Collier's Encyclopedia*, 1981, XX, 376.

This entry characterizes "Salinger's work ... [as] marked by a profound sense of craftsmanship, a keen ear for dialogue, and a deep awareness of the frustrations of contemporary life in America.

389.   "Salinger ..., Jerome David (1919-)." *Encyclopedia International*, 1976, XVI, 128.

One-paragraph summary of Salinger's works.

390.   "Salinger, J(erome) D(avid)." *The New Encyclopedia Britannica: Micropaedia*, 15th ed, VIII, 811.

General survey "of Salinger's work [which] has

to do with characters who struggle to protect or
regain the honesty and spontaneity of childhood in
a world of adult hypocrisy and conformity."

391. Seymour-Smith, Martin. *Funk & Wagnalls Guide to
     Modern World Literature*. New York: Funk & Wag-
     nalls, 1973, pp. 140-141.

     Praising *The Catcher* as a work which caught "the
     exact tone and flavour of post-war middle-class,
     adolescent alienation," Seymour-Smith finds Salin-
     ger's later works inferior to *The Catcher*: "these
     tend to be cute and to fall back not on any kind of
     mellowness or comprehension of the real nature of
     the world, but on pseudo-religiosity."

392. ————. "Salinger, J.D." *Who's Who in Twentieth
     Century Literature*. New York: Holt, Rinehart and
     Winston, 1976, p. 452.

     Seymour-Smith provides a brief descriptive dis-
     cussion of Salinger's works with the criticism that
     "the Glass family is unreal (possesses no vitality),
     and the writing has become increasingly mystical and,
     in fact, meaningless."

393. ————. "Salinger, J.D." *Novels and Novelists: A
     Guide to the World of Fiction*. New York: St.
     Martin's Press, 1980, pp. 210-211.

     Brief survey of Salinger's fiction: "He is ex-
     ceptionally fluent and elegant, yet he has shown
     great integrity in not publishing what he feels
     does not fulfil his requirements."

394. Spiller, Robert E., et al., eds. *Literary History
     of the United States: History*. 4th ed. rev. New
     York: Macmillan, 1974, pp. 1418, 1462.

     The Catcher is mentioned as a book which "sought
     meaning in the most private gestures of irony, love,
     or rebellion," and Salinger's contribution to Amer-
     ican literature is summarized in one paragraph.

395. Straumann, Heinrich. *American Literature in the
     Twentieth Century*. 3rd rev. ed. New York: Har-
     per & Row, 1965, pp. 125-126.

     The Catcher is a good example of a novel with a
     teenage hero and "light" symbolism.

396. Ward, A.C. "Salinger, J.D." *Longman Companion to
     Twentieth Century Literature*. 2nd ed. London:
     Longman, 1975, p. 472.

Brief biographical information and list of Salinger's major works.

397. Watts, Harold H. "Salinger, J(erome) D(avid)." In
      Contemporary Novelists. Ed. James Vinson. New
      York: St. Martin's Press, 1972, pp. 1086-1088;
      2nd ed., 1976, pp. 1191-1193.

      Brief biography, a list of Salinger's books, and
      a commentary on Salinger's fiction, which for Watts
      "in terms of subject-matter ... falls into two
      groups"--Holden Caulfield and the Glass family.
      "It is undoubtedly the merging of Eastern and West-
      ern religious wisdom--the solution of the 'mystery'
      of existence--that gives the work of Salinger its
      particular elan."

                    d. Book-length Works

      Book-length studies of Salinger fall into three types:
five collections of criticism, six monographs, and two issues of scholarly journals devoted to Salinger. Included
below are reviews of the critical collections and the monographs. Entries for the books provide cross-references to
the appropriate reviews and to the locations where the annotations for the collected materials occur. The reviews
include cross-references to the entries for the books being reviewed. All of the entries are arranged alphabetically.

398. "At-a-Glance." [Review of French's *J.D. Salinger*]
      School Library Journal, 23 (October 1976), 126.

      Three-and-a-half line review of the revised edi-
      tion of French's book and another book. See item
      403.

399. Balbert, Peter. "Configurations of the Ego: Studies
      of Mailer, Roth, and Salinger." [Review of Lund-
      quist's *J.D. Salinger*] *Studies in the Novel*, 12
      (Spring 1980), 73-81.

      In a review of Robert Merrill's *Norman Mailer*,
      Bernard Rodgers' *Philip Roth*, and James Lundquist's
      J.D. Salinger, Balbert finds Lundquist's commentary
      on *The Catcher* "a competent reading," his "analysis
      of *Nine Stories* ... easily the best and most orig-
      inal section," and the "discussion of the longer
      Glass fictions ... not nearly as persuasive as his
      criticism of the earlier." See item 414.

400. Belcher, William F., and James W. Lee, eds. *J.D.
      Salinger and the Critics*. Belmont, California:

Wadsworth Publishing Company, 1962.

Designed for college students writing essays a-
bout Salinger's work, the book contains an introduction to Salinger by Jack Skow and the editors
of *Time* and critical material divided into two sec-
tions--*The Catcher in the Rye* and "The Stories and
General Criticism." The material in Part I, arranged chronologically from 1954 to 1961, shows
developing critical attitudes toward the novel.
The material in Part II, "arranged to point up con-
trasting views," covers Salinger's work in general.
A brief third section includes both possible topics
for essays relevant to the material reprinted in the
collection and a short bibliography with some annotations. For works which are included in this collection in either full form or excerpts, see items
241, 288, 407, 472, 492, 515, 530, 555, 565, 678,
681, 692, 708, 712, 728, 751, 768, 771, 809, 872,
901, 970, and 985. For a review of this collection,
see item 410.

401. Butscher, E. [Review of Lundquist's *J.D. Salinger*]
      Booklist, 1 March 1979, p. 1032.

      Lundquist's book "makes a competent attempt to
      place Salinger's achievement with a firm personal
      and historical context and has the added value of
      stressing the evolutionary aspect of that achieve-
      ment." See item 414.

402. Dempsey, David. "Secret of Seymour and Esmé." [Re-
      view of Grunwald's *Salinger: A Critical and Per-
      sonal Portrait*] *Saturday Review*, 30 June 1962,
      p. 19.

      Dempsey writes that Grunwald's book "foreshadows"
      that as Salinger "moves away from the simple, early
      stories to longer, introspective 'prose home movies'
      ... he will acquire too many 'students of Salinger.'"
      See item 404.

403. French, Warren. *J.D. Salinger*. New York: Twayne,
      1963; Rev. ed. Boston: G.K. Hall, 1976.

      The text of French's work is divided into eleven
      chapters: Salinger's life, a suggestion of a unify-
      ing theme, six chapters on Salinger's short stories,
      one on *The Catcher*, one on the Glass family works,
      and a summary. In both editions, French includes
      a checklist of Salinger's writings and a brief bib-
      liography of criticism. The two editions are es-
      sentially the same except for revisions in the bib-
      liography. French writes that the first edition
      "was to serve parents and teachers especially as

'a guide for those who, bedeviled by the inscruta-
bility of the younger generation are not content
to throw up their hands in despair but wish to understand'" and that the second edition, with minor
corrections, "may now introduce a younger generation to what their parents of the 'silent generation' of the 1950s read with enthusiasm because
they thought Salinger voiced their views of the
'phony' world." Rpt. in 385. For reviews of this
book, see items 398, 406, 419, and 420.

404. Grunwald, Henry Anatole, ed. *Salinger: A Critical
      and Personal Portrait*. New York: Harper & Row,
      1962.

      Grunwald's collection of critical and biographi-
cal materials includes both a lengthy introduction
to the volume and an introduction to each of the
twelve sections. In addition to Grunwald's introduction, the volume contains one previously unpublished essay by a college student. Users of this
book will find a helpful index. For works which
are included in this collection in either full form
or excerpts, see items 235, 241, 288, 407, 438,
466, 472, 480, 492, 504, 513, 530, 554, 555, 564,
570, 571, 678, 708, 872, 950, 1020, 1023, 1034,
and 1059. For the previously unpublished essay,
see item 754. For reviews of this collection, see
items 402, 405, 409, 411, 417, 421, 422, and 423.

405. Gutwillig, Robert. "The Art Is Seen Dimly as a The-
      ory-Riddled Effigy." [Review of Grunwald's *Sal-
      inger: A Critical and Personal Portrait*] *New
      York Times*, 1 July 1962, Sec. 7, pp. 4, 21.

      While praising Salinger, "along with Saul Bellow
and possibly two or three others, [as] one of the
best writers of his generation," Gutwillig finds
Grunwald's collection of articles "a pretty depress-
ing performance." See item 404.

406. Gwynn, Frederick L. [Review of French's *J.D. Salin-
      ger*] *American Literature*, 36 (March 1964), 103.

      "This latest single study of a popular writer is
lively, judicious, and detailed, and as such is not
likely to be replaced until the subject's corpus of
fiction is vastly increased." See item 403.

407. Gwynn, Frederick L., and Joseph L. Blotner. *The
      Fiction of J.D. Salinger*. Pittsburgh: University
      of Pittsburgh Press, 1958.

      In the first monograph about Salinger's fiction,
Gwynn and Blotner discuss Salinger's work in three

chronological periods--"The Apprentice Period"
(1940-1948), "The Classic Period" (1948-1951), and
"Religion Through Satire (1953-1957)--except for
an introductory chapter on "The High Point of Salinger's Art," "For Esmé--with Love and Squalor."
The study includes a checklist of Salinger's fiction and a bibliography of criticism. Rpt. in 400,
404, 413, 415, and 428.

408.   Hamilton, Kenneth. *Jerome David Salinger: A Criti-
       cal Essay*. Grand Rapids, Michigan: Eerdmans,
       1967.

       In a four-chapter pamphlet, which is a part of
       a series entitled "Contemporary Writers in Chris-
       tian Perspective," Hamilton discusses (1) Salinger's
       fascination with "the paradox that nothing fails
       like success or succeeds like failure," (2) the con-
       nections between Salinger's life and his works, (3)
       Salinger writing about love, and (4) the quality of
       Salinger's religious vision.

409.   Hardwick, Elizabeth. "The New Books." [Review of
       Grunwald's *Salinger: A Critical and Personal Por-
       trait*] *Harper's*, 225 (July 1962), 92.

       Praising and criticizing the collection of crit-
       icism, Hardwick feels that Grunwald "does not quite
       seem to understand what the critics of Salinger are
       about" and "does not want to take seriously some of
       the problems represented by Salinger's strange pre-
       sentation of the Glass family." See item 404.

410.   Hill, Hamlin. [Review of Belcher and Lee's *J.D. Sal-
       inger and the Critics*] *College English*, 24 (March
       1963), 491-492.

       "This volume deserves to find a large audience
       in courses using *The Catcher*; it is an excellent
       supplementary volume. I mean, it really is." See
       item 400.

411.   Jackson, Robert B. [Review of Grunwald's *Salinger:
       A Critical and Personal Portrait*] *Library Jour-
       nal*, 1 June 1962, p. 2140.

       The reviewer suggests that "this collection of
       preliminary evaluation and comment should be includ-
       ed in most public library [sic] and all college and
       university literature collections. See item 404.

412.   "J.D. Salinger Number." *Modern Fiction Studies*, 12
       (Autumn 1966), 297-391.

       This collection of seven essays and a bibliography

includes essays on Salinger's fiction in general,
on his stories, and on *The Catcher*. For works
which are included in this issue, see items 337,
434, 478, 543, 677, 897, 974, and 983.

413. Laser, Marvin, and Norman Fruman, eds. *Studies in
       J.D. Salinger: Reviews, Essays, Critiques of
       "The Catcher in the Rye" and Other Fiction*. New
       York: Odyssey Press, 1963.

       With "the primary focus of the book ... on *The
       Catcher in the Rye*," Laser and Fruman have reprinted
       several articles, essentially "in their original
       order of publication," in order for "a reader to
       trace the development of Salinger's reputation, the
       character of the original interest in Salinger among
       critics, and the broadening circle of critical at-
       tention." The editors include "suggested topics
       for writing" both short and long papers and a check-
       list of Salinger's fiction. For works which are in-
       cluded in this collection in either full form or ex-
       cerpts, see items 183, 235, 241, 292, 407, 462, 472,
       492, 525, 530, 554, 564, 566, 571, 678, 699, 708,
       712, 771, 809, 848, 863, 872, 877, 878, 899, 901,
       970, 985, 1020, 1023, 1041, and 1059.

414. Lundquist, James. *J.D. Salinger*. New York: Ungar,
       1979.

       As one in the series of Modern Literature Mono-
       graphs, Lundquist's study examines Salinger's fic-
       tion in four phases, which parallel the first four
       chapters in Lundquist's book: (1) "His early sto-
       ries generally portray characters who feel estranged
       and marooned because of World War II"; (2) "*The
       Catcher in the Rye* and Salinger's attempt ... to
       deal with estrangement and isolation through a Zen-
       inspired awakening and lonely benevolence"; (3)
       "*Nine Stories* ... bringing together the principles
       of Zen art and the tradition of the short story";
       (4) "Salinger's work becomes more and more experi-
       mental, resulting in the philosophical mood of his
       last two books." A fifth and final chapter consid-
       ers the development of Salinger's "patterns" of
       writing. Lundquist includes an unannotated but ex-
       tensive bibliography. Rpt. in 385. For reviews of
       this book, see items 399, 401, and 424.

415. Marsden, Malcolm, ed. *If You Really Want to Know:
       A "Catcher" Casebook*. Chicago: Scott, Foresman,
       1963.

       Marsden's casebook is divided into four sections:
       book reviews of *The Catcher*, articles presenting
       "conflicting views of Holden," materials about "the

craft of J.D. Salinger," and comparisons between
Salinger's work and Twain's. This volume includes
thirty-five study questions and a list of Salinger's
publications and a brief bibliography of material not
included in this book. For works which are included
in this collection in either full form or excerpts,
see items 407, 438, 472, 492, 513, 515, 525, 554,
555, 564, 570, 591, 597, 606, 609, 613, 615, 617,
628, 629, 661, 678, 682, 685, 692, 708, 711, 723,
728, 731, 751, 768, 771, 809, 863, 872, 899, 901,
and 935.

416. Miller, James E., Jr. *J.D. Salinger*. Minneapolis:
University of Minnesota Press, 1965.

In one of the series of University of Minnesota
Pamphlets on American Writers, Miller presents forty-
five pages of commentary on the corpus of Salinger's
fiction and provides a short bibliography. Miller
concludes that "no serious history of post-World
War II American fiction can be written without a-
warding him a place in the first rank, and even,
perhaps, the pre-eminent position." Rpt. in 380
and 385. For reviews of this book, see items 425
and 427.

417. Morton, Robert. [Review of Grunwald's *Salinger: A
Critical and Personal Portrait*] *Show*, 2 (August
1962), 95.

The reviewer wonders if criticism slows Salinger
up, "what Mr. G.'s motivation could be in collecting so much of it in one easily accessible place."
See item 404.

418. Peterson, Clair. "Editor's Choice." [Review of Rosen's *Zen in the Art of J.D. Salinger*] *Books
West*, 1 (October 1977), 39.

Brief mention of publication of Rosen's study of
Salinger. See item 426.

419. [Review of French's *J.D. Salinger*] *Choice*, 13 (September 1976), 821.

These "191 pages of bland and sometimes superficial commentary" are "a non-revision"; there is
no need to replace the first edition. See item
403.

420. ———. *Library Journal*, 15 June 1964, p. 2674.

Calling French's book a "critical, sometimes
carping study" that discusses "Salinger's worlds
of the 'phony' and the 'nice,'" the reviewer grants

that "the insights into Salinger's philosophy, popularity, and purpose seem valid." See item 403.

421. [Review of Grunwald's *Salinger: A Critical and Per-
      sonal Portrait*] *Christian Science Monitor*, 5
      July 1962, p. 11.

      Mention of the publication of Grunwald's book.
      See item 404.

422. ————. *Kirkus*, 15 April 1962, p. 415.

      Grunwald's book, "a handbook for his [Salinger's]
      cult, for literature studies and classes ... will
      be of interest in its current comprehensive cover-
      age." See item 404.

423. ————. *Library Journal*, 15 September 1962, p. 3216.

      The reviewer recommends this book, but criticizes
      its lack of balance in selections and warns teachers
      that students who read the critical essays will not
      need to read Salinger. See item 404.

424. [Review of Lundquist's *J.D. Salinger*] *Choice*, 16
      (September 1979), 834.

      The reviewer criticizes Lundquist's book for its
      out-of-date biographical material and its reliance
      on "Alan Watts as a key commentator on Zen." The
      book is valuable for "accurate plot summaries of
      difficult-to-find early stories" and for review of
      "critical reception." See item 414.

425. [Review of Miller's *J.D. Salinger*] *Choice*, 3 (May
      1966), 210.

      This "short but most useful [book] to undergrad-
      uates" is "responsive both to Salinger's mystic
      tendency and to his rejection of much of 20th-cen-
      tury American culture." See item 416.

426. Rosen, Gerald. *Zen in the Art of J.D. Salinger.*
      Berkeley: Creative Arts Book Company, 1977.

      The title of Rosen's work explains the topic of
      his fifty-page work, which he concludes as follows:
      "Ultimately, the problems faced by Holden and the
      Glass children have no 'answer' that *we* can hold on
      to. But we must be careful not to ask Salinger (or
      anyone else) to provide us with this illusory 'an-
      swer.'" For a review of this book, see item 418.

427. Russell, H.K. [Review of Miller's *J.D. Salinger*]
      South Atlantic Quarterly, 66 (Spring 1967), 275-
      278.

In a review of several of the University of Minnesota Pamphlets on American Writers, Russell says
that "Miller writes an accurate and valuable criti-
que of Salinger's masterpieces." See item 416.

428. Simonson, Harold P., and Philip E. Hager, eds. *Sal-
    inger's "Catcher in the Rye": Clamor vs. Criti-
    cism*. Lexington, Massachusetts: D.C. Heath, 1963.

As the title of this collection of essays suggests, the editors divide the material into two
groups--the clamor and the criticism, the latter
"subdivided into sections representing typical critical approaches"--the text, psychological approach,
socio-literary American tradition, and the author
on the literary scene. The material within each
section is presented chronologically. At the end
of the volume appears a bibliography arranged around
specific topics: reviews, censorship and controversy,
biographical information on Salinger, humor, adoles-
ence, psychological and sociological approaches, and
"Salinger as an author on the contemporary literary
scene." For works which are included in this collection in either full form or excerpts, see items
235, 285, 407, 438, 445, 609, 613, 628, 661, 678,
708, 723, 728, 731, 732, 751, 759, 768, 771, 809,
819, 820, 822, 824, 831, 837, 849, 853, 863, 869,
872, 878, and 901. This collection includes a portion of an article not printed elsewhere (see item
733).

429. "Special Number: Salinger." *Wisconsin Studies in
    Contemporary Literature*, 4 (Winter 1963), 5-149.

Except for two book reviews, this issue is devoted entirely to ten pieces about Salinger's work.
For works which are included in this issue, see
items 342, 440, 442, 463, 470, 489, 545, 557, 992,
and 1104.

e. References, Articles, Chapters

The criticism cited in this subsection includes studies of Salinger's fiction in general, studies of more than
one of Salinger's specific works--for example, similar
themes in *The Catcher* and *Nine Stories*; examination of
works which concern the Glass family--and brief summarizing comments about Salinger's fiction. All entries appear
alphabetically.

430. Ahrne, Marianne. "Experience and Attitude in *The
    Catcher in the Rye* and *Nine Stories* by J.D. Sal-
    inger." *Moderna Språk*, 61, No. 3 (1967), 242-263.

Ahrne writes that *The Catcher* has the same theme
as all of Salinger's fiction: love ("of mankind,
resulting in a specific, personal gesture") and
squalor ("the mundane, the petty, the mendacious");
in *Nine Stories*, Salinger finds the "answers to the
conflicts in which his characters are involved ...
[in] Eastern religion and mysticism."

431.   Aksynov, V[asily]. "An Unusual American." In *Soviet
       Criticism of American Literature in the Sixties*.
       Ed. and Trans. Carl R. Proffer. Ann Arbor, Michi-
       gan: Ardis, 1972, pp. 12-14.

       In a somewhat rambling commentary on Salinger's
       works, Aksynov contrasts Hemingway and Salinger and
       concludes that Salinger "is a real American writer
       of our time, an unusual American."

432.   Alsen, Eberhard. "The Role of Vedanta Hinduism in
       Salinger's Seymour Novel." *Renascence*, 33 (Win-
       ter 1981), 99-116.

       "Seymour's teachings reflect those of the *Bhaga-
       vad Gita*," Alsen explains, and the Glass stories
       are "seen as an exposition of and a commentary on
       the teachings of Vedanta Hinduism."

433.   ————. "Seymour: A Chronology." *English Record*,
       29 (Fall 1978), 28-30.

       In order to interpret Seymour's character, Alsen
       lists in chronological order the events in Seymour's
       life (1917-1948); this chronology shows, according
       to Alsen, that Seymour "was a near-saint only in
       his youth and that he deteriorated spiritually as
       he reached adulthood."

434.   Antico, John. "The Parody of J.D. Salinger: Esmé
       and the Fat Lady Exposed." *Modern Fiction Stud-
       ies*, 12 (Autumn 1966), 325-340.

       Antico's purpose is "to show that the usual in-
       terpretations [of "For Esmé--with Love and Squalor"
       and "Zooey"] do not do full justice to the art of
       J.D. Salinger"--more specifically, that his stories
       "can best be appreciated as irony and parody"; "'For
       Esmé' is a parody of the typical war story"; "the
       Fat Lady speech in 'Zooey' is not intended seriously
       but as an absurdity which awakens Franny's 'third
       eye' and makes her *see*."

435.   Avni, Abraham. "The Influence of the Bible on Amer-
       ican Literature: A Review of Research from 1955
       to 1965." *Bulletin of Bibliography*, 27 (October-
       December 1970), 101-106.

Lists and annotates Hamilton's study of the influence of the Bible on Salinger (see item 485).

436. Balakian, Nona. "The Prophetic Vogue of the Antiheroine." *Southwest Review*, 47 (Spring 1962), 134-141.

Modern "anti-heroines" of writers like Salinger and others display a contrast of what is and what ought to be the relationship of men and women.

437. Barr, Donald. "Ah, Buddy: Salinger." In *The Creative Present: Notes on Contemporary American Fiction*. 2nd ed. Eds. Nona Balakian and Charles Simmons. New York: Gordian Press, 1973, pp. 27-62.

Barr investigates "Salinger and his audiences" and concludes that "for nearly ten years he has been writing for an audience of converts."

438. ————. "Saints, Pilgrims and Artists." *Commonweal*, 25 October 1957, pp. 88-90; rpt. *On Contemporary Literature*. Ed. Richard Kostelanetz. New York: Avon Books, 1964, pp. 537-543.

Barr, viewing Salinger's career in three phases, comments that the personality of each of Salinger's characters "is always at grips with a problem which is almost too strong for it. The problem is always love." Rpt. in 378, 404, 415, and 428.

439. ————. "The Talent of J.D. Salinger." *Commonweal*, 30 October 1959, pp. 165, 167.

Barr calls Salinger "one of the most powerful talents now practicing the short story."

440. Baskett, Sam S. "The Splendid / Squalid World of J.D. Salinger." *Wisconsin Studies in Contemporary Literature*, 4 (Winter 1963), 48-61.

"Even if no more is forthcoming," Baskett defends Salinger's fiction of the Glass family because, "as they now stand the Glass family stories represent an exciting and original attempt to deal with the American experience as the several protagonists enact in a specifically American context and what Wallace Stevens expresses as 'The poem of the mind in the act of finding / What will suffice.'" Rpt. in 380.

441. Bellman, Samuel Irving. "New Light on Seymour's Suicide: Salinger's 'Hapworth 16, 1924.'" *Studies in Short Fiction*, 3 (Spring 1966), 348-351.

After recounting the usual explanations of Seymour

Glass' suicide in "A Perfect Day for Bananafish"
with references to "Seymour: An Introduction," Bellman explains that Salinger's "Hapworth 16, 1924"
offers another explanation.

442.   Blotner, Joseph L. "Salinger Now: An Appraisal."
       Wisconsin Studies in Contemporary Literature,
       4 (Winter 1963), 100-108.

       Reviewing Salinger's works and the criticism of
them, Blotner wishes "almost for a moratorium now
on Salinger criticism as well as for evidence that
this gifted writer has assimilated the influences
which have both informed and swamped his later work,
evidence that he is ready to break through from a
minor phase to a major one." He further wishes
that more critical attention might be paid "to Nathanael West and W.C. Williams, to Conrad Aiken and
E.E. Cummings."

443.   Booth, Wayne C. "Distance and Point-of-View: An
       Essay in Classification." *Essays in Criticism*,
       11 (January 1961), 60-79; rpt. *The Rhetoric of
       Fiction*. Chicago: University of Chicago Press,
       1961, pp. 66, 155, 171, 213, 287; rpt. *The Novel:
       Modern Essays in Criticism*. Ed. Robert Murray
       Davis. Englewood Cliffs, New Jersey: Prentice-
       Hall, 1969, pp. 172-191.

       Booth makes the following references to Salinger:
concerning authors' objectivity, Booth quotes Sal-
inger--"An ecstatically happy prose writer ... can't
be moderate or temperate or brief ... He can't be
detached"; mentions the narrator of *The Catcher* as
one who is aware of himself as a writer; refers the
reader to Salinger's "Zooey" "for other narrative
uses of what Salinger's narrator calls 'the aesthetic evil of a footnote'"; points out that "many more
mature readers have found themselves feeling" the
way Holden did about calling an author whose work
"really knocks ... [you] out"; mentions Salinger in
a lament that there is "no careful study of the many
kinds of quest-novels."

444.   Bostwick, Sally. "Reality, Compassion, and Mysticism
       in the World of J.D. Salinger." *Midwest Review*,
       5 (1963), 30-43.

       In a detailed discussion of Salinger's works,
Bostwick calls him "one of the more dazzling satirical stylists of the day, whose presentation of the
profound and the shallow, the ugly and the sublime,
and the schism between ideals and actions, place[s]
him in the top rank of American moderns."

445.   Bowen, Robert O. "The Salinger Syndrome: Charity
       Against Whom?" *Ramparts*, 1 (May 1962), 52-60.

       Bowen characterizes "Salinger's fiction ... [as]
       catty and snide and bigotted in the most thorough
       sense" and calls for "those of us who are Christian
       and who love life [to] lay the book aside as the
       weapon of an enemy." Rpt. in 428.

446.   Bowen, Robert O., Warren Hinckle, and Edward M.
       Keating. "A Symposium on J.D. Salinger." *Ram-
       parts*, 1 (May 1962), 47-66.

       A collection of three articles, one by each of
       the above authors. See items 445, 499, and 508.

447.   Breslow, Paul. "The Support of the Mysteries: A
       Look at the Literary Prophets of the Beat Mid-
       dle Class." *Studies on the Left*, 1 (Fall 1959),
       15-28.

       In a section subtitled "The Message of Compro-
       mise," Breslow reads *The Catcher* "as a beat alle-
       gory of the middle-class American reconciling him-
       self to a non-sensical existence"; Breslow comments
       briefly on other Salinger fiction.

448.   Browning, Preston M., Jr. "Flannery O'Connor and
       the Grotesque Recovery of the Holy." In *Adver-
       sity and Grace*. Ed. Nathan A. Scott, Jr. Chi-
       cago: University of Chicago Press, 1968, pp. 133-
       161.

       Even though O'Connor writes about adolescents,
       her work does not have "that seemingly narcissistic
       preoccupation with adolescence" found in Salinger
       and John Updike.

449.   Bryan, James E. "J.D. Salinger: The Fat Lady and
       the Chicken Sandwich." *College English*, 23 (De-
       cember 1961), 226-229.

       Bryan relates the stories of the Glass family
       to those in *Nine Stories*: the Fat Lady in "Zooey"
       and the chicken sandwich in "Just Before the War
       with the Eskimos" are Christian symbols.

450.   ―――――. "Salinger's Seymour's Suicide." *College
       English*. 24 (December 1962), 226-229.

       Bryan compares Seymour's "symptoms" to other Sal-
       inger characters and concludes that "whether his
       suicide represents abject defeat or a limited vic-
       tory, a salvaging of something in escaping from
       'the Fedder's fetters' to the next generation, can-
       not yet be determined."

451. Bufithis, Philip. "J.D. Salinger and the Psychia-
      trist." *West Virginia University Bulletin: Phil-
      ological Papers*, 21 (December 1974), 67-77.

      Bufithis' thesis is that "the primary themes in
      the novels of such widely diverse writers as Vladi-
      mir Nabokov, William Burroughs, J.D. Salinger [*The
      Catcher*, "Franny," "Raise High the Roof Beam, Car-
      penters," "Zooey," and "Seymour: An Introduction"],
      Saul Bellow, Norman Mailer, John Barth, James Purdy,
      and Ken Kesey are embodied in the protagonist-psy-
      chiatrist relationship." In the Glass stories,
      "Salinger has expressed the belief that American
      society is looking in the wrong direction--that the
      artist, not the psychiatrist, can truly tell us who
      and what we are."

452. Burgess, Anthony. "The Postwar American Novel: A
      View from the Periphery." *American Scholar*, 35
      (Winter 1965-66), 150, 152, 154, 156.

      "For Esmé--with Love and Squalor" adumbrates
      the "theme of innocence"; *The Catcher* was impor-
      tant because "it gave us a dialect of candid and
      innocent protest," but as Salinger writes the
      Glass stories, Burgess wonders "how genuine Holden
      is."

453. Burnett, Hallie, and Whit Burnett. *Fiction Writer's
      Handbook*. New York: Harper and Row, 1975, pp.
      10, 11, 65, 71, 105, 129-130, 134; rpt. Barnes
      and Noble, 1979.

      Among the several references to Salinger, the
      Burnetts comment on Salinger's characterization
      and titles: "J.D. Salinger created characters so
      completely visual that one critic stated he had to
      distrust Salinger the man, because if his charact-
      ers were *not* real, in the sense of having actual
      birth certificates and Social Security numbers,
      then what sort of liar was Salinger that he made us
      believe in them so profoundly?" For titles, "Sal-
      inger started with the most obvious, and to our
      minds the most successful."

454. Bury, Richard. "Salinger." *Books and Bookmen*, 7
      (June 1962), 8.

      Bury notes Salinger's desire for privacy, sum-
      marizes his biography, and concludes that Salin-
      ger's writing is more "romantic" and "sentimental"
      than "realistic": "the most significant thing about
      Salinger's heroes and heroines is that they *are*
      good people and that, in contrast to most contemp-
      orary fiction characters, they are full of hope and
      optimism for the future."

455. Cecile, Sister Marie, S.S.J. "J.D. Salinger's Circle
     of Privacy." *Catholic World*, 194 (February 1962),
     296-301.

     With comment on pertinent parts of Salinger's
     fiction, Sister Cecile discusses Salinger's with-
     drawal and privacy" as "the key to peace and the key
     to Salinger's thinking."

456. "The Characteristic Form: A Distinct Predilection
     for the Short Story." *Times Literary Supplement*,
     6 November 1959, p. xv.

     "Salinger's stories seem to be a series of nar-
     rations on a theme from *Hamlet*--'whether 'tis bet-
     ter in the mind to suffer.'"

457. Chester, Alfred. "Salinger: How to Love Without
     Love." *Commentary*, 35 (June 1963), 467-474.

     Chester criticizes Salinger's early works for
     being shallow and dated and judges his later works
     on the basis of Salinger's technique of contrast in
     characterization. Rpt. in 380.

458. Coles, Robert. "Reconsideration: J.D. Salinger."
     New Republic, 28 April 1973, pp. 30-32.

     In 1973, Coles, reconsidering *The Catcher* and
     Franny and Zooey, "wonder[s] once more how to do
     justice to his [Salinger's] sensibility: his wide
     and generous responsiveness to religious and phil-
     osophical ideas, his capacity to evoke the most
     poignant of human circumstances vividly and honestly,
     and with a rare kind of humor, both gentle and teas-
     ing." Rpt. in 381.

459. Cotter, James Finn. "Religious Symbols in Salinger's
     Shorter Fiction." *Studies in Short Fiction*, 15
     (Spring 1978), 121-132.

     Cotter investigates "the way in which Salinger
     employs three symbols--the Fat Lady, the glass, and
     the ashtray--to support his theistic vision, ex-
     pressed by Teddy in the last of the *Nine Stories*."

460. Cowie, Alexander. *American Writers Today*. Stock-
     holm: Radiotjänst, 1956, pp. 156-165.

     In a brief introduction to Salinger's writing,
     Cowie explains that in *The Catcher*, Salinger of-
     fers "an unflinching examination of that murky,
     potentially-explosive isthmus between childhood
     and maturity known as adolescence" and in *Nine Sto-
     ries*, "Salinger specializes in precocious, unpre-
     dictable juvenile characters who alternate in

behavior between the innocently angelic and the innocently diabolical." Cowie includes an excerpt
from *The Catcher* of Holden with the prostitute.

461. Cowley, Malcolm. "American Myths, Old and New."
       Saturday Review, 1 September 1962, pp. 6-8, 47.

       Reference to "Salinger's troubled adolescents in
       a world where every mature person is a phony."

462. Davis, Tom. "J.D. Salinger: The Identity of Sergeant
       X." *Western Humanities Review*, 16 (Spring 1962),
       181-183.

       Davis identifies Sergeant X as Seymour Glass.
       See items 549 and 560.

463. ————. "J.D. Salinger: 'The Sound of One Hand Clap-
       ping.'" *Wisconsin Studies in Contemporary Lit-
       erature*, 4 (Winter 1963), 41-47.

       Davis' purpose in this essay is "to discuss the
       two central aspects of Zen thought, and to show,
       by contrasting 'For Esmé--with Love and Squalor'
       with 'Zooey' that Salinger is deeply--perhaps harm-
       fully--influenced by Zen."

464. Deer, Irving, and John H. Randall, III. "J.D. Sal-
       inger and the Reality Beyond Words." *Lock Haven
       Review*, No. 6 (1964), 14-29.

       For "Holden Caulfield, Franny Glass, Sergeant X,
       de Daumier-Smith, and the Chief in 'The Laughing Man'
       ... their greatest aim is to achieve a communion be-
       yond language, a reality beyond words."

465. DeMott, Benjamin. "Dirty Words?" *Hudson Review*, 18
       (Spring 1965), 31-44; rpt. *You Don't Say*. New
       York: Harcourt, Brace and World, 1965; rpt. *The
       American Novel Since World War II*. Ed. Marcus
       Klein. Greenwich, Connecticut: Fawcett, 1969,
       pp. 210-223.

       DeMott compares Iris Murdoch's theme in *Under
       the Net* with that of Salinger's fiction: "the theme
       of silence as both strategy and therapy--the one
       means by which writers can effect the emasculation
       of their oppressors and the restoration of their
       own potency." Rpt. in 379.

466. Fiedler, Leslie A. "The Eye of Innocence: Some Notes
       on the Role of the Child in Literature." In *No!
       in Thunder: Essays on Myth and Literature*. Bos-
       ton: Beacon Press, 1960, pp. 172, 251-291.

Fiedler makes passing references to Salinger and repeats the articles from *The New Leader* (see items 688, 977, and 978). Rpt. in 404.

467. ————. *Love and Death in the American Novel*. New York: Criterion, 1960; Rev. ed. New York: Stein and Day, 1966, pp. 289-290, 333.

Salinger's works contain examples of the "Good Good Girl": Phoebe, Esmé, and Sybil.

468. Finkelstein, Sidney. *Existentialism and Alienation in American Literature*. New York: International Publishers, 1965, pp. 219-234.

Besides commenting that the alienation in Salinger's work has its "roots ... in present-day society, and the alienation is between one entire generation and another," Finkelstein discusses the Zen Buddhism in the Glass family stories.

469. Flaker, Aleksandar. "Salinger's Model in East European Prose." In *Fiction and Drama in Eastern and Southeastern Europe: Evolution and Experiment in the Postwar Period*. Eds. Henrik Birnbaum and Thomas Eekman. Columbus, Ohio: Slavica Publishers, 1980, pp. 151-160.

Flaker's purpose is to explore "some features of Salinger's work that are also found in the works of Central and East European authors."

470. French, Warren. "The Phony World and the Nice World." *Wisconsin Studies in Contemporary Literature*, 4 (Winter 1963), 21-30.

French uses Salinger's "Uncle Wiggily in Connecticut" as the "central document that provides a focal point from which the others may be viewed." In this story, he finds the "basic concepts of the perishability of the 'nice' world and the 'phoniness' of the persisting world provide ... the warp on which Salinger subsequently weaves in *The Catcher in the Rye* and the stories of the Glass family the intricate, colorful patterns devised by a craftsman's fancy."

471. Galloway, David D. *The Absurd Hero in American Fiction: Updike, Styron, Bellow, Salinger*. Austin: University of Texas Press, 1966; Rev. ed., 1970; 2nd rev. ed., 1981.

Salinger examines what "is perhaps the most acute problem of our age": "to act with morality and love in a universe in which God is dead (or, at least,

in which historical preconceptions of God frequently
seem invalid)." Salinger's fiction shows a "pro-
gression from early stories in which the misfit hero
can find genuine love only in children to the later
stories in which mysticism is rejected in favor of
an absurd love stance." Each of Galloway's editions
contains a bibliography. Rpt. in 385.

472. Geismar, Maxwell. "J.D. Salinger: The Wise Child
      and the *New Yorker* School of Fiction." In *Amer-
      ican Moderns: From Rebellion to Conformity*. Ed.
      Maxwell Geismar. New York: Hill and Wang, 1958,
      pp. 195-209.

      Salinger, like other *New Yorker* writers, writes
      about a "pre-Edenite community of yearned-for bliss,
      where knowledge is again the serpent of all evil:
      but a false and precocious show of knowledge, to be
      sure, which elevated without emancipating its in-
      nocent and often touching little victims." Rpt.
      in 385, 400, 404, and 415.

473. Geller, Bob. "'Dear Benjamin.'" *English Journal*,
      58 (March 1969), 423-425.

      Geller contrasts Salinger's Holden, Seymour and
      Buddy Glass, Sergeant X, and Franny with Ben in
      The Graduate.

474. Giles, Barbara. "The Lonely War of J.D. Salinger."
      Mainstream, 12 (February 1959), 2-13.

      Giles criticizes Salinger because "Holden has
      still to discover that to care nothing at all about
      the approbation of one's fellowmen is itself a form
      of vanity" and because "such sublimity as the Glass-
      es achieve, cut off from the living tissue of human
      relationships, is as suspect as the armor on any
      Hollywood knight."

475. Glazier, Lyle. "The Glass Family Saga: Argument
      and Epiphany." *College English*, 27 (December
      1965), 248-251.

      Glazier regards "the poetic epiphany ... [as]
      the soul of Salinger's excellence, for Salinger like
      Seymour is essentially a poet."

476. Goldhurst, William. "The Hyphenated Ham Sandwich of
      Ernest Hemingway and J.D. Salinger." In *Fitzger-
      ald/Hemingway Annual 1970*. Eds. Matthew J. Bruc-
      coli and C.E. Frazer Clark, Jr. Washington, D.C.:
      NCR/Microcard Eds., 1970, pp. 136-150.

      Goldhurst examines the interrelationships of

influence of Twain, Hemingway, and Salinger, specifically "that the Saga of the Salinger hero is a
latter-day recapitulation of the adventures of Nick
Adams."

477. Goldstein, Bernice, and Sanford Goldstein. "Some
      Zen References in Salinger." *Literature East and
      West*, 15, No. 1 (1971), 83-95.

      In contrast to their earlier article (see item
      478), the Goldsteins in this piece "take a much
      more specific look at Salinger's compiling of and/
      or awareness of Zen materials and their application
      in his stories" and illustrate that his "use of Zen
      and related Eastern experience ... cannot be dis-
      missed as pedantic and obtrusive, but emerges ...
      as a driving force behind much of his writing, be-
      hind the conflict and tension and partial enlighten-
      ment of his Glass children."

478. ———. "Zen and Salinger." *Modern Fiction Studies*,
      12 (Autumn 1966), 313-324.

      In a brief survey of some of Salinger's major
      works, the Goldsteins suggest that "the importance
      of the present moment, the long search and struggle
      in which reason, logic, cleverness, and intellect
      prove ineffectual; the inadequacy of judgment and
      criticism which reinforce and stimulate the arti-
      ficial boundary between self and other; and some de-
      gree of enlightenment which results from the non-
      rational and spontaneous blending of dualities, an
      enlightenment which permits experience that is com-
      plete and unadulterated and makes the moment and,
      in effect, life non-phoney--all these aspects of
      Zen can be found in Salinger's world." See item
      477. Rpt. in 380.

479. Green, Martin Burgess. "American Rococo: Salinger
      and Nabokov." In *Re-Appraisals: Some Common-
      Sense Readings in American Literature*. New York:
      Norton, 1965, pp. 211-229.

      Labeling it "rococo realism," Green describes
      Salinger's writing as "characterized by its exuber-
      ant and recondite vocabulary, highly literary and
      highly technical ... lavish of foreign phrases,
      commercial terms, academic turns of speech ... e-
      laborate, sometimes formal in its phrasing and
      sentence-structure, but far from pompous." Rpt. in
      385.

480. ———. "Cultural Images in England and America."
      In *A Mirror for Anglo-Saxons*. Ed. Martin Burgess
      Green. New York: Harper and Brothers, 1960, pp.
      85-88.

Salinger "passes every test the reader's mind
imposes, and enters it deeply enough to act upon
the faculties of self-creation. The more you read
him, the more original you find his meanings; the
more he points out to you what you had not seen in
your daily life, the finer and more vital his taste
and tact are, the more exciting his intelligence
and his complex tension of values." Rpt. in 558.

481.   ————. "*Franny and Zooey*." In *Re-Appraisals: Some
        Common-Sense Readings in American Literature*.
        New York: Norton, 1965, pp. 197-210.

After comparing the reception of Salinger and
D.H. Lawrence, Green concludes that in their "au-
tonomy, independent life, power to outreach ...
[their] creator," Holden and Zooey are superior to
Tolstoy's Kostya Levin and Pierre Bezukhov.

482.   Gross, Theodore L. "J.D. Salinger: Suicide and Sur-
        vival in the Modern World." *South Atlantic Quar-
        terly*, 68 (Autumn 1969), 454-462; rpt. *Represen-
        tative Men: Cult Heroes of Our Time*. Ed. Theo-
        dore L. Gross. New York: Free Press, 1970, pp.
        230-239; rpt. *The Heroic Ideal in American Lit-
        erature*. New York: Free Press, 1971, pp. 262-
        271.

Gross examines the reasons Salinger "has interested and often obsessed more readers than any other
serious American author since the Second World War,
why he has been, as Mailer himself admits, 'everybody's favorite.'" Rpt. in 381 and 385.

483.   ————. "Literature." In *Representative Men: Cult
        Heroes of Our Time*. Ed. Theodore L. Gross. New
        York: Free Press, 1970, pp. 212-213.

"Each of them [Norman Mailer, J.D. Salinger,
Robert Lowell, Allen Ginsberg, and Edward Albee]
... has been particularly concerned with the central issue of our time: the conflict between human
possibility and institutional power, between hope
and violence, between idealism and authority."

484.   Hamilton, Kenneth. "J.D. Salinger's Happy Family."
        Queen's Quarterly, 71 (Summer 1964), 176-187.

For Hamilton, Salinger preaches "in a hundred
different ways" that the Glasses "are a happy family." That preaching, Hamilton suggests, is becoming tiring and ineffective.

485.   ————. "One Way to Use the Bible: The Example of
        J.D. Salinger." *Christian Scholar*, 47 (Fall 1964),
        243-251.

Taking up what he sees ás a "neglected aspect"
of Salinger, Hamilton believes "that Salinger uses
the Bible ... as a mirror to reflect light derived
from other sources."

486. Handy, William J. *Modern Fiction: A Formalist Ap-
      proach*. Carbondale, Illinois: Southern Illinois
      University Press, 1971, pp. 119-120, 128.

"For Hemingway, man's problem was how to main-
tain a stoic self-discipline in a world which was
ultimately malevolent," Handy writes, "but for Salinger, Bellow, and Malamud ... the problem ... [was]
the individual's determination to discover, amid a
welter of inner as well as outer determining forces,
a self which could be accepted and affirmed."

487. Harmon, William. "'Anti-Fiction' in American Humor."
      In *The Comic Imagination in American Literature*.
      Ed. Louis D. Rubin, Jr. New Brunswick, New Jer-
      sey: Rutgers University Press, 1973, pp. 373-
      384.

Harmon mentions that in Salinger often times
"there is patently some sort of 'fiction' but not
very much to satisfy an old-fashioned ordinary concept of 'story.'" In "Hapworth 16, 1924," Salinger
uses a narrator conscious of himself as writer.

488. Harper, Howard M., Jr. "J.D. Salinger--Through the
      Glasses Darkly." In *Desperate Faith: A Study of
      Bellow, Salinger, Mailer, Baldwin, and Updike*.
      Chapel Hill: University of North Carolina Press,
      1967, pp. 65-95.

In a discussion of *The Catcher*, *Nine Stories*, and
the Glass family stories, Harper finds Salinger,
despite opinion to the contrary, a major writer with
"a rich comic sense, his vision ... of the utmost
seriousness." Rpt. in 380.

489. Hassan, Ihab H. "Almost the Voice of Silence: The
      Later Novelettes of J.D. Salinger." *Wisconsin
      Studies in Contemporary Literature*, 4 (Winter
      1963), 5-20.

Hassan writes that Salinger's "Raise High the Roof
Beam, Carpenters," "Zooey," and "Seymour: An Introduction" display a "sur-real" form, which "makes use
of all the resources of language, including accident
or distortion, to convey an unmediated vision of
reality." In Salinger's fiction, we hear "the voice
of steadfast love struggling with the locutions of
art--the sacred and the profane intermingling--and
making itself audible in new ways."

490.   ————. "The Character of Post-War Fiction in Ameri-
        ca." *English Journal*, 51 (January 1962), 1-8.

        Hassan uses Salinger's works as examples and
        says that *The Catcher* "is perhaps the classic of
        post-war fiction."

491.   ————. "The Idea of Adolescence in American Fic-
        tion." *American Quarterly*, 10 (Fall 1958), 312-
        324.

        In *The Catcher* and *Nine Stories*, "the image of
        adolescence throws a new light on that perennial
        conflict between the self and the world to which
        Freud assigned a decisive role in any culture."

492.   ————. "Rare Quixotic Gesture: The Fiction of J.D.
        Salinger." *Western Review*, 21 (Summer 1957),
        261-280; rpt. *Radical Innocence: Studies in the
        Contemporary American Novel*. Princeton, New Jer-
        sey: Princeton University Press, 1961, pp. 259-
        289.

        In a five-part discussion of several of Salin-
        ger's works, Hassan writes that when Salinger recon-
        ciles "the redeeming powers of outrage and compas-
        sion," he comes through as "an American poet, his
        thin and intelligent face all but lost among the
        countless faces of the modern city, his vision, for-
        ever lonely and responsive, troubled by the dream of
        innocence and riddled by the presence of both love
        and of squalor. What saves Salinger's vision from
        sentimentality is the knowledge ... that no man can
        give an object more tenderness than God accords it."
        Rpt. in 385, 400, 404, 413, and 415.

493.   Hayes, Ann L. "J.D. Salinger: A Reputation and a
        Promise." In *Lectures on Modern Novelists*. Ed.
        A. Fred Sochatoff, Beckman W. Cottrell, and Ann
        L. Hayes. Pittsburgh: Carnegie Institute of Tech-
        nology, 1963, pp. 15-24.

        At the end of a review of Salinger's published
        fiction, Hayes ponders the possibility of Salinger's
        "find[ing] the full statement of what the world of
        the Glass family is, the full statement of what all
        the parts mean ... how it is possible not only to
        be oneself, but to live in the world with others."

494.   Hendin, Josephine. "Experimental Fiction." In *Har-
        vard Guide to Contemporary American Writing*. Ed.
        Daniel Hoffman. Cambridge, Massachusetts: Belk-
        nap Press, 1979, pp. 243, 269-270.

        According to Hendin, "Salinger's men are too

good for this world. These blessed boys cannot
grow up; if they do they kill themselves; if they
marry they often find death is preferable. They
yearn, as Holden longs for Allie, for the life before puberty, before responsibility."

495. ————. *Vulnerable People: A View of American Fiction Since 1945*. New York: Oxford University
Press, 1978, pp. 113-115.

In a chapter entitled "The Victim Is a Hero,"
Hendin comments that "Salinger's gentle, brilliant
boys [Holden Caulfield and Seymour Glass] cannot
grow up: if they do, they die. If they marry, they
can keep their specialness only by suicide. In
death they remain ideals of tenderness, sweetness,
unworldliness."

496. Herndl, George C. "Golding and Salinger: A Clear
Choice." *Wiseman Review*, No. 502 (1964), 309-
322.

Lord of the Flies "exposes ... the inescapable
or 'natural' sanctions of an historically accreted
and inherited civility, of the 'artificially' struc-
tured community, as the only milieu in which man
creates his humanity"; in contrast, "Salinger exposes springs of evil not in man but in urban soci-
ety--in the city."

497. Hicks, Granville. "The Quest in a Quiet Time." *Saturday Review*, 28 November 1959, p. 20.

Reference to Salinger: "With J.D. Salinger ...
the search for love merges with the search for wisdom."

498. Hinchliffe, Arnold P. *The Absurd*. London: Methuen,
1974, p. 96.

Brief reference to Galloway's work (see item
471), which examines "four examples (Updike, Styron, Saul Bellow, and J.D. Salinger) of *optimistic*
chroniclers of the Absurd, who share a belief that
man can establish values in an Absurdist world."

499. Hinckle, Warren. "J.D. Salinger's Glass Menagerie."
Ramparts, 1 (May 1962), 48-51.

Hinckle finds "a consistent strain of anguish
running through Salinger's fiction" and concludes
that in the Glass stories "Salinger has ... begun
to pick apart the callouses of our emotionally sub-
erized society."

500. Hipkiss, Robert A. *Jack Kerouac, Prophet of the New*

Romanticism: A Critical Study of the Published
Works of Kerouac and a Comparison of Them to
Those of J.D. Salinger, James Purdy, John Knowles,
and Ken Kesey. Lawrence, Kansas: The Regents
Press of Kansas, 1976, pp. 97-105, passim.

Generally, Salinger's characters are concerned
with *caritas* ... a deeply felt, honest expression
of responsibility"; Kerouac's "characters are generally too self-concerned, too inward in their experience of life, to really feel responsibility for
other specific people for more than a few fleeting
moments."

501.   Hoffman, Frederick J. *The Modern Novel in America*.
       Chicago: Henry Regnery, 1951, pp. 233-234.

       While remarking in a footnote that *The Catcher*
       is "a 'minor classic,'" Hoffman nevertheless writes
       that "Salinger's fiction ... is beginning to seem
       as tedious as the persons Salinger wishes to cari-
       cature actually are."

502.   Howe, Irving. "The Salinger Cult." In *Celebrations*
       and Attacks: Thirty Years of Literary and Cul-
       tural Commentary. New York: Horizon Press, 1979,
       pp. 93-96.

       "As the priest of an underground cult," Salin-
       ger, Howe writes, portrays characters of "inner
       emigration." Howe praises Salinger for his person-
       al privacy.

503.   Hyman, Stanley Edgar. "J.D. Salinger's House of
       Glass." *Standards: A Chronicle of Books of Our*
       Time. New York: Horizon Press, 1966, pp. 123-
       127.

       Calling Salinger "the most talented fiction writ-
       er in America," Hyman criticizes "the direction Sal-
       inger's writing has taken in the Glass stories."
       Rpt. in 385.

504.   Jacobsen, Josephine. "The Felicity of J.D. Salinger."
       Commonweal, 26 February 1960, pp. 589-591.

       Salinger's work needs to be studied carefully
       because he creates characters who are "sensitive to
       suffering and forms of evil ... [but he] can recur
       to the clear note of joy, and sustain it." Rpt. in
       404.

505.   Jessey, Cornelia. "Creative Fulfillment." *Critic*,
       22 (October-November 1963), 24-31.

Jessey sees Salinger's characters as "modern pilgrims [who] are not only lost in a maze of paths and
do not know where they are, they do not know where
they came from, where they were before they got lost,
and are confused about where they are going." As a
result, they "look for an Emergency Station": Holden
cannot find one; Franny and Zooey find it "right in
the heart of the family."

506. Karlstetter, Klaus. "J.D. Salinger, R.W. Emerson
     and the Perennial Philosophy." *Moderna Språk*,
     63, No. 3 (1969), 224-236.

     Reacting to what he calls the critics' lack of
     a "clear definition of the pattern beneath Salin-
     ger's work or of the way in which Salinger fits into
     the stream of American literature," Karlstetter
     demonstrates that Salinger's life and "philosophy
     of life" are similar to those of Emerson and Tho-
     reau and that Salinger "explores a problem of global
     and cosmic significance: Man's search for the ex-
     istence of a universal truth."

507. Kazin, Alfred. *Bright Book of Life: American Novel-
     ists and Storytellers from Hemingway to Mailer*.
     Boston: Little, Brown, 1973, pp. 114-119, passim.

     "Salinger's Holy [Glass] Family stand out from
     the great mass of unvalued, unregarded and unde-
     scribed individuals in contemporary fiction. *His*
     people will last." Rpt. in 381 and 385.

508. Keating, Edward M. "Salinger: The Murky Mirror."
     Ramparts, 1 (May 1962), 61-66.

     After mentioning the difficulties involved in
     the study of Salinger, Keating examines Salinger's
     works and finds that Salinger causes pain because
     he presents "ourselves and our values, ourselves
     and our failings, ourselves and our responsibili-
     ties."

509. Kinney, Arthur F. "J.D. Salinger and the Search
     for Love." *Texas Studies in Literature and Lang-
     uage*, 5 (Spring 1963), 111-126.

     "Salinger's greatest achievement so far," Kinney
     writes, "is 'For Esmé--with Love and Squalor'"; in
     The Catcher, Salinger "established love as a saving
     grace in a society of convention, immorality, phoni-
     ness."

510. Krassner, Paul. "An Impolite Interview with Alan
     Watts." *Realist*, December 1960-January 1961,
     pp. 1, 8-11.

Watts says that the members of Salinger's Glass
family are his "kind of people" and that in Salinger's writing "Christ is always the unexpected reve-
lation of the divine where you didn't think you'd
find it."

511. Lakin, R.D. "D.W.'s: The Displaced Writer in Ameri-
      ca." *Midwest Quarterly*, 4 (Summer 1963), 295-
      303.

      Salinger creates "a *world*, however precarious,
      for his characters to inhabit," and "he provides a
      more coherent view of our world than most of the
      competition."

512. Leer, Norman. "Escape and Confrontation in the Short
      Stories of Philip Roth." *Christian Scholar*, 49
      (Summer 1966), 132-146.

      Roth thinks that "the suicide of Seymour Glass
      and the madness of Holden Caulfield ... become the
      ultimate forms of escape."

513. Leitch, David. "The Salinger Myth." *Twentieth Cen-
      tury*, 168 (November 1960), 428-435.

      Leitch discusses Salinger's appeal to his read-
      ers: "the idea of the unfallen preadolescent";
      "while the beats express their revolt dramatically,
      so that all the squares in the world can see, the
      whimsical rebels for whom Salinger writes will be
      content to live theirs in a mental world of escape
      and disaffiliation." Rpt. in 404 and 415.

514. Levin, Beatrice. "Everybody's Favorite: Concepts of
      Love in the Work of J.D. Salinger." *Motive*, 22
      (October 1961), 9-11.

      Quoting Archibald MacLeish's statement "The crime
      against life, the worst of all crimes, is NOT to
      feel," Levin examines Salinger's works and concludes
      that "Salinger has told us what it is to suffer from
      lack of love and the inability to express love ...
      warning us against the pretenses of affection ...
      asking US to *feel*."

515. Levine, Paul. "J.D. Salinger: The Development of
      the Misfit Hero." *Twentieth Century Literature*,
      4 (October 1958), 92-99.

      Salinger's heroes are "a reflection of a moral
      code arising out of a cult of innocence, love, al-
      ienation, and finally redemption." In addition to
      "Raise High the Roof Beam, Carpenters," "Zooey,"
      and some of the stories later included in *Nine*

Stories, Levine uses several early, uncollected stories to show how Salinger's "heroes form a particularly adolescent troupe of spiritual non-conformists,
though-minded and fragile, humorous and heartbreak-
ing," who face "the most significant and complex
moral problems we face today." Rpt. in 385, 400,
and 415.

516. Livingston, James T. "J.D. Salinger: The Artist's
      Struggle to Stand on Holy Ground." In *Adversity
      and Grace*. Ed. Nathan A. Scott, Jr. Chicago:
      University of Chicago Press, 1968, pp. 113-132.

      As an artist, Salinger "manages to make us see
      beyond the natural object--the enamel basins, the
      broken watch, Holden's red hunting hat, the chick-
      en soup, the Fat Lady--to sacred presences."

517. Lodge, David. "Family Romances." *Times Literary Sup-
      plement*, 13 June 1975, p. 642.

      Ascribing "economy, the delicacy, the artful mim-
      icry, the tenderly ironic domesticity, the goddam
      reticence ... of vintage Salinger" to his early sto-
      ries, Lodge notes similarities between Salinger's
      uncollected stories and his later, better known
      works and prefers Salinger's work to that of the
      present.

518. ———. *The Novelist at the Crossroads and Other
      Essays on Fiction and Criticism*. Ithaca, New
      York: Cornell University Press, 1971, pp. 17,
      23-24.

      Lodge lists parallels between "Salinger's Glass
      stories" and *Tristram Shandy*.

519. Lorch, Thomas M. "J.D. Salinger: The Artist, the
      Audience, and the Popular Arts." *South Dakota
      Review*, 5 (Winter 1967-1968), 3-13.

      Lorch claims that because Salinger has "deeply
      ambivalent feelings about his audience ... it seems
      likely that Salinger will continue to produce in-
      ferior work."

520. Lowrey, Burling. "Salinger and the House of Glass."
      New Republic, 26 October 1959, pp. 23-24.

      Criticizes Salinger for his in-depth investiga-
      tion of the Glass family: "Seymour" is "a crashing
      bore."

521. Malin, Irving. *New American Gothic*. Carbondale, Il-
      linois: Southern Illinois University Press, 1962,
      passim.

Malin makes many references to Salinger's works.
He stresses that Seymour Glass' first name is more
important symbolically than his last in that "in
every story this saint *sees* things in a new way."

522.   Martin, Augustine. "A Note on J.D. Salinger." *Stud-*
        ies: An Irish Quarterly Review, 48 (Autumn 1959),
        336-345.

        In a commentary on *The Catcher* and the British
        edition of *Nine Stories*, Martin concludes that these
        two books by Salinger "affirm in profane terms of
        their environment that there is in man something
        godlike, an innocence that is indestructible, and
        that this innocence is just as real as sin."

523.   Matthews, James F. "J.D. Salinger: An Appraisal."
        University of Virginia Magazine, 1 (Spring 1956),
        52-60.

        Commenting on both the strengths and defects in
        Salinger's writing, Matthews finds a universal theme:
        "the protagonists of all of Salinger's stories are
        thoughtful and sensitive, misunderstood by this world
        of materialism and convention, a world into which
        they don't quite fit, but in some way transcend in
        their insight into and rebellion against it."

524.   May, Keith M. "Attack on the Unconscious: Sartre
        and the Post-War American Novel." In *Out of the*
        Maelstrom: Psychology and the Novel in the Twen-
        tieth Century. New York: St. Martin's Press,
        1977, pp. 78-97.

        May calls Holden Caulfield "an existential hero
        in embryo" and sees "Franny Glass ... in a position
        not unlike Holden Caulfield's."

525.   McCarthy, Mary. "J.D. Salinger's Closed Circuit."
        Harper's, 225 (October 1962), 46-48; rpt. *The*
        Writing on the Wall and Other Literary Essays.
        New York: Harcourt, Brace and World, 1970, pp.
        35-41.

        With "a good deal of natural style, a cruel ear,
        a dislike of ideas (the enemy's intelligence sys-
        tem), a toilsome simplicity, and a ventriloquist's
        knack of disguising his voice," Salinger may be "a
        fake." Rpt. in 385, 413, and 415.

526.   McSweeney, Kerry. "Salinger Revisited." *Critical*
        Survey, 20 (Spring 1978), 61-68.

        For McSweeney, *Nine Stories* contains "profession-
        al pieces of work, textbook examples of the short-

story form," and *The Catcher* "belong[s] on permanent
display in the gallery of classic American fiction."

527. Miller, James E., Jr. *Quests Surd and Absurd: Essays
       in American Literature*. Chicago: University of
       Chicago Press, 1967.

       Besides reprinting his essay written with Arthur
       Heiserman, "J.D. Salinger: Some Crazy Cliff" (see
       item 708), Miller mentions Salinger several times:
       Sergeant X, Holden Caulfield, Franny, Zooey, and
       Buddy Glass, "although suffering from acute spiri-
       tual nausea ... (unlike Seymour Glass) make some
       kind of separate peace with themselves and with the
       world"; Salinger, Flannery O'Connor and John Updike
       are "religious writers" with "some measure of af-
       firmation ... expressed in some kind of spiritually
       transcendental terms, however vague or faint"; *The
       Catcher* is a book "in which an episode of crucial
       seriousness is alleviated--or intensified--by a
       comic mode"; Salinger is one of four (Flannery O'Con-
       nor, Saul Bellow, and Wright Morris) who "have made
       serious claims for some kind of permanent recogni-
       tion"; Faulkner praised *The Catcher* "as the 'best
       one' he had read."

528. Milton, John R. "The American Novel: The Search for
       Home, Tradition, and Identity." *Western Humani-
       ties Review*, 16 (Spring 1962), 169-180.

       James Farrell and Salinger present "a typical
       American experience ... a houselessness within a
       house."

529. Mizener, Arthur. "The American Hero as Poet: Sey-
       mour Glass." In *The Sense of Life in the Modern
       Novel*. Boston: Houghton Mifflin, 1964, pp. 227-
       246.

       "Salinger's vision of the heroic life ... con-
       sists in a struggle that ... American heroes have
       been going through for the last hundred years of
       our literature."

530. ————. "The Love Song of J.D. Salinger." *Harper's*,
       218 (February 1959), 83-90.

       Even though there are "certain limitations--both
       of subject matter and of technique--" in Salinger's
       fiction, "Salinger's achievement is not that he has
       grasped an abstract idea of American experience,
       important as that idea may be in itself; it is that
       he has seen this idea working in the actual life of
       our times, in our habitual activities, in the very
       turns of our speech, and has found a way to make us

see it there, too." Rpt. in 378, 385, 400, 404,
and 413.

531. Murphy, Carol. "Some Last Puritans." *Approach*, No.
         53 (Fall 1964), 38-43.

         Murphy sees a similarity between the Glass fam-
      ily and Oliver Arlen from George Santayana's *The
      Last Puritan*.

532. Noland, Richard W. "The Novel of Personal Formula:
         J.D. Salinger." *University Review*, 33 (Autumn
         1966), 19-24.

         Looking at Salinger's work embodying "a very
      definite world view," Noland concludes that "Sal-
      inger's place in the history of the American novel
      is not at all assured" because "he must either ac-
      cept the material which is offered him by life, or
      he must successfully embody his mystical vision in
      an as yet unachieved form, a form which is by no
      means certain to fiction."

533. O'Connor, Frank. *The Lonely Voice: A Study of the
         Short Story*. Cleveland: World Publishing, 1962,
         pp. 23, 42-45.

         O'Connor dubs Salinger "the most typical of mod-
      ern American storytellers" because "though his
      theme is still human loneliness the loneliness is
      specific instead of generalized."

534. Oldsey, Bernard. "Salinger and Golding: Resurrec-
         tion or Repose." *College Literature*, 6 (Spring
         1979), 136-144.

         Oldsey recounts the fact that Salinger and Gold-
      ing were once "overvalued"; he now fears that "we
      may overreact and undervalue their work." Their
      works (*The Catcher, Nine Stories; Lord of the Flies,
      The Inheritors*) "deserve ... to be re-read and of-
      fered to a new generation of college students who
      can help us decide the case for resurrection or re-
      pose."

535. Padovano, Anthony T. *The Estranged God: Modern Man's
         Search for Belief*. New York: Sheed and Ward,
         1966, pp. 138-149, 154, 157-159.

         Besides a brief contrast of the views of Salin-
      ger and Golding toward evil, Padovano discusses *The
      Catcher* and *Franny and Zooey* and sees Salinger's
      "predominant, if not exclusive theme ... [as] the
      human need for innocence and sincerity."

536.   Peden, William. *The American Short Story: Continu-
       ity and Change 1940-1975*. Boston: Houghton Miff-
       lin, 1975, pp. 13, 19, 53, 123-124, 153.

       Peden compares Salinger's Glass family to "Faulk-
       ner's Snopeses or Compsons and Hemingway's Nick Ad-
       ams and Salinger's own Holden Caulfield ... [as]
       part of our national mythology"; all of Peden's com-
       ments about Salinger's fiction are positive.

537.   ————. *The American Short Story: Front Line in the
       National Defense of Literature*. Boston: Houghton
       Mifflin, 1964, passim.

       With comments on several of Salinger's stories,
       Peden describes Salinger's fiction as "frequently
       threatened by a curious kind of shadowy, lurking
       tendency toward cuteness."

538.   Rees, Richard. "The Salinger Situation." In *Con-
       temporary American Novelists*. Ed. Henry T. Moore.
       Carbondale, Illinois: Southern Illinois Univer-
       sity Press, 1964, pp. 95-105.

       Rees refutes "the criticism of Salinger ... but-
       ton-holing the reader and enticing him into a cosy
       club of tender and sympathetic souls who see them-
       selves as the only 'real' people in a world full of
       pathetic phoneys, or as human beings among a herd
       of pachyderms."

539.   Romano, John. "Salinger Was Playing Our Song." *New
       York Times Book Review*, 3 June 1979, pp. 11,
       48-49.

       Trying to ignore "our careless, unrecast affec-
       tion" for Salinger, Romano examines Salinger's
       works from a fresh point of view to determine the
       quality of his work and finds, among other positive
       conclusions, that the children in Salinger are "a-
       mong the few unmistakably genius-made literary crea-
       tures of our time."

540.   Rot, Sandor. "J.D. Salinger's Oeuvre in the Light of
       Decoding Stylistics and Information-Theory."
       Studies in English and American, 4 (1978), 85-
       129.

       Rot's essay claims "to give an objective and im-
       partial assessment to the real value of" Salinger's
       works by examining them with "decoding stylistics
       and the theory of information."

541.   Roth, Philip. "Writing American Fiction." *Commen-
       tary*, 31 (March 1961), 223-233; rpt. *The American*

Novel Since World War II. Ed. Marcus Klein.
Greenwich, Connecticut: Fawcett, 1969, pp. 142-
158; rpt. *Reading Myself and Others*. New York:
Farrar, Straus, and Giroux, 1975, pp. 117-135.

Roth sees "in Salinger ... an increasing desire
to place the figure of the writer himself directly
in the reader's line of vision" and "the suggestion
that mysticism is a possible road to salvation."
Rpt. in 385.

542. Rupp, Richard H. "J.D. Salinger: A Solitary Litur-
      gy." In *Celebration in Postwar American Fiction,
      1945-67*. Coral Gables, Florida: University of
      Miami Press, 1970, pp. 113-131, et passim.

Salinger's *The Catcher* and a few of his stories
are, for Rupp, good fiction, but "the legend of
Seymour ... is a dead end"; "the Glass stories are
increasingly slack, tedious, and mendacious affirma-
tions of an illusory reality. Ultimately his litur-
gy denies life and love by denying the earth on
which they occur." Rpt. in 381.

543. Russell, John. "Salinger's Feat." *Modern Fiction
      Studies*, 12 (Autumn 1966), 299-311.

Russell states that his purpose is "to show that
the entire canon of Salinger's mature fiction, story by story, yields meaning in terms of human feet."

544. Schulz, Max F. "Epilogue to *Seymour: An Introduction*:
      Salinger and the Crisis of Consciousness." *Stud-
      ies in Short Fiction*, 5 (Winter 1968), 128-138;
      rpt. as "J.D. Salinger and the Crisis of Con-
      sciousness." In *Radical Sophistication: Studies
      in Contemporary Jewish-American Novelists*. Ath-
      ens, Ohio: Ohio University Press, 1969, pp. 198-
      217, passim.

Salinger's "receptivity to" the problem of communication "mirrors a crisis of consciousness in
J.D. *Buddy*frannyzooeyseymour-Salinger, whose exacer-
bated sensibility seems to be reflecting ever multiple refraction of reality, with infinity apparently the end in mind."

545. Schwartz, Arthur. "For Seymour--with Love and Judg-
      ment." *Wisconsin Studies in Contemporary Litera-
      ture*, 4 (Winter 1963), 88-99.

Working with the dilemma of "keeping insight,
emotion, and expression reasonably commensurate with
one another," Salinger, "in his most benign moments
... as much as says [(] *i.e.*, Buddy does, or

Seymour, or Zooey) that salvation is open to all--
Lane Coutell, Mrs. Edie Burwick, Mrs. Fedder."

546. Scott, Nathan A., Jr. *The Broken Center: Studies in
      the Theological Horizon of Modern Literature*.
      New Haven, Connecticut: Yale University Press,
      1966, pp. 106, 220, 223, 226.

      Shakespeare's Falstaff is similar to Huck Finn
      and Holden Caulfield in lying; the "essential core
      of what Salinger's Holden ... has to say" is "the
      whole burden of the embittered deliverance"; *Franny
      and Zooey* is "committed to the registration of the
      tremors of the self's experience of its own inward-
      ness in an adverse world."

547. Shechner, Mark. "Jewish Writers." In *Harvard Guide
      to Contemporary American Writing*. Ed. Daniel
      Hoffman. Cambridge, Massachusetts: Belknap Press,
      1979, p. 220.

      A short reference to "Salinger, whose novels are
      all about 'manners,' albeit crudely defined as
      forms of dullness and masks for social fraud."

548. Simms, L. Moody, Jr. "Seymour Glass: The Salinger-
      ian Hero as Vulgarian." *Notes on Contemporary
      Literature*, 5 (November 1975), 6-8.

      Simms suggests that Seymour's "attempt to merge
      with Vulgarian society through the sacrifice of per-
      sonal values failed because those values were too
      much a portion of his essential being to be denied."

549. Slabey, Robert M. "Sergeant X and Seymour Glass."
      Western Humanities Review, 16 (Autumn 1962),
      376-377.

      Slabey provides more parallels between Sergeant
      X and Seymour Glass than Davis (see item 462) does,
      but also gives "several significant and irrefutable
      differences [that] make it infeasible to identify
      these two characters." See item 560.

550. ————. "Salinger's 'Casino': Wayfarers and Spiri-
      tual Acrobats." *English Record*, 14 (February
      1964), 16-20.

      Salinger's works demonstrate that "the failure
      of human love ... brings about squalor, suffering,
      misunderstanding and war."

551. Slavitt, David R. "Poetry, Novels and Critics: A
      Reply." *Yale Review*, 51 (Spring 1962), 502-504.

Slavitt objects to Lewis' pronouncement (see item 722) of the prominence of novels over poetry and his choice of novelists including Salinger.

552. Slethaug, G[ordon] E. "Form in Salinger's Shorter Fiction." *Canadian Review of American Studies*, 3 (Spring 1972), 50-59.

In "The Laughing Man," *Franny and Zooey*, and *Raise High the Roof Beam, Carpenters and Seymour: An Introduction*, "form versus individual expression constitutes both the crisis and the elements of the resolution for poetry and life, for art and nature."

553. ———. "Seymour: A Clarification." *Renascence*, 23 (Spring 1971), 115-128.

Rather than labeling Seymour "negative and irresponsible," Slethaug argues that "within the Glass world created by Salinger, Seymour's particular sort of spiritual insight and suicide form the most dedicated commitment to a divinely ordained pattern of life."

554. Steiner, George. "The Salinger Industry." *Nation*, 14 November 1959, pp. 360-363.

Noting that Salinger is "a gifted and entertaining writer," Steiner recounts the critical attention given to Salinger and sees it as excessive and misguided. Rpt. in 404, 413, and 415.

555. Stevenson, David L. "J.D. Salinger: The Mirror of Crisis." *Nation*, 9 March 1957, pp. 215-217.

Salinger superbly presents characters in crisis: "a beautifully deft, professional performer who gives us a chance to catch quick, half-amused, half-frightened glimpses of ourselves and our contemporaries, as he confronts us with his brilliant mirror images." Rpt. in 378, 400, 404, and 415.

556. Stone, Edward. "Naming in Salinger." *Notes on Contemporary Literature*, 1 (March 1971), 2-3.

Some of Salinger's characters have literary predecessors: Ramona in "Uncle Wiggily in Connecticut" is related to *Ramona* by Helen Hunt Jackson; Lee in "Pretty Mouth and Green My Eyes" is related to Flaubert's Leon.

557. Strauch, Carl F. "Salinger: The Romantic Background." *Wisconsin Studies in Contemporary Literature*, 4 (Winter 1963), 31-40.

Reviewing the criticism of Salinger's works, particularly as it is represented in Grunwald's *Salinger: A Critical and Personal Portrait* (see item 404), Strauch concludes that "Salinger's characters make a cult of vulnerability, of 'amateurism in life'; and in Salinger, as in the Romantics, this vulnerability, this capacity to feel and suffer is representative of the human condition."

558. Tanner, Tony. "Afterword: Wonder and Alienation-- The Mystic and the Moviegoer." In *The Reign of Wonder: Naivety and Reality in American Literature*. Cambridge: Cambridge University Press, 1965, pp. 336-361.

Tanner is critical of Salinger for trying "to solve his problems by having recourse to the easy unearned generalization." Salinger and the Transcendentalists cease to be artists for the same reason: "generalizations satisfied them more than reality challenged them."

559. ————. "Pigment and Ether: A Comment on the American Mind." *British Association for American Studies Bulletin*, NS, No. 7 (December 1963), 40-45.

Mentions that in his later works Salinger uses "facile generalisations, sombre or uplifting as taste decides."

560. Tosta, Michael R. "'Will the Real Sergeant X Please Stand Up?'" *Western Humanities Review*, 16 (Autumn 1962), 376.

Tosta refutes Tom Davis (see item 462) that Sergeant X is Seymour Glass. See item 549.

561. Turner, Decherd, Jr. "The Salinger Pilgrim." *Seventeenth Annual Conference: American Theological Library Association*. Austin, Texas: Episcopal Theological Seminary of the Southwest, 1963, pp. 59-69.

Turner examines Salinger's use of letters and diaries, the telephone, luggage, the demonic, words, moments of truth through children, and sources. Turner's conclusion is that Salinger's "magnificent failure" occurs when his work "forgives"; "it ceases to be poetry and becomes a cheap theology."

562. Vogel, Albert W. "J.D. Salinger on Education." *School and Society*, 91 (Summer 1963), 240-242.

Vogel insists that Salinger points out the often

ignored "truth ... that ultimately education must
be concerned with the spiritual unity of creation
and man's relation to it and that through education
man must seek wisdom as well as material benefit."

563.   Voss, Arthur. *The American Short Story: A Critical
       Survey*. Norman, Oklahoma: University of Oklahoma
       Press, 1973, pp. 284, 302, 318-326.

       Voss' survey of Salinger's short stories con-
       cludes that his "themes have been significant and
       his ability to give them artistic expression impres-
       sive, but whether he will add meaningfully to his
       achievement seems ... problematical."

564.   Wakefield, Dan. "Salinger and the Search for Love."
       New World Writing, No. 14. New York: New Ameri-
       can Library, 1958, pp. 68-85; rpt. *Discussions
       of the Short Story*. Ed. Hollis Spurgeon Summers.
       New York: Heath, 1963, pp. 110-118.

       The major concern of Salinger's writing is his
       search for love. According to Wakefield, what Sal-
       inger has written "is the history of human trouble
       and the poetry of love." Rpt. in 385, 404, 413,
       and 415.

565.   Walzer, Michael. "In Place of a Hero." *Dissent*, 7
       (Spring 1960), 156-162.

       Salinger's "theme is childhood lost, his conclu-
       sion is a half-mystic, half-sentimental resignation,"
       and "he is successful, appealing and comforting be-
       cause he suggests a kind of reconciliation with the
       adult world which is at the same time an evasion of
       worldliness." But Walzer wonders what his charac-
       ters' "love [will] come to, and what their goodness,
       if they do not calculate and take risks?" Rpt. in
       385 and 400.

566.   Way, Brian. "'Franny and Zooey' and J.D. Salinger."
       New Left Review, No. 15 (May-June 1962), 72-82.

       While *Franny and Zooey* "is sickeningly inept," *The
       Catcher* "is the classic novel of adolescence," but
       its "greatness [is] flawed by the denouement and
       rests on those earlier scenes of adolescence where
       there is no falsity of observation, lapse of con-
       sciousness, or failure of control." Rpt. in 413.

567.   Weber, Daniel B. "Society and the American Novel,
       1920-1960." *Diliman Review*, 13 (October 1965),
       366-379.

       Weber briefly discusses Salinger's works, along

with those of Joseph Heller, Ralph Ellison, Bernard
Malamud, James Baldwin, Saul Bellow, Flannery O'Connor, Jack Kerouac, and Norman Mailer, as a group
"which seems to deny society as meaningful for man's
self-knowledge."

568. Weinberg, Helen. "J.D. Salinger's Holden and Sey-
      mour and the Spiritual Activist Hero." *The New
      Novel in America*. Ithaca, New York: Cornell Uni-
      versity Press, 1970, pp. 141-164.

      Objecting to much Salinger criticism, Weinberg
      sees the major idea in Salinger's works as "the po-
      tential of the spiritual self, and the elusiveness
      of that self, which is always ahead of the movement
      of the particular moment." The problem for Salin-
      ger's characters is that the "inner self is forever
      out of reach."

569. Westbrook Max Roger. "J.D. Salinger (1919-   )."
      In *The Modern American Novel: Essays in Criti-
      cism*. Ed. Max Roger Westbrook. New York: Random
      House, 1966, pp. 209-211.

      In a summary of Salinger's works, Westbrook calls
      "Salinger's attempt to discover man's 'spiritual
      mechanism' through a rhetoric of slang ... one of
      the boldest attempts of our times." Rpt. in 385.

570. Wiegand, William. "J.D. Salinger's Seventy-eight
      Bananas." *Chicago Review*, 11 (Winter 1958), 3-
      19; rpt. *Recent American Fiction: Some Critical
      Views*. Ed. Joseph J. Waldmeir. Boston: Houghton
      Mifflin, 1963, pp. 252-264.

      Wiegand justifies Salinger's significance because
      of "the coherence of his particular vision of the
      world" as seen in "Holden Caulfield, Seymour Glass,
      Teddy, Franny, Daumier Smith." Salinger seems to
      ask "why these intelligent, highly sensitive, af-
      fectionate beings fight curious, gruelling battles,
      leaderless and causeless, in a world they never
      made." Rpt. in 385, 404, and 415.

571. ———. "The Knighthood of J.D. Salinger." *New Re-
      public*, 19 October 1959, pp. 19-21.

      In a brief analysis of Salinger's writing and its
      appeal, Wiegand's assessment is that "the body of
      Salinger's work has been an exploration chiefly of
      the problem of loss and mutability, free from the-
      ories about how a solution may be found. Inasmuch
      as poets have largely lost interest in such quests
      since about the time of Tennyson's *In Memoriam* and
      that it has made few real inroads into English or

American fiction (unlike French and German) since
Tennyson, the Salinger vogue is not surprising. It
answers a need for a different kind of treatment of
experience." Rpt. in 404 and 413.

572. ———. "Salinger and Kierkegaard." *Minnesota Re-
      view*, 5 (May-July 1965), 137-156.

Wiegand explores "the influence of Kierkegaard
on Salinger ... in 'Franny' and 'Zooey,' in 'Raise
High the Roof Beam, Carpenters,' and in 'Seymour.'"
Specifically, he examines these questions: "What is
Franny's problem?" "What is Zooey's existential
relation to Franny, and how does he treat her problem?" "What is Seymour's problem, and what is Buddy's existential relation to Seymour?"

f. Uncollected Stories

A few critical pieces concern Salinger's uncollected
short stories, both individually and collectively. Those
studies are cited alphabetically below.

573. Gehman, Richard, ed. "Introduction." *The Best from
      Cosmopolitan*. New York: Avon Books, 1961, pp.
      xiii-xxvii.

Gehman mentions that editor Arthur Gordon printed Salinger's "The Inverted Forest" including "a
cover page heralding it as one of the most distinguished pieces of fiction the magazine [*Cosmopolitan*] ever had given its readers ... Gordon was
swamped with letters of protest and from that point
on ... he refused to publish anything in which the
story-line was not clear-cut and definite."

574. Goldstein, Bernice, and Sanford Goldstein. "Ego and
      'Hapworth 16, 1924.'" *Renascence*, 24 (Spring
      1972), 159-167.

Salinger's last published story, "Hapworth 16,
1924," the Goldsteins find, is Salinger's "attempt
[at] a portrait of his guru at an early age—a
Seymour already enlightened at the age of seven."
For the Goldsteins, the story shows "a compassion-
ate and enlightened Seymour struggling to deepen
his level of awareness."

575. Newlove, Donald. "'Hapworth 16, 1924.'" *The Village
      Voice*, 22 August 1974, p. 27.

Newlove's review of Salinger's last published
story gives it a high rating: "Salinger's finest

work and a perfection among great short novels by
20th century Americans--as strong as "The Old Man
and the Sea," "The Great Gatsby," the best of Henry James, Stephen Crane, and Faulkner." Rpt. in
385.

576. Quagliano, Anthony. "*Hapworth 16, 1924*: A Problem
        in Hagiography." *University of Dayton Review*,
        8 (Fall 1971), 35-43.

        Quagliano believes that Salinger's latest Glass
        family story is part of the author's attempt at
        "enriching the improbable characterization of his
        contemporary American saint."

577. Ray, David. "Preface: A Past Worth Remembering."
        New Letters, 45 (Fall 1978), 4.

        Salinger's "story reprinted here ["Go See Eddie"]
        should show *The University Review* did not neglect
        fiction--this was one of the very first appearances
        of a then unknown writer."

578. Stone, Elizabeth. "Books: Salinger Comes Up Short."
        Crawdaddy, February 1975, pp. 87-88.

        Shortly after the publication of the pirated
        volumes of Salinger's uncollected stories, Stone
        shows how the early stories are preparation for Sal-
        inger's later more significant works.

g. Dissertations and Theses

    Salinger's works have been the subject of master's
theses and doctoral dissertations, which examine individual works and groups of Salinger's writings. Some concentrate on Salinger exclusively, and other consider Salinger's works in relation to works by other authors. One
master's thesis is the first extensive Salinger bibliography. These academic documents are listed alphabetically.

579. Brinkley, Thomas Edwin. "J.D. Salinger: A Study of
        His Eclecticism--Zooey as Existential Zen Thera-
        pist." Diss. Ohio State 1976.

        "In addition to the Oriental context, I believe
        that there are at least four other major frameworks
        which, while none alone will suffice for an ade-
        quate understanding of Salinger's eclecticism, will,
        when applied simultaneously with the Oriental frame-
        work prove to be the best combination of interpre-
        tive materials offered to date for the explication
        of Salinger's work. These are Kierkegaard's theory

of the stage of life (aesthetic, ethical, and religious); existential analysis and psychotherapy;
the psychosocial context, with special emphasis on
the formulations of Fromm, Erikson, and Keniston;
and, more narrowly with respect to *The Catcher in
the Rye*, Buber's existential communion."

580.   Bryan, James Edward. "Salinger and His Short Fic-
       tion." Diss. Virginia 1968.

       "A critical summary of Salinger's fiction is
       followed by analyses of five stories: 'A Perfect
       Day for Bananafish,' 'Uncle Wiggily in Connecti-
       cut,' 'Just Before the War with the Eskimos,' 'For
       Esmé--with Love and Squalor,' and 'Teddy.' Recur-
       ring themes are discussed, but the emphasis is on
       interpreting and showing methods of development in
       the individual works."

581.   Daniell, Angelane Beth. "Visionary Innocence: The
       Child-Figure in Wordsworth and Salinger." Thesis.
       Georgia State 1973.

       "What seems to be of enduring value in both
       Wordsworth's and Salinger's treatment of the child
       is the reaffirmation of what we often forget: that
       the human experience is a unified whole not to be
       fragmented by arbitrary periods of time or space."

582.   DeGaetano, Madelyn. "An Explication of 'Seymour,
       An Introduction' by J.D. Salinger." Thesis.
       Ohio 1962.

       DeGaetano examines the Glass stories in order
       "to make 'sense' of Seymour's suicide ... to formu-
       late into a cohesive whole the philosophy by which
       Seymour Glass sought and failed to guide his life
       and to analyze the effect of Seymour and of his
       philosophy upon his family."

583.   Erwin, Kenneth J. "An Analysis of the Dramatic and
       Semantic Use of Altruism in the Writings of J.D.
       Salinger." Diss. Texas at Austin 1968.

       Erwin investigates Salinger's "conceptualization
       and dramatization of altruism as a norm of morality:
       in six of the *Nine Stories*, in *The Catcher*, and in
       Franny and Zooey.

*   Fiene, Donald M. "A Bibliographical Study of J.D.
       Salinger: Life, Work and Reputation." Thesis.
       Louisville 1962.

       Cited above as item 341.

584. Harper, Howard M., Jr. "Concepts of Human Destiny
     in Five American Novelists: Bellow, Salinger,
     Mailer, Baldwin, Updike." Diss. Pennsylvania
     State 1965.

     "The study shows that these five writers believe
     that traditional values and views of man are inade-
     quate to explain the experience, especially the ir-
     rationality and violence, of our time. Each writ-
     er, therefore, has tried to find a philosophy which
     is true to the facts of his experience. For Sal-
     inger this philosophy is an amalgam of Christianity
     and Zen Buddhism."

585. Howell, John Michael. "The Waste Land Tradition in
     the American Novel." Diss. Tulane 1963.

     Howell studies "the influence of T.S. Eliot's
     The Waste Land" on Fitzgerald's *The Great Gatsby*,
     Hemingway's *The Sun Also Rises*, Faulkner's *The
     Sound and the Fury*, and Salinger's *The Catcher*.
     In an environment of "spiritual sterility ... Holden
     Caulfield ... seeks stasis ... His quest ends in a
     mental institution, the 'arid plain' still behind
     him."

586. Mirza, Humayun Ali. "The Influence of Hindu-Buddhist
     Psychology and Philosophy on J.D. Salinger's
     Fiction." Diss. New York at Binghamton 1976.

     "Salinger uses Eastern thought as a form of ulti-
     mate truth, and in his fiction this philosophical
     mode functions as the Absolute Standard against
     which human experience in time is measured. From
     this perspective, American middle-class values are
     satirized because, in terms of Absolute Conscious-
     ness (Brahman), this value-system is adjudged as
     deficient and dehumanizing, with the result that it
     perverts life's 'valid pursuits' and ideals."

587. Paniker, Sumitra. "The Influence of Eastern Thought
     on 'Teddy' and the Seymour Glass Stories of J.D.
     Salinger." Diss. Texas at Austin 1971.

     "The Eastern influence in Salinger passes finally
     from content to form. Inspired by the Eastern in-
     sistence on the limitation of language, Salinger's
     stories become an effort to exhaust all the possi-
     bilities of language and thus discover a mode of
     communication beyond language."

588. Pickering, John K. "J.D. Salinger: Portraits of Al-
     ienation." Diss. Case Western Reserve 1968.

     "According to Salinger's vision, man is alienated

both because inherently he is unable to know himself and because he must live within a society which
denies him the opportunity to be himself. The two
causes, however, are not separable. Dissociation
from self in a metaphysical sense and dissociation
from society play upon each other, and are both
cause and effect of each other."

589. Pickard, Linda Kay Haskovec. "A Stylo-Linguistic
      Analysis of Four American Writers." Diss. Texas
      Woman's 1974.

      From a study of "Ernest Hemingway in the Nick
      Adams stories and Katherine Anne Porter in the Mir-
      anda literature" in contrast with Salinger's *The
      Catcher* and Sylvia Plath's *The Bell Jar*, Pickard
      concludes that "writing may not be so much mascu-
      line and feminine as a matter of conditioning."

590. Pomeranz, Regina Esther. "The Search for Self in
      the Adolescent Protagonist in the Contemporary
      American Novel: A Method of Approach for the Col-
      lege Teacher of Literature." Diss. Columbia 1966.

      "Based on psychological criteria of self-actuali-
      zation developed by Abraham Maslow in his study of
      both modern and historical figures," Pomeranz stud-
      ies *The Catcher* in order for college teachers "to
      undertake the teaching of the contemporary novel to
      college students and thus awaken them to this type
      of novel of self as a source of insight for the ma-
      turing individual."

591. Saha, Winifred M. "J.D. Salinger: The Younger Writ-
      er and Society." Diss. Chicago, Divinity School
      1957.

      "Holden has uncompromising ideals--ideals about
      other people and about what the world should be.
      It is these ideals which are so disturbing for the
      adult reader and which are such easy targets for the
      common dismissal of Holden as 'an immature kid who
      needs to grow up and face reality.' It is these
      same ideals and Holden's rage against the impossi-
      bility of attaining the ideals which have so en-
      deared Holden to adolescent readers of those young
      adults who still fondly recall their 'initiation
      into evil.'"

592. Symula, James F. "Censorship of High School Litera-
      ture: A Study of Incidents of Censorship Involv-
      ing J.D. Salinger's *The Catcher in the Rye*."
      Diss. New York at Buffalo 1969.

      "The review of the studies of censorship and the

in-depth look at one particular incident point out
that censorship is not indigenous to a particular
locale, and that even the possibility that a book
may be censored is enough in many instances to limit
the use of it partially or totally. These studies
also suggest that parents are trying to protect
their children from the evils of the language and
vulgarity in *The Catcher in the Rye*. Finally, the
studies indicate the need for schools to adopt book
selection policies and formal procedures for han-
dling a complaint against a book."

593. Withey, Lawrence M. "Treatment of the Rootless Man
      in the Short Stories of Hemingway, Salinger,
      Stafford, and Welty." Thesis. Wesleyan 1957.

Salinger's characters "do not have satisfactory
roots"; they lack "real culture ... solid love ...
religion ... contact with the land ... admirable
wife-husband or parent-child relationship ... adult
affinity with childhood." The four authors studied
portray characters "in the grip of forces which ag-
gravate or cause rootlessness and which are beyond
their control"--in Salinger, "the forces at work
are the city and city society."

2. *The Catcher in the Rye*

This section of secondary sources on *The Catcher* is
divided into three subsections: reviews; study and teaching aids; and, references, articles, and chapters. For
other studies of *The Catcher*, see the subsections above on
reference works (items 336-397), on book-length works (i-
tems 398-429), on miscellaneous references, articles, and
chapters (items 430-572), and on dissertations and theses
(items 579-593).

a. Reviews

This subsection of secondary sources related to *The
Catcher* lists the reviews of Salinger's novel that appeared
in various periodicals soon after the publication of the
novel in 1951. In general, these reviews present a cursory
examination of *The Catcher* in contrast to later, more detailed studies (see items 654-938). The reviews are listed
alphabetically. A few of the reviews are not annotated.

594. B., M. *Saturday Night*, 28 August 1951, p. 29.

595. Behrman, S.N. "The Vision of the Innocent." *New
      Yorker*, 11 August 1951, pp. 64-68.

In a most positive review, Behrman concludes

that, "on the basis of Holden's unorthodox literary
test" for authors, Salinger is successful. Behrman
"would certainly like to call *him* [Salinger] up."

596.   Bowen, Elizabeth. "Books of 1951: Some Personal
         Choices." [London] *Observer*, 30 December 1951,
         p. 71.

         In one sentence about *The Catcher*, Bowen writes
         that the novel is "the novel about adolescence to
         end all: here the potential of tragedy is given an
         enchantingly comic sheath."

597.   Breit, Harvey. "Reader's Choice." *Atlantic*, 188
         (August 1951), 82-85.

         Holden Caulfield and Huck Finn are similar. *The
         Catcher* "has sufficient power and cleverness to
         make the reader chuckle and--rare indeed--even laugh
         aloud." Rpt. in 415.

598.   *British Book News*, No. 216 (August 1958), 566-567.

599.   Brooke, Jocelyn. "New Novels." *News Statesman and
         Nation*, 18 August 1951, pp. 184-185.

         The reviewer calls *The Catcher* "an odd, tragic
         and at times an appallingly funny book, with a taste
         of its own."

600.   *The Bulletin*, 10 September 1958, p. 58.

601.   Burger, Nash K. "Books of *The Times*." *New York Times*,
         16 July 1951, p. 19.

         With "the unconscious humor, the repetitions,
         the slang and profanity, the emphasis, all ... just
         right," *The Catcher* presents Holden Caulfield, with
         whom "there is nothing ... that a little understand-
         ing and affection, preferably from his parents,
         couldn't have set right."

602.   Canby, Henry Seidel, et al. "Concurrence [with Clif-
         ton Fadiman]." *Book-of-the-Month Club News*, July
         1951, p. 4.

         Other members of the editorial board of the Book-
         of-the-Month Club agree with Clifton Fadiman (see
         item 607) about *The Catcher*, "a source of wonder
         and delight--and concern," a book which "reaches
         far deeper into reality" than "the comedies and
         tragedies of Booth Tarkington's *Seventeen*."

603.   "*The Catcher in the Rye*." *Montreal Star*, 29 Septem-
         ber 1951, p. 20.

"The whole book is literally plastered with slang colored by indecencies."

604. Charques, R.D. "Fiction." *Spectator*, 17 August 1951, p. 224.

"Intelligent, humorous, acute and sympathetic in observation, the tale is rather too formless to do quite the sort of thing it was evidently intended to do."

605. "A Dark Horse." *Kirkus*, 15 May 1951, p. 247

The reviewer calls *The Catcher* "tender and true, and impossible, in its picture of the old hells of young boys, the lonesomeness and tentative attempts to be mature and secure, the awful block between youth and being grown-up, the fright and sickness that humans and their behavior cause the changeling, the dramatization of the big bang."

606. Engle, Paul. "Honest Tale of Distraught Adolescent." *Chicago Sunday Tribune Magazine of Books*, 15 July 1951, p. 3.

In a positive review, Engle calls *The Catcher* "engaging and believable ... full of right observations and sharp insight, and a wonderful sort of grasp of how a boy can create his own world of fantasy and live form." Rpt. in 415.

607. Fadiman, Clifton. *Book-of-the-Month Club News*, July 1951, pp. 1-4.

Fadiman, a member of the editorial board for Book-of-the-Month Club, writes glowingly about *The Catcher*: "That rare miracle of fiction has again come to pass: a human being has been created out of ink, paper and the imagination. See item 602.

608. "Fiction." *Booklist*, 15 July 1951, p. 401.

"An unusual book on a pertinent theme ... [that] will not appeal to everyone but is certainly worth attention for its sensitive insight into a currently important topic, as well as for the quality of the writing."

609. Goodman, Anne L. "Mad About Children." *New Republic*, 16 July 1951, pp. 20-21.

Goodman writes a mixed review: *The Catcher* "is a brilliant tour-de-force"; "the final scene ... is as good as anything that Salinger has written"; but "the reader wearies of ... explicitness, repetition ... and adolescence"; "in a writer of Salinger's

undeniable talent one expects something more." Rpt.
in 415 and 428.

610. Hartley, L.P. *The Sunday Times*, 5 August 1951, p. 3.

611. House, Vernal. "Growing Pains." *Globe and Mail*, 17
      November 1951, p. 10.

      "Of its kind, it is a minor masterpiece."

612. Hughes, Riley. "New Novels: *The Catcher in the Rye*."
      Catholic World, 174 (November 1951), 154.

      "Not only do some of the events stretch probabil-
      ity, but Holden's character as iconoclast, a kind
      of latter-day Tom Sawyer or Huck Finn, is made mo-
      notonous and phony by the formidably excessive use
      of amateur swearing and coarse language."

613. Jones, Ernest. "Case History of All of Us." *Nation*,
      1 September 1951, p. 176.

      Reflecting "something not at all rich and strange
      but what every sensitive sixteen-year-old since Rous-
      seau has felt," *The Catcher*, Jones writes, "as a
      whole is predictable and boring." Rpt. in 415 and
      428.

614. Laski, Marghanita. *The Observer*, 29 July 1951, p. 7.

615. Longstreth, T. Morris. "New Novels in the News."
      Christian Science Monitor, 19 July 1951, p. 11.

      Thankful that there are not many Holdens in the
      world, Longstreth fears "that a book like this given
      wide circulation may multiply his kind--as too eas-
      ily happens when immorality and perversion are re-
      counted by writers of talent whose work is counte-
      nanced in the name of art or good intention." Rpt.
      in 415.

616. Neal, S.M. "'Catcher in the Rye' Story of Unruly
      Boy." *Springfield* [Massachusetts] *Republican*,
      22 July 1951, p. 5D.

      In a generally favorable review, Neal writes
      that "the struggle through these pages is repaid
      by the outcome."

617. Peterson, Virgilia. "Three Days in the Bewildering
      World of an Adolescent." *New York Herald Tribune
      Book Review*, 15 July 1951, p. 3.

      In *The Catcher* "lies the implication that our
      youth today has no moorings, no criterion beyond

instinct, no railing to grasp along the steep as-
cent to maturity. This is the importance of 'The
Catcher in the Rye,' and it is upon the integrity
of this portrait of a so-called privileged American youth that Mr. Salinger's novel stands or falls."
Rpt. in 415.

618. Poster, William. "Tomorrow's Child." *Commentary*, 13
      (January 1952), 90-92.

      "The ennui, heartburn, and weary revulsions of
      The Catcher in the Rye are the inevitable actions,
      not of an adolescent, however disenchanted, but of
      a well-paid satirist with a highly developed tech-
      nique, no point of view, and no target to aim at
      but himself."

619. Price, R.G. "Booking Office." *Punch*, 15 August 1951,
      p. 192.

      "The weakness of the novel is its sentimental-
      ity."

620. "Problem Boy." *Newsweek*, 16 July 1951, pp. 89-90.

      Essentially a summary of the plot with little
      comment.

621. *Prospect*, 2 (January 1959), 25-27.

622. Ritt, Thomas Francis. "The Catcher in the Rye."
      America, 11 August 1951, pp. 463-464.

      A negative review which criticizes the use of
      "four-letter words" and suggests that "Salinger
      would do well to remain in the field of the short
      story."

623. Rodriquez, J.S. "Youth-American Style." [Montreal]
      Gazette, 22 September 1951, p. 25.

      A negative review which calls Holden an "unap-
      pealing young neurotic."

624. Roth, Harold L. "Salinger, J.D. *The Catcher in the
      Rye*." *Library Journal*, 86 (July 1951), 1125-1126.

      "This may be a shock to many parents who wonder
      about a young man's thought and actions, but its
      effect can be a salutary one. An *adult* book (very
      frank) and highly recommended."

625. Russell, John. *The Listener*, 30 August 1951, p. 355.

626. Schrapnel, Norman. *The Guardian*, 10 August 1951,
      p. 4.

627. *The Scotsman*, 2 August 1951, p. 7.

628. Smith, Harrison. "Manhattan Ulysses, Junior." *Saturday Review*, 14 July 1951, pp. 12-13.

Among many positive comments about the novel, Smith sums up the character of Holden: "moral revulsion against anything that was ugly, evil, cruel, or what he called 'phoney' and his acute responsiveness to beauty and innocence, especially the innocence of the very young, in whom he saw reflected his own lost childhood." Rpt. in 415 and 428.

629. Stern, James. "Aw, the World's a Crumby Place." *New York Times*, 15 July 1951, Sec. 7, p. 5.

Written in Holden's vernacular, this review indirectly praises *The Catcher* and Salinger for his characterization of children. Rpt. in 415.

630. *The Sydney Morning Herald*, 23 August 1958, p. 13.

631. Urquhart, Fred. *Books of Today*, NS, No. 4 (September 1951), 12.

632. Wain, John. "Holden and Huck." *The Observer*, 8 June 1958, p. 17.

633. Wickendan, Dan. "Clear-Sighted Boy." *The Freeman*, 10 September 1951, p. 798.

Finding Holden Caulfield as hypnotic as the Ancient Mariner, Wickendan calls *The Catcher* a modern picaresque novel similar to *Huckleberry Finn* and thinks that it may become a classic.

634. "With Love & 20-20 Vision." *Time*, 16 July 1951, p. 97.

"The prize catch in *The Catcher in the Rye* may be Novelist Salinger himself. He can understand the adolescent mind without displaying one."

635. Yaffe, James. "Outstanding Novels." *Yale Review*, 41 (Autumn 1951), viii, xii, xiv, xviii, xx, xxii.

"Salinger has written a book with life, feeling, and lightheartedness--very rare qualities nowadays."

636. "Young Minds." *Times Literary Supplement*, 7 September 1951, p. 60.

"The boy is really very touching; but the endless

stream of blasphemy and obscenity in which he talks,
credible as it is, palls after the first chapter."

b. Study and Teaching Aids

Aids for the study of and the teaching of *The Catcher*
have appeared in a variety of forms in print and non-print
media. The list, arranged alphabetically, includes pam-
phlet-size study guides, lesson plans, study questions,
writing assignments, cassette tapes, filmstrips, and posters.

637. Alexander, Charlotte A. *J.D. Salinger's "The Catch-
      er in the Rye": A Critical Commentary*. New York:
      Monarch Press, 1965.

      This pamphlet-size study guide contains six chap-
      ters: biography of Salinger, *The Catcher*, charac-
      ters, commentary, test questions, and bibliography.

638. Angney, Mark N. *Novel Ideas Literature/Reading
      Learning Packet: "Catcher in the Rye."* Little-
      ton, Massachusetts: Sundance, 1980.

      This teaching guide provides a teacher's guide
      and twenty-five spiritmaster activity sheets for
      teaching *The Catcher*.

639. Austin, Deborah S., Ralph W. Condee, and Chadwick
      C. Hansen. *Modern Fiction: Form and Idea in the
      Contemporary Novel and Short Fiction*. University
      Park, Pennsylvania: Center for Continuing Lib-
      eral Education, Pennyslvania State University,
      1959, pp. 90-95.

      In a course guide for sixteen pieces of modern
      fiction, the authors present twenty-six study ques-
      tions for *The Catcher*.

640. Bonheim, Helmut W. "An Introduction to J.D. Salin-
      ger's *The Catcher in the Rye*." *Exercise Exchange*,
      4 (April 1957), 8-11.

      Bonheim provides twenty-five study questions on
      The Catcher for use in a freshman or sophomore col-
      lege class in composition or introduction to liter-
      ature.

641. Coles, William E., Jr. "Assignment 19: J.D. Salin-
      ger." In *The Plural "I": The Teaching of Writing*.
      New York: Holt, Rinehart and Winston, 1978, pp.
      163-172.

      Coles illustrates and explains the following

assignment he gives on a passage from Chapter 3 of
*The Catcher: "Describe the voice you hear speaking
in this passage ... and its ideal audience. What
is it you call professional here? What do you call
amateur?*

642. *Eight Masters* [Fitzgerald, Hemingway, Wolfe, Bald-
      win, Salinger, McCullers, Faulkner, Steinbeck]
      of Modern Fiction. New York: Scholastic Book
      Service.

      Set of eight pictures, 15 x 20 inches each.

643. *Famous Author Super Posters: J.D. Salinger.* Logan,
      Iowa: The Perfection Form Company.

      23 x 29 inch picture of Salinger.

644. Hampton, Judith D., ed. *American Redi-Notes Litera-
      ture Series: "The Catcher in the Rye."* Topeka,
      Kansas: American Econo-Clad Services, 1977.

      This eight-page pamphlet, to be used as a teach-
      ing guide, includes biographical information about
      Salinger, a plot summary of *The Catcher*, instruc-
      tional objectives, discussion questions with sug-
      gested answers, student activities, test questions,
      and a five-item bibliography.

645. Kaplan, Robert B. *"The Catcher in the Rye" Notes.*
      Lincoln, Nebraska: Cliff's Notes, 1965.

      As a study guide, this pamphlet contains several
      sections: biographical material on Salinger, an in-
      troduction to the novel, "general plot summary,"
      list of characters, summaries of and commentaries
      on each chapter, an essay relating Holden to other
      Salinger works, and lists of study questions and
      essay topics.

646. Lettis, Richard. *J.D. Salinger: "The Catcher in the
      Rye."* Woodbury, New York: Barron's Educational
      Series, 1964.

      This pamphlet in the series of "Barron's Studies
      in American Literature" contains an introduction,
      a brief biography of Salinger, a detailed analysis
      of Holden Caulfield, extensive study questions for
      each chapter in the novel, a list of "general ques-
      tions," excerpts from critics, and a bibliography.

647. Light, James F. *Salinger's "The Catcher in the Rye":
      A Critical Commentary.* New York: Barrister Pub-
      lishing Company, 1966.

      As a part of the "Bar-Notes Literature Study

and Examination Guides," this booklet has nine major
sections: the author and the book, analysis of *The
Catcher*, guide to main action and location, characters, meaning, review of criticism, identification, index to questions, and selected bibliography.

648. MacDonald. *The Catcher in the Rye*. Topeka, Kansas:
      American Econo-Clad Services, 1977.

      A 23 x 35 inch poster with a yellow and orange
      drawing of a young profile looking over the New
      York City skyline with a quarter rainbow in the
      background.

649. Miller, James E., Jr. *20th Century American Novel:
      The Catcher in the Rye*. Deland, Florida: Everett/
      Edwards.

      Twenty-nine-minute cassette with Miller comment-
      ing briefly on the popularity of *The Catcher*, read-
      ers' identification with Holden, the language of
      the novel and at length on Salinger's characteriza-
      tion of Holden.

650. *The Modern Novel: The Catcher in the Rye*. Great
      Neck, New York: Educational Dimension Corpora-
      tion.

      Nineteen-minute color filmstrip with either rec-
      ord or tape.

651. Printz, Mike. *American Redi-Notes Book Talk: "Catch-
      er in the Rye."* Topeka, Kansas: American Econo-
      Clad Services, 1978.

      Narrated by Randy Jordon, this ten-minute cas-
      sette provides an introduction to *The Catcher* for
      high school students. Jordon reads two lengthy
      passages from the novel.

652. Roberts, Edgar V. *Writing Themes About Literature*.
      Englewood Cliffs, New Jersey: Prentice-Hall,
      1964, pp. 51, 134, 148-150.

      In a textbook for students of composition and
      literature, Roberts includes three references to
      Salinger's works: (1) suggestion of "a comparison
      of *The House of Mirth* by Edith Wharton" and *The
      Catcher* as "The Treatment of the 'Outsider' or Cor-
      rosive Influences of an Affluent Society on the In-
      dividual or The Basis of Social Criticism," (2)
      suggestion to study Holden Caulfield to understand
      how "the *persona* of the piece will create the nature
      of the diction," (3) a sample of a "theme of evalua-
      tion," which is a five-paragraph essay entitled "An

Evaluation of *The Catcher in the Rye*."

2nd ed., 1969, pp. 53-54, 72, 159, 186-187.

To the three references in the first edition, Roberts adds a fourth about the symbolic nature of children in Salinger's fiction.

3rd ed., 1973, pp. 55, 60, 80, 111, 205.

Omitting the sample theme of evaluation about *The Catcher* and retaining the references to Salinger from the second edition of his textbook, Roberts mentions Salinger as a writer who has paid attention "to voices and narrators and to the means by which detail is authenticated."

653. *United States Authors: J.D. Salinger*. Logan, Iowa: Perfection Form Company.

An 8 1/2 x 11 inch picture of Salinger.

c.   References, Articles, Chapters

Because more material has been written about *The Catcher* than about any other of Salinger's works, the entries in this subsection have been further categorized into the following groups: general studies; studies of censorship, controversy, and problems in the classroom; and, the relationship of *The Catcher* to other literary works and authors.

(1.) General Studies

The entries in this category refer to studies of *The Catcher* that are shorter than book-length and that are not included in either of the two following categories (censorship or the relationship of *The Catcher* to other works and authors).   The entries are listed alphabetically.   For other studies of *The Catcher*, see the subsections above on reference works (items 336-397), on book-length studies (items 398-429), on miscellaneous references, articles, and chapters (items 430-572), and on dissertations and theses (items 579-593).

654.   "Accused Lennon Slayer Sentenced." *Facts on File*, 28 August 1981, pp. 626-627.

Mark Chapman reads a passage from *The Catcher* before he is sentenced.   Chapman says this passage is his "final spoken words."

655. Agee, Hugh. "Adolescent Initiation: A Thematic Study
      in the Secondary School." *English Journal*, 58
      (October 1969), 1021-1024.

      In addition to *The Catcher*, Agee uses works by
      Carson McCullers, Truman Capote, Jean Stafford, and
      Saul Bellow in the classroom so that "the adolescent
      in our society, unlike his fictional counterpart,
      need not find the transition from childhood to a-
      dulthood a traumatic, trial-and-error process."

656. Alley, Alvin D. "Puritanism: Scourge of Education?"
      Clearing House, 38 (March 1964), 393-395.

      Alley's students identify with Holden Caulfield
      because "they see in him, not the ideal young man,
      but a young man in search of himself, in search of
      his place in the human scheme of things, and in con-
      flict with the narrowness of the society in which
      he lives." See items 709 and 745.

657. Amur, G.S. "Theme, Structure, and Symbol in *The
      Catcher in the Rye*." *Indian Journal of American
      Studies*, 1 (1969), 11-24.

      Salinger's theme ("Holden's search for genuine
      and satisfying personal relationships"), structure
      ("a movement which involves the beginning of a psy-
      chological crisis in Holden, the deepening of this
      crisis ... and his final recovery"), and symbols
      (hat, Allie's baseball mitt, and other "private
      symbols"), Amur writes, "are ... the choice of a
      firm controlling intention ... [which] give us a
      fuller insight into the nature of his [Holden's]
      struggle, more than his words and actions do, and
      add depth and concreteness to the novel, which in
      its form is essentially an organisation of memories."

658. Bank, Stanley. "A Literary Hero for Adolescents:
      The Adolescent." *English Journal*, 58 (October
      1969), 1013-1020.

      Bank demonstrates the relevance of *The Catcher*
      and Holden Caulfield for adolescent students.

659. Baumbach, Jonathan, Jr. "The Saint as a Young Man:
      A Reappraisal of *The Catcher in the Rye*." *Modern
      Language Quarterly*, 25 (December 1964), 461-472;
      rpt. "The Saint as a Young Man: *The Catcher in
      the Rye* by J.D. Salinger." In *The Landscape of
      Nightmare: Studies in the Contemporary American
      Novel*. New York: New York University Press, 1965,
      pp. 55-67.

      After recounting the objections to *The Catcher*,

Baumbach calls Salinger's major work enduring, "full
of insights," "almost perfectly achieved," "an important minor novel," and "near perfection." Rpt.
in 380 and 385.

660. Bennett, James R. "Style in Twentieth Century Brit-
        ish and American Fiction: A Bibliography." *West
        Coast Review*, 2 (Winter 1968), 43-51.

Lists Donald Costello's article (see item 678)
about Salinger's language in *The Catcher*.

661. Bhaerman, Robert D. "Rebuttal: Holden in the Rye."
        College English, 23 (March 1962), 508.

Bhaerman objects to Bernard Oldsey's claim (see
item 751) about Holden's name. Salinger's use of
Caulfield, Bhaerman points out, predates the 1947
movie of William Holden and Joan Caulfield." Rpt.
in 415 and 428.

662. Blessing, Richard A. "For Pookie, with Love and Good
        Riddance: John Nichols' *The Sterile Cuckoo*."
        Journal of Popular Culture, 7 (Summer 1973), 124-
        135.

Blessing mentions that "we" have misread Holden:
"We loved Holden, not because he was struggling to
come to manhood, but because he loved the museum
and the carousel."

663. "Books in 1965." *Facts on File*, 11 May 1966, pp.
        167-168.

The Catcher is listed as one of ten "leading
mass market paperback bestsellers in 1965."

664. "Books in 1967." *Facts on File*, 18 December 1968,
        pp. 545-546.

The Catcher is listed as one of "the leading 25
bestsellers since 1895."

665. Bratman, Fred. "Holden, 50, Still Catches." *New
        York Times*, 21 December 1979, p. 35A; rpt.
        "Holden Caulfield, Now 50, Still Attracts Us."
        Chicago Tribune, 25 December 1979, Sec. 4, p. 4,
        col. 1.

In the month of the fiftieth anniversary of
Holden's birthday, Bratman reminisces about his
identification with Holden, "a teenager who sees
people for what they really are, and can laugh at
his own troubles."

666. Brower, Brock. "Notes on an Illustrated Childhood."

Esquire, 81 (March 1974), 116-117, 180.

In contrast to some earlier works, Salinger's *The Catcher* portrays "childhood ... [as] its own reward, cerebrally isolate, a private pursuit that is no longer so broadly--in the way I mean--illustratable."

667. Bruccoli, Matthew J. "Some Transatlantic Texts: West to East." In *Bibliography and Textual Criticism: English and American Literature 1700 to the Present*. Eds. O.M. Brack, Jr. and Warner Barnes. Chicago: University of Chicago Press, 1969, pp. 244-255.

Bruccoli points out the changes made in a British edition of *The Catcher*: "the removal of 225 italic words" and bowdlerizations.

668. Bryan, James. "The Psychological Structure of *The Catcher in the Rye*." *PMLA*, 89 (October 1974), 1065-1074.

Bryan's introduction states that "an examination of the structure, scene construction, and suggestive imagery reveals a pattern of aggression and regression, largely sexual, which is suggested in the Pencey Prep section, acted out in the central part of the novel, and brought to a curious climax in the Phoebe chapters."

669. Bryant, Jerry H. *The Open Decision: The Contemporary American Novel and Its Intellectual Background*. New York: Free Press, 1970, pp. 236-240.

Bryant illustrates Holden's "refusal ... to enter manhood and affirm the human condition." Caulfield's vision of life is short-sighted.

670. Burack, Boris. "Holden the Courageous." *CEA Critic*, 27 (May 1965), 1.

In response to Deane Warner (see item 933), Burack argues that "Holden has courage ... a courage different from that of a generation ago." See item 755.

671. Burd, Van Akin. "The Theme of the Quest in Thoreau, Melville, Mark Twain, and J.D. Salinger: An Approach to Stimulate Critical Teaching and Reading of Four Important Writers." *English Record*, 8 (Winter 1957), 2.

Burd writes an introduction to four essays on the idea of quest, "man's search for his identity and an understanding of himself":

Kennedy, Richard S. "The Theme of Quest: Melville's
Use of the Quest Theme in 'Moby Dick,'" pp. 2-7.

Cady, Edwin H. "The Theme of Quest: The Quest for
Identity in 'Huckleberry Finn,'" pp. 8-10.

Dodge, Stewart. "The Theme of Quest: In Search of
'The Fat Lady,'" pp. 10-13. Cited below as item
685.

Westbrook, Perry D. "The Theme of Quest: In Thoreau," pp. 13-17.

672.   Burgess, Anthony. *The Novel Now: A Guide to Contemporary Fiction*. New York: W.W. Norton, 1967,
pp. 150-151, 153.

In his chapter entitled "A Sort of Rebels," Burgess calls *The Catcher* "one of the key-books of the
post-war period ... the culminating work of a series
of stories, most of which carried the theme of a
sick mind's redemption through the innocence of a
child." Rpt. in 385.

673.   Burrows, David J. "Allie and Phoebe: Death and Love
in J.D. Salinger's 'The Catcher in the Rye.'"
In *Private Dealings: Modern American Writers in
Search of Integrity*. Eds. David J. Burrows, Lewis
M. Dabney, Milne Holton, and Grosvenor E. Powell.
Rockville, Maryland: New Perspectives, 1974, pp.
106-114.

In an effort to "explain the deep and lasting effect the book has had," Burrows examines "a series
of related images" of falling (death) and concludes
that "the responsibility he [Holden] assumes toward
her [Phoebe], as well as the freedom he realizes
she requires, provides a starting point from which
he can learn to accept the world's pervasive muta-
bility."

674.   Cagle, Charles. "*The Catcher in the Rye* Revisited."
Midwest Quarterly, 4 (Summer 1963), 343-351.

Cagle meticulously summarizes the critical approaches taken toward *The Catcher* and decides "that
the essence of *Catcher* is really the distilled and
heady vibration of our own time, the same unquiet
beating of restless feet which Fitzgerald heard
thirty years ago when the world was caught between
social change and economic disaster."

675.   Cahill, Robert. "J.D. Salinger's Tin Bell." *Cadence*,

14 (Autumn 1959), 20-22.

Cahill examines the popularity of *The Catcher*
and illustrates that there are two common themes
in which its significance does not lie and three
reasons for its importance: Salinger's "prosodic
achievement," children, and humor.

676.   Carpenter, Frederic I. "Fiction and the American
       College." *American Quarterly*, 12 (Winter 1960),
       443-456.

In making the point that "there are no first-
rate fictions describing life in any American (or
British) university," Carpenter cites *The Catcher*
as an excellent novel "dealing with adolescent and
high school years."

677.   Cohen, Hubert I. "'A Woeful Agony Which Forced Me
       to Begin My Tale': *The Catcher in the Rye*."
       Modern Fiction Studies, 12 (Autumn 1966), 355-
       366.

In an examination of "the way Holden tells things
as well as ... the matter of his tale," Cohen finds
that Holden's story is "a means of coming to grips
with his experiences, but ... for Salinger ... the
process which Holden is going through ... is anal-
ogous to the process the artist ... undergoes as
he begins to look carefully and critically at his
family, his friends, his society's conventions and
facades, and his own illusions."

678.   Costello, Donald P. "The Language of 'The Catcher
       in the Rye.'" *American Speech*, 34 (October 1959),
       172-181.

At the end of a detailed analysis of Holden's
and Salinger's use of language, "only one part of
an artistic achievement," Costello calls this language "an authentic artistic rendering of a type of
informal, colloquial, teenage American speech ...
strongly typical and trite, yet often somewhat individual ... crude and slangy and imprecise, imita-
tive yet occasionally imaginative, and affected toward standardization by the strong efforts of
schools." Rpt. in 400, 404, 415, and 428.

679.   Costello, Patrick. "Salinger and 'Honest Iago.'"
       Renascence, 16 (Summer 1964), 171-174.

Just as Othello allows "'honest Iago' to infect
... [him] with his insanity," Holden has been in-
fected with the thinking of people like Carl Luce.
Salinger criticizes "this poisoning of Holden's

judgment by adult society," which causes Holden to repulse "the one person who is willing and apparently able to help him, the one man who treats him as a person, a human being yearning for a grasp of real adulthood."

680. Costelloe, M. Joseph, S.J. "Sex in Contemporary Literature." *Homiletic and Pastoral Review*, 41 (November 1960), 145-154.

Because *The Catcher* "is one continuous round of drinking, fighting, necking and, though Holden loses heart when the prostitute starts to undress," Costelloe "do[es] not see how this and other episodes narrated would not be a source of serious temptation to youthful readers."

681. Creeger, George R. "'Treacherous Desertion': Salinger's *The Catcher in the Rye*." Middleton, Connecticut: Graduate Summer School for Teachers Wesleyan University, 1961.

In "this address given ... August 10, 1961, at a luncheon meeting of Summer School students," Creeger approaches *The Catcher* through two phrases from William Wordsworth's *The Prelude*: "unjust tribunals" and "treacherous desertion." The former describes what *The Catcher* "has had to face" and the latter "is the best brief description ... of the work's theme." Rpt. in 400.

682. Davis, Tom. "J.D. Salinger: 'Some Crazy Cliff' Indeed." *Western Humanities Review*, 14 (Winter 1960), 97-99.

Davis suggests that "the source for the 'catcher in the rye' image is the bodhisattva figure of Mahayana Buddhism ... [which] provides a unification of technique which has been so sadly lacking in Salinger's later fiction." Rpt. in 415.

683. DeJovine, F. Anthony. *The Young Hero in American Fiction: A Motif for Teaching Literature*. New York: Appleton-Century-Crofts, 1971, pp. 23-28, 32, 39, 77, 98, 100, 115, 133, 142, 149, 157-158.

DeJovine discusses characterization, symbolism, irony, romanticism, lack of humor, structure, and language in *The Catcher*.

684. DeLuca, Geraldine. "Unself-Conscious Voices: Larger Contexts for Adolescents." *The Lion and the Unicorn*, 2 (Fall 1978), 89-108.

"*The Catcher in the Rye* is the one book that the

adolescent novel comes from." Salinger's literary
"descendants" imitate "the idiosyncracies--not to
say excesses--of his style, along with his simpli-
fications and his celebration of innocence." Rpt.
in 385.

685. Dodge, Stewart. "The Theme of Quest: In Search of
      'The Fat Lady.'" *English Record*, 8 (Winter 1957),
      10-13.

      Dodge uses Salinger's story "Zooey" for "a way
of better understanding Holden['s] ... pilgrimage:
he struck through the mask of pretension everywhere;
though revolted and hurt, he continued in pursuit
of people; he sought the genuine, the sincere, the
pure, the innocent, the beautiful; he tried to puri-
fy himself; he gave himself in large handfuls; he
refused to be normal, when to be normal was to be
phony but safe; he found out what he could be--some-
thing non-utilizable and necessary and, for him,
right: a catcher in the rye." See item 671. Rpt.
in 415.

686. Edwards, Duane. "Holden Caulfield: 'Don't Ever Tell
      Anybody Anything.'" *Journal of English Literary
      History*, 44 (Fall 1977), 554-565.

      Edwards demonstrates a negative side of Holden:
those who "idealize Holden" overlook the fact "that
Holden shares in the phoniness he loathes; that he
lives by his unconscious needs and not the values
he espouses; that he withdraws from rather than
faces the challenge of personal relationships."

687. Ely, Mary. "A Cup of Consecrated Chicken Soup."
      Catholic World, 202 (February 1966), 298-301.

      Ely is convinced that Holden, despite his lan-
guage, belongs in the classroom: "Holden is a crazy
mixed-up kid, but he is the teen's true brother,
the legitimate offspring of the twisted age."

688. Fiedler, Leslie A. "Boys Will Be Boys!" *New Leader*,
      28 April 1958, pp. 23-26.

      Fiedler calls Holden an example of a "Good Bad
Boy" who "comes to the end of ineffectual revolt in
a breakdown out of which he is impelled to fight
his way by the Good Good Girl in the guise of the
Pure Little Sister." See item 468.

689. Fleissner, Robert F. "Salinger's Caulfield: A Re-
      fraction of Copperfield and his Caul." *Notes on
      Contemporary Literature*, 3 (May 1973), 5-7.

Citing the comments of Bernard Oldsey (see item
751) and Robert Bhaermann (see item 661) about the
origin of Holden's last name, Fleissner insists that
it is related to Copperfield and that there is more
influence of Charles Dickens on Salinger than anyone has ever pointed out.

690.   Fogel, Amy. "Where the Ducks Go: *The Catcher in the
       Rye.*" *Ball State Teachers' College Forum*, 3
       (Spring 1962), 75-79.

       In this "prize essay of the *Atlantic* 1960-61
       Contests for High School and Private School Stu-
       dents," Fogel defends the place of *The Catcher* in
       the high school classroom.

691.   Foran, Donald J., S.J. "A Doubletake on Holden Caul-
       field." *English Journal*, 57 (October 1968), 977-
       979.

       Foran "propose[s] to prove, by careful textual
       scrutiny of several key episodes in the novel, that
       Holden most often lives in a world-proof 'world' of
       his own making; and, secondly, that Phoebe Caul-
       field is Holden's closest tie to reality, the one
       catalyst in his struggle for maturity."

692.   Fowler, Albert. "Alien in the Rye." *Modern Age*, 1
       (Fall 1957), 193-197.

       Salinger's portrayal of Holden "reflects the
       idea propounded by Rousseau and the disciples of
       naturalism of the individual born good and corrupt-
       ed by his institutions." Fowler uses a statement
       by Freud to show the modern expression of this
       theme.   Rpt. in 400 and 415.

693.   French, Warren. "Holden's Fall." *Modern Fiction
       Studies*, 10 (Winter 1964-1965), 389.

       In response to J.D. O'Hara (see item 747), French
       argues that it is clear when Holden abandons the
       idea of "becoming a catcher in the rye."

694.   Friedberg, Barton C. "The Cult of Adolescence in
       American Fiction." *Nassau Review*, 1 (Spring
       1964), 26-35.

       The searching experience by Holden in *The Catch-
       er* and other adolescent protagonists in American
       literature parallels the search of the nation it-
       self.

695.   Friedrich, Gerhard. "Perspective in the Teaching
       of American Literature." *College English*, 20

(December 1958), 122-128.

Mentions *The Catcher* as an example of contemporary distinctively American literature.

696. Glasser, William. *"The Catcher in the Rye." Michigan Quarterly Review*, 15 (Fall 1976), 432-457.

For Glasser, "Holden Caulfield undergoes a startling transformation: from an existence in which his
nature is dangerously divided, to a remarkably in-
tegrated state of being." Holden's journey is a
positive one so that "he offers his narration of
The Catcher in the Rye as a record of his troubles
for anyone who might wish to learn from his experience." Rpt. in 385.

697. Greenburg, Dan. "Catcher Her in the Oatmeal." *Esquire*, 49 (February 1958), 46-47; rpt. *Twentieth Century Parody, American and British*. Ed.
Burling Lowrey. New York: Harcourt, Brace, 1960,
pp. 103-104.

Greenburg parodies the style of *The Catcher* by
retelling the story of "Goldilocks and the Three
Bears" in the vernacular of Holden Caulfield.

698. Guerin, Wilfred L., Earle Labor Lee Morgan, and
John R. Willingham. *A Handbook of Critical Approaches to Literature*. 2nd ed. New York: Harper and Row, 1979, p. 82.

In the chapter on "The Formalist Approach," the
authors emphasize the importance of the narrator
in the view of the world presented in *The Catcher*.

699. Gutwillig, Robert. "Everybody's Caught 'The Catcher in the Rye.'" *New York Times*, 15 January
1961, Sec. 7, pp. 38-39.

Gutwillig reviews the appeal, popularity, ac-
claim, and notoriety that *The Catcher* has had in
ten years.

700. Hainsworth, J.D. "Maturity in J.D. Salinger's 'The
Catcher in the Rye.'" *English Studies*, 48 (October 1967), 426-431.

Hainsworth's article centers on these questions:
"Is he [Holden] just an immature teenager with a
teenager's attitude to the adult world, or are we
supposed to see him as more mature than his society?" Hainsworth's answer is that "Holden's ex-
cesses" show immaturity, but "he does have some
measure of maturity--has, in fact, precisely those

aspects of it which the novel has shown society to
be most lacking in--integrity, spontaneity, moral
sensitivity and knowledge of good and evil."

701. Hall, James. "Play, the Fractured Self, and Ameri-
      can Angry Comedy: From Faulkner to Salinger."
      In *The Lunatic Giant in the Drawing Room: The
      British and American Novel Since 1930*. Blooming-
      ton: Indiana University Press, 1968, pp. 56-77.

      Finding *The Catcher* unsurpassed "as American An-
      gry," Hall writes that Salinger was "the first to
      find a scene, language and action for impatience
      with the more vigorous adolescence which postwar
      hopes demanded." Rpt. in 385.

702. Handa, Takuya. "On Interpretations of J.D. Salinger's
      The Catcher in the Rye." *Kyushu American Litera-
      ture*, 21 (June 1980), 42-53.

      Handa summarizes his essay as follows: "The main
      source of confusion in interpreting *The Catcher*
      lies in that ... many critics have failed to grasp
      the ethical implications of the novel, forming two
      extreme interpretations--namely, optimistic and
      pessimistic ones--and that these extremists have
      committed errors by overlooking or underestimating
      Holden's ambivalent feelings, his experiences of
      love, and the momentariness of his relief.

703. Hassan, Ihab H. "The Character of Post-War Fiction
      in America." In *On Contemporary Literature*. Ed.
      Richard Kostelanetz. New York: Avon Books, 1964,
      pp. 36-47.

      The Catcher contains "naturalism and symbolism,
      comedy and tragedy, picaresque and romance, even
      surrealism"; it is "the classic of post-war fic-
      tion."

704. ————. "Laughter in the Dark: The New Voice in
      American Fiction." *American Scholar*, 33 (Autumn
      1964), 636-638, 640.

      Hassan remarks that "even in such zany and gen-
      uinely humorous 'picaresques' as Salinger's *The
      Catcher in the Rye* ... laughter trails into a wist-
      ful tremor."

705. ————. "The Victim: Images of Evil in Recent Amer-
      ican Fiction." *College English*, 21 (December
      1959), 140-146.

      Hassan mentions that Holden Caulfield "remains
      a solitary victim to innocence, to an ideal which
      society must continually betray."

706. Hays, Peter L. "Runaways on a One-Way Ticket, or
     Dropouts in Literature." *Arizona Quarterly*, 31
     (Winter 1975), 301-310.

     Hays mentions Holden Caulfield as a "recent ad-
     olescent dropout" in showing that the "pattern of
     retreat and withdrawal from conventional life ...
     is plainly present in much of American literature."

707. Hazard, Eloise Perry. "Eight Fiction Finds." *Sat-
     urday Review*, 16 February 1952, pp. 16-18.

     Brief biography and comments on the success of
     The Catcher and Salinger's reaction.

708. Heiserman, Arthur, and James E. Miller, Jr. "J.D.
     Salinger: Some Crazy Cliff." *Western Humanities
     Review*, 10 (Spring 1956), 129-137; rpt. Miller,
     James E., Jr. *Quests Surd and Absurd*. Chicago:
     University of Chicago Press, 1967, pp. 31-40.

     Heiserman and Miller analyze *The Catcher* in "the
     tradition of the Quest"; Holden "needs to go home
     and he needs to leave it." The authors conclude
     that "to 'cure' Holden, he must be given the con-
     tagious, almost universal disease of phony adult-
     ism; he must be pushed over that 'crazy cliff.'"
     Rpt. in 385, 400, 404, 413, 415, and 428.

709. Held, George. "The Ideals of Holden Caulfield."
     Clearing House, 40 (January 1966), 295-297.

     In refuting John Mulholland's objections (see
     item 745), Held hopes "that young people will con-
     tinue to read *The Catcher in the Rye* and to make
     the kind of identification with its hero that the
     students of Alvin Alley [see item 659] have made."

710. Howe, Irving. "Mass Society and Post-Modern Fiction."
     Partisan Review, 26 (Summer 1959), 420-436; rpt.
     The American Novel Since World War II. Ed. Mar-
     cus Klein. Greenwich, Connecticut: Fawcett, 1969,
     pp. 124-141.

     "The precocious and bewildered boy in J.D. Sal-
     inger's *The Catcher in the Rye* expresses something
     of the moral condition of adolescents today--or so
     they tell us; but clearly his troubles are not
     meant to refer to his generation alone."

711. Jacobs, Robert G. "J.D. Salinger's *The Catcher in
     the Rye*: Holden Caulfield's 'Goddam Autobiogra-
     phy.'" *Iowa English Yearbook*, No. 4 (Fall 1959),
     9-14.

     After a brief review of criticism of *The Catcher*

and comments on its style, character, plot, Holden's
sickness, criticism of adulthood, concepts of himself, and the curse of adulthood, Jacobs concludes
that "the reader cannot, finally, identify himself
with Holden Caulfield, for Holden is hilariously,
ridiculously sick, and the reader lives in a world
where adulthood is health." Rpt. in 415.

712. Kermode, Frank. "Fit Audience." *The Spectator*, 30
        May 1958, pp. 705-706.

        Acknowledging much to admire in *The Catcher*,
Kermode finds "something phoney" in it. He rejects
it as "a 'key' book, because it is not designed for
the smart-common reader." Rpt. in 385, 400, and
413.

713. Kinney, Arthur F. "The Theme of Charity in *The
        Catcher in the Rye*." *Papers of the Michigan
        Academy of Science, Arts, and Letters*, 48 (1963),
        691-702.

        Kinney's thematic interpretation of *The Catcher*
states that the "idea of charity--that the highest
love is selfless devotion to all men, friend and
enemy alike, a love valid only when practiced, is
the sermon Salinger preaches in this novel."

714. Kinnick, Bernard C. "Holden Caulfield: Adolescents'
        Enduring Model." *High School Journal*, 53 (May
        1970), 440-443.

        To Kinnick, "Holden Caulfield represents the u-
niqueness in man in a world which has lost its spirit for the idealism so often expressed in man's
past search for Utopia."

715. Klein, Marcus. "Introduction." In *The American Novel
        Since World War II*. Ed. Marcus Klein. Greenwich,
        Connecticut: Fawcett, 1969, pp. 9-23.

        Mentions *The Catcher* as one of the major novels
since World War II.

716. Kostelanetz, Richard. "Contemporary Literature." In
        On Contemporary Literature. Ed. Richard Kostelan-
        etz. New York: Avon Books, 1964, pp. xv-xxvii.

        Kostelanetz mentions that Salinger's Holden Caul-
field and other modern protagonists "are all faced
with the possibility of death, but their awareness
of their possible extinction only inspires them to
draw strength from their deepest sources of resil-
ience and to salvage their lives."

717. Laser, Marvin. "Character Names in *The Catcher in
        the Rye*." *California English Journal*, 1 (Winter
        1965), 29-40.

        Some of the names Salinger gives to several char-
        acters in *The Catcher* are used as "character tags,
        others to suggest a leading trait, others for ironic
        humor, a few for symbolic purposes, and several for
        broad or ribald comedy."

718. Lee, Charles. *The Hidden Public: The Story of the
        Book-of-the-Month Club*. Garden City, New York:
        Doubleday, 1958, p. 184.

        For 1951, "J.D. Salinger's *The Catcher in the
        Rye* (not especially liked, however, by the member-
        ship) shared honors as a discovery with *The Cruel
        Sea* (very well liked), the first big seller by
        Nicholas Monsarrat."

719. Lerner, Laurence. "City Troubles: Pastoral and Sat-
        ire." In *The Uses of Nostalgia: Studies in Pas-
        toral Poetry*. London: Chatto and Windus, 1972,
        pp. 130-148.

        By looking at *The Catcher* "outwards from the
        book's attitudes towards a literary form it has
        not actually assumed," Lerner judges Salinger's
        novel to be "a pastoral satire."

720. Lettis, Richard. "Holden Caulfield: Salinger's 'I-
        ronic Amalgam.'" *American Notes & Queries*, 15
        (November 1976), 43-45.

        With a review of attempts to explain Holden Caul-
        field's name (see items 661, 732, and 751), Lettis
        interprets it as follows: "He *holds in the caul
        field*--tries to prevent children, including him-
        self from growing up."

721. Leverett, Ernest. "The Virtues of Vulgarity--Rus-
        sian and American Views." *Carleton Miscellany*,
        1 (Spring 1960), 29-40.

        Leverett cites Holden as an example of the "buf-
        foon and hero all at once" and compares him to Gats-
        by.

722. Lewis, R.W.B. "Adam as Hero in the Age of Contain-
        ment." In "Epilogue: The Contemporary Situation."
        In *The American Adam: Innocence, Tragedy and
        Tradition in the Nineteenth Century*. Chicago:
        University of Chicago Press, 1955, pp. 197-200.

        The Catcher is a novel in which "the hero ["an

unstable adolescent"] is willing, with marvelously
inadequate equipment, to take on as much of the
world as is available to him, without ever finally
submitting to any of the world's determining categories."

723.   Light, James F. "Salinger's *The Catcher in the Rye*."
       Explicator, 18 (June 1960), Item 59.

       In a comment on the ducks in *The Catcher*, Light
       writes that Holden's questions "where do the ducks
       go?" and "what is the meaning of death?" are "really
       the same question." See item 780. Rpt. in 415 and
       428.

724.   "The Limits of the Possible: Accepting the Reality
       of the Human Situation." *Times Literary Supple-
       ment*, 6 November 1959, p. xvi.

       The Catcher "is indeed a work of almost magical
       charm, though charm is not a quality its hero-nar-
       rator would approve of."

725.   Lipton, Lawrence. "The Barbarian Is at the Gates."
       In *The American Novel Since World War II*. Ed.
       Marcus Klein. Greenwich, Connecticut: Fawcett,
       1969, pp. 177-185.

       "It is not difficult for the beat generation
       youth to identify itself with the book's hero,
       Holden Caulfield. He not only *sounds* right to them
       but the things he says are often the things they
       say."

726.   ————. "Disaffiliation and the Art of Poverty."
       Chicago Review, 10 (Spring 1956), 53-79.

       "Caulfield's father belongs to F. Scott Fitzger-
       ald's Jazz Age Twenties. Young Caulfield belongs
       to the generation" of Lizzie in George Mandel's
       Flee the Angry Strangers.

727.   Love, Glen A. "Ecology in Arcadia." *Colorado Quart-
       erly*, 21 (Autumn 1972), 175-185.

       "We have found the pattern of regenerative na-
       ture frequently reasserted not only in Heminway,
       but ... in the yearnings of an Eastern sophisti-
       cate like Salinger's Holden Caulfield to go west
       and 'build me a little cabin somewhere right near
       the woods.'"

728.   MacLean, Hugh. "Conservatism in Modern American
       Fiction." *College English*, 15 (March 1954),
       315-325.

Reads *The Catcher* as "entirely negative, an 'Everlasting No.'" Rpt. in 400, 415, and 428.

729. Marcus, Fred H. *"The Catcher in the Rye*: A Live Circuit." *English Journal*, 52 (January 1963), 1-8.

Not often studied in the secondary classroom at the time of this article, *The Catcher*, Marcus writes, "merits detailed study."

730. Margolis, John D. "Salinger's *The Catcher in the Rye*." *Explicator*, 22 (November 1963), Item 23.

Margolis proclaims that the "carrousel scene" at the end of *The Catcher* shows symbolically that "Holden has undergone a decided change in the course of the novel."

731. Marks, Barry A. "Rebuttal: Holden in the Rye." *College English*, 23 (March 1962), 507.

Marks objects to Peter Seng's reading (see item 768) of *The Catcher*, which, according to Marks, "dramatizes ... ultimate issues rather than ultimate judgments." Rpt. in 415 and 428.

732. Martin, Dexter. "Rebuttal: Holden in the Rye." *College English*, 23 (March 1962), 507-508.

Objecting to statements by Peter Seng (see item 768), Martin claims "that what ails Holden is the death of his brother, Allie ('All'), plus parental neglect." Rpt. in 428.

733. ————. [Unpublished portion of] "Rebuttal [to Old-sey]." In *Salinger's "Catcher in the Rye": Clamor vs. Criticism*. Eds. Harold P. Simonson and Philip E. Hager. Lexington, Massachusetts: D.C. Heath, 1963, pp. 45-46.

Martin suggests that "Salinger's primary reason for selecting [the name] Caulfield is obviously the fact that it means 'cold field'" and that Jane is "soul-sick, like Holden." See items 732 and 751.

734. Matle, John. "Calling Miss Aigletinger." *CEA Critic*, 39 (March 1977), 18-20.

After a review of other readers who have commented on names in *The Catcher* (see items 661, 711, 732, and 768), Matle suggests a possible connection between Miss Aigletinger and an Aigeltinger in a poem by William Carlos Williams.

735. McCarthy, Mary. "Characters in Fiction." *Partisan*

Review, 28 (March-April 1961), 171-191; rpt. *On the Contrary: Articles of Belief*. New York: Farrar, Strauss, Cudahy, 1961, pp. 271-292.

The Catcher is a dramatic monologue.

736. McNamara, Eugene. "Holden as Novelist." *English Journal*, 54 (March 1965), 166-170.

McNamara investigates Holden's "whole complex set of attitudes towards and assumptions about the universe he exists in."

737. McWhirter, J. Jeffries. "Understanding the Adolescent Through Catcher in the Rye." *Counselor Education and Supervision*, 9 (Winter 1970), 139-142.

McWhirter suggests that counselors might better understand certain areas of human behavior--communication, acceptance, conformity, and values--with a study of *The Catcher*.

738. Meral, Jean. "The Ambiguous Mr. Antolini in Salinger's *Catcher in the Rye*." *Caliban*, 7 (1970), 55-58.

Despite Antolini's own problems and his being a phony, Holden benefits from the encounter with him in that Antolini "precipitates Holden's fall into manhood."

739. Miles, Donald. *The American Novel in the Twentieth Century*. New York: Harper and Row, 1978, p. 109.

In his chapter entitled "Fantasy," Miles mentions "Salinger's amusing but superficial *Catcher in the Rye* where the real problem of the adolescent hero, Holden Caulfield, is that there is no fantasy world enduring enough to afford him the excitement that his imagination craves."

740. Miller, James E., Jr. "*Catcher* in and out of History." *Critical Inquiry*, 3 (Spring 1977), 599-603.

Miller criticizes Carol and Richard Ohmann's "Marxist or neo-Marxist approach" (see item 748) for wanting "to carry Holden out of baffling, muddled history into a tidy and clear-cut ideology." See item 749.

741. Millgate, Michael. *American Social Fiction: James to Cozzens*. Edinburgh: Oliver and Boyd, 1964, pp. 203, 204.

"American literature is rich in images of

isolated escape: its typical figures are ... Holden
Caulfield planning to act deaf-mute and live in a
hut on the edge of the woods."

742. Montgomery, Paul L. "Lennon Murder Suspect Prepar-
        ing Insanity Defense." *New York Times*, 9 Febru-
        ary 1981, p. 12B.

        In a note to the *New York Times*, Mark Chapman,
        the accused murderer of John Lennon, urges people
        to read *The Catcher* in order "'to understnad what
        has happened.'"

743. Moore, Robert P. "The World of Holden." *English
        Journal*, 54 (March 1965), 159-165.

        Moore's analysis of Holden's character yields
        "the innocent youth in a world of cruel and hypo-
        critical adults ... the twentieth-century, unroman-
        tic version of Melville's Billy Budd."

744. Moss, Adam. "Catcher Comes of Age." *Esquire*, 96
        (December 1981), 56-58, 60.

        On the thirtieth anniversary of the publication
        of *The Catcher*, Moss presents many bits of infor-
        mation about the novel: details of its appearance
        in print, the various editions and numbers of cop-
        ies printed and sold, quotations called "The Wit
        and Wisdom of Holden Caulfield" on subjects like
        mothers, women, courage, etc., John Updike's, Peter
        DeVries', and Tom Wolfe's "lasting impressions,"
        biographical material about Salinger, "*Catcher*" in
        the News" (1951-1980), and Holden's genesis in ear-
        lier Salinger fiction.

745. Mulholland, John F. "Puritanism: A Needed Ingredi-
        ent in Education." *Clearing House*, 39 (January
        1965), 268-270.

        Responding to Alvin Alley's statement (see item
        656) about students identifying with Holden, Mulhol-
        land objects to *The Catcher*, not because of the
        language, but because students do identify with
        Holden, "the failure, the misunderstood, the de-
        feated, the rejected." See item 709.

746. Murry, John Middleton. *The London Magazine*, 3 (De-
        cember 1956), 69-72.

        In a review of John Lehmann's *The Craft of Let-
        ters in England*, Murry mentions that *The Catcher*
        "is the only absolutely modern novel which has moved
        me deeply. Its power of spiritual reverberation is
        subtle and persistent."

747.   O'Hara, J.D. "No Catcher in the Rye." *Modern Fiction
       Studies*, 9 (Winter 1963-64), 370-376; rpt. *The
       Modern American Novel: Essays in Criticism*. Ed.
       Max Roger Westbrook. New York: Random House,
       1966, pp. 211-220.

       O'Hara focuses on "such simple questions as
       these: at the end of the book, is Holden a catcher?
       How does Salinger feel about the idea of a catcher
       in the rye?"

748.   Ohmann, Carol, and Richard Ohmann. "Reviewers, Crit-
       ics, and *The Catcher in the Rye*." *Critical In-
       quiry*, 3 (Autumn 1976), 15-37.

       Repudiating the idea that Holden rejects "an im-
       moral world, the inhumanity of the world, the adult
       world, the predicament of modern life, the human
       condition, the facts of life, evil," the Ohmanns
       suggest that Holden actually rejects the particular
       "time and place" in which he lives. *The Catcher*
       "is ... a serious critical mimesis of bourgeois
       life in the Eastern United States, ca. 1950." See
       items 740 and 749. Rpt. in 385.

749.   ————. "Universals and the Historically Particu-
       lar." *Critical Inquiry*, 3 (Summer 1977), 773-
       777.

       The Ohmanns respond that "Miller's reading [see
       item 740] is inadequate to *Catcher*." See item 748.

750.   Olderman, Raymond M. *Beyond the Waste Land: A Study
       of the American Novel in the Nineteen-Sixties*.
       New Haven, Connecticut: Yale University Press,
       1972, p. 33.

       Holderman views the end of *The Catcher* as "the
       end of American quests for the pure Utopia. Now
       the novel of the sixties begins where Holden left
       off--at the end of adolescence and in the waste
       land asylum, hoping to move beyond."

751.   Oldsey, Bernard S. "The Movies in the Rye." *College
       English*, 32 (December 1961), 209-215.

       Oldsey demonstrates the effects of movies on
       Holden and Salinger's theme in *The Catcher*: "the-
       matically, the novel is intent on exposing the
       phoniness of life in these United States, the tawd-
       riness of a Barnum-and-Bailey world remade by Metro-
       Goldwyn-Mayer." Even the major character's name
       may be "an ironic amalgan of the last names of mov-
       ie stars William Holden and Joan Caulfield." See
       items 661, 689, 720, and 732. Rpt. in 400, 415,
       and 428.

752. Orel, Harold. "What They Think About Teen-Agers in
        Books." *College English*, 23 (November 1961),
        147-149.

        The Catcher was one "of the books that dealt
        with the problems of teen-agers and young men and
        women" that Orel used in a class of freshmen in
        1961. The students were critical of Holden. Rpt.
        in 415.

753. Panova, Vera. "On J.D. Salinger's Novel." In *Soviet
        Criticism of American Literature in the Sixties*.
        Ed. and Trans. Carl R. Proffer. Ann Arbor, Mich-
        igan: Ardis, 1972, pp. 4-10.

        Calling Holden "a loafer, a petty liar, a swag-
        gering dandy, a strange, unlucky young creature,"
        Panova nevertheless finds in *The Catcher* "many fe-
        licitous discoveries, magnificent details, and
        brilliant dialogue."

754. Parker, Christopher. "'Why the Hell *Not* Smash All
        the Windows?'" In *Salinger: A Critical and Per-
        sonal Portrait*. Ed. Henry Anatole Grunwald. New
        York: Harper and Row, 1962, pp. 254-258.

        In what he calls "a crazy kid's view of a crazy
        kid," Parker, a college student, explains "the phe-
        nomenal success of *The Catcher* among college stu-
        dents ... [as] little more than a kind of myth wor-
        ship--like Jimmy Dean." See item 404.

755. Peavy, Charles D. "Holden Courage Again." *CEA Crit-
        ic*, 28 (October 1965), 1, 6, 9.

        In the discussion between Deane Warner (see item
        933) and Boris Burack (see item 670), Peavy sees
        Holden as "he represents not so much a courageous
        rebel as a frightened, pathetic Peter Pan."

756. Pilkington, John. "Mummie and Ducks." *University of
        Mississippi Studies in English*, OS 6 (1965),
        15-22.

        "Holden identifies himself with the ducks" be-
        cause "they escape"; similarly, "the Egyptians had
        actually been able to keep something from change
        or rot," as Holden mentioned earlier in his exam
        for Spencer.

757. Piper, Henry Dan. "Modern American Classics." *Sat-
        urday Review*, 17 February 1962, p. 20.

        Piper asked a group of college English instruc-
        tors in California the following questions: "Of the

literary works by American writers published since
1941, which have already begun to attain the stature of modern classics? What books published during the last two decades deserve to be included in
a college course in American literature?" With the
results of the survey tallied by writer and title,
Salinger and *The Catcher* appeared at the top of
both lists. See item 773.

758. Ralston, Nancy C. "Holden Caulfield: Super-Adoles-
cent." *Adolescence*, 6 (Winter 1971), 429-432.

Ralston illustrates that in Holden Caulfield
Salinger has created a universal adolescent; if the
novel were written today, "only the external and
none of the internal factors of the story would
need revision."

759. Reiman, Donald H. "Rebuttal: Holden in the Rye."
College English, 23 (March 1962), 507.

Reiman objects to Peter Seng's overstating Hold-
en's "immaturity" (see item 768) and Bernard Oldsey's overstressing "his virtues" (see item 715).
Rpt. in 428.

760. ———. "Salinger's *The Catcher in the Rye*, Chapters 22-26." *Explicator*, 21 (March 1963), Item
58.

"Holden's fundamental choice has been between a
dead, museum realm of Being and the imperfect, tem-
poral world of Becoming. At the end of the novel
he has chosen as his model of human life his sister
Phoebe--living, learning, reading, perhaps falling--
rather than his dead brother, Allie, doomed to e-
ternal childhood." See item 778.

761. Riedel, Walter E. "Some German Ripples of Holden
Caulfield's 'Goddam Autobiography': On Trans-
lating and Adapting J.D. Salinger's *The Catcher
in the Rye*." *Canadian Review of Comparative
Literature*, 7 (Spring 1980), 196-205.

Riedel finds that Heinrich Böll, in his German
translation of *The Catcher*, has rendered "the original in the translator's own image depending on
such aspects as his interpretation, his background
of experience, his perception of nuances as well as
his judgment in matters pertaining to public taste,
and, perhaps, his adherence to guidelines from the
publisher."

762. Romanova, Elena. "Reviews and News: What American
Novels do Russians Read?" *Soviet Literature*,

No. 7 (July 1961), 178-182.

During a visit to the United States, Romanova
was surprised to learn that even presumably know-
ledgeable Americans did not know which American
writers had been translated into Russian. She explains that *The Catcher* appeals to Russian readers
because "'a book which makes us think, which makes
us worry about the hero and wish him well is a good
book.'"

763. Roper, Pamela E. "Holden's Hat." *Notes on Contempo-
      rary Literature*, 7 (May 1977), 8-9.

      Roper sees Holden's hat "as a caul," which "does
      not keep him from being drenched by reality, but he
      is at least preserved from drowning in the down-
      pour."

764. Rosen, Gerald. "A Retrospective Look at *The Catch-
      er in the Rye*." *American Quarterly*, 29 (Winter
      1977), 547-562.

      Rosen sees the story of Holden Caulfield as sim-
      ilar to that of the Buddha: "he is confronted with
      old age, sickness, and death. They so shake him he
      decides to leave the shelter of his surroundings
      and the distractions of his involvement in his ev-
      eryday life in order to wander in the world in
      search of a guide."

765. Salisbury, Harrison E. "'Lost Generation' Baffles
      Soviet; Nihilistic Youths Shun Ideology." *New
      York Times*, 9 February 1962, pp. 1, 4.

      "The more sophisticated members of the 'lost
      generation' prefer J.D. Salinger"; *The Catcher* "has
      become almost a status symbol among the university
      generation."

766. Scott, Nathan. *Modern Literature and the Religious
      Frontier*. New York: Harper and Brothers, 1958,
      pp. 90-94, 102.

      The Catcher presents the idea "that perhaps the
      best way of surviving this present time is for us
      to become 'catchers in the rye,' to seek self-def-
      inition in and through the most primitive realities
      of our human togetherness, and to talk to one an-
      other about our lives."

767. Seligmann, Jean, and Michael Reese. "Favorite Books
      in English Class." *Newsweek*, 30 April 1979, p.
      95.

      A report on a poll by *English Journal* that high

school English teachers "select some modern books
of special interest to young people--among them,
'Roots,' 'The Catcher in the Rye,' and 'To Kill a
Mockingbird.'"

768. Seng, Peter J. "The Fallen Idol: The Immature World
      of Holden Caulfield." *College English*, 32 (De-
      cember 1961), 203-209.

      Seng emphasizes the importance of the relation-
ship between Holden and Mr. Antolini, Holden's
former teacher whose "saving advice ... has been
rendered useless because the idol who gave it has
fallen." According to Seng, Holden's survival de-
pends on his ability to have compassion for what
he finds in this world and to follow the advice
Antolini gives him. See items 731, 732, 734, and
759. Rpt. in 400, 415, and 428.

769. Sherr, Paul C. "'The Catcher in the Rye' and the
      Boarding School." *Independent School Bulletin*,
      26 (December 1966), 42-44.

      Recognizing that his male students in a board-
ing school find *The Catcher* "an exciting work and
respect it," Sherr plans "to offer some suggestions
as to what is meaningful from their point of view
and to propose that they misread the book, a fact
that makes it an extremely effective teaching de-
vice in all secondary schools, and especially in a
boarding school for boys."

770. Slabey, Robert M. "*The Catcher in the Rye*: Christian
      Theme and Symbol." *College Language Association
      Journal*, 6 (March 1963), 170-183.

      Slabey examines "the Christian materials" of
"the Advent season, the Original Sin, and Redemption" in *The Catcher* and illustrates that "the pattern of religious quest and conversion is recurrent
in Salinger's works."

771. Strauch, Carl F. "Kings in the Back Row: Meaning
      Through Structure--A Reading of Salinger's *The
      Catcher in the Rye*." *Wisconsin Studies in Con-
      temporary Literature*, 2 (Winter 1961), 5-30.

      In a long article, Strauch writes "that Salinger
has employed neurotic deterioration, symbolic death,
spiritual awakening, and psychological self-cure as
the inspiration and burden of an elaborate pattern--
verbal, thematic, and episodic, that yields the
meaning as the discursive examination of Holden's
character and problem out of metaphoric context can
never do. Structure *is* meaning." *The Catcher*,

Strauch says, ends affirmatively. Rpt. in 385, 400, 413, 415, and 428.

772. Stretch, Linda. *Time*, 30 May 1960, p. 4.

Stretch reports teaching *The Catcher* "because it is well written, and we learned a lot from discussing Holden Caulfield's problems."

773. Sublette, Jack R. "Modern American Classics (1941-1970) in Colleges of Illinois." *Illinois English Bulletin*, 59 (November 1972), 13-15.

In an update of Henry Piper's survey (see item 757), Sublette finds that among professors in colleges and universities in Illinois Salinger and *The Catcher* rank second behind Ralph Ellison and *Invisible Man* in response to the questions "Which books by American authors published during the last three decades (1941-70) deserve to be included in a college course in American literature?" and "Which have already begun to attain the stature of modern classics?"

774. Sykes, Richard E. "American Studies and the Concept of Culture: A Theory and Method." *American Quarterly*, 15 (Summer 1963, Part 2), 253-270.

Sykes asks if Salinger's choice of a narrator in *The Catcher* "helps the author express meanings he could not otherwise easily express."

775. Tanner, Tony. *City of Words: American Fiction 1950-1970*. New York: Harper and Row, 1971, p. 416.

Brief mention that Salinger unsuccessfully "reexamined the premises underlying this age-old suspicion and repudiation of society by the American writer and his hero."

776. Tarinaya, M. "Salinger: *The Catcher in the Rye*." *Literary Half-Yearly*, 7 (July 1966), 49-60.

Calling *The Catcher* "a remarkable achievement in fiction," Tarinaya criticizes Salinger for not "bring[ing] out the best in his hero's character" and for lack of "a comprehensive general design"; the message of the novel seems to be "that if America is to fulfil her destiny and make the New World also the New Jerusalem, the kingdom of heaven brought within reach of man, the American people must be aware of their deficiencies and must not forget the great tradition handed down to them by Lincoln, Whitman, Emerson and Thoreau."

777. Theroux, Joseph. "Holden Caulfield Comes to Samoa."
      English Journal, 70 (September 1981), 42-46.

      A teacher in Pago Pago, American Samoa, Theroux
      briefly explains the Samoan educational system and
      his difficulties and joys in teaching *The Catcher*
      to a class of twelfth grade boys.

778. Tirumalai, Candadai K. "Salinger's *The Catcher in
      the Rye.*" *Explicator*, 22 (March 1964), Item 56.

      Note that Donald Reiman (see item 760) fails to
      distinguish between "*two* distinct museums, the Mu-
      seum of Natural History (Chap. 16) *and* the Museum
      of Art (Chap. 25)."

779. Toynbee, Philip. "Experiment and the Future of the
      Novel." In *The Craft of Letters in England*. Ed.
      John Lehmann. Boston: Houghton Mifflin, 1957,
      pp. 60-73.

      Toynbee finds *The Catcher* as "the best modern
      example ... of a novel which combines a concern for
      the modern world with a conscious attempt to do
      something new."

780. Travis, Mildred K. "Salinger's *The Catcher in the
      Rye.*" *Explicator*, 21 (December 1962), Item 36.

      In contrast to James Light's interpretation (see
      item 723), Travis believes "that it is the accep-
      tance rather than the rejection of the 'catcher'
      role that involves Holden's insight."

781. Trowbridge, Clinton W. "Salinger's Symbolic Use of
      Character and Detail in *The Catcher in the Rye.*"
      Cimarron Review, No. 4 (June 1968), 5-11.

      If one views *The Catcher* as "Salinger's depic-
      tion of Holden Caulfield as symbolizing the plight
      of the idealist in the modern world," then this
      novel "stands on every count as one of the master-
      pieces of symbolist fiction" because the "minor
      character," "the concrete details," and "the major
      and minor emphases" are all "symbolic extensions
      of the protagonist."

782. ———. "The Symbolic Structure of *The Catcher in
      the Rye.*" *Sewanee Review*, 74 (July-September
      1966), 681-693.

      Trowbridge summarizes the "structural pattern"
      of *The Catcher*: "as a result of a frighteningly
      clear vision of the disparity between what is and
      what ought to be both in the world and in himself

and because of an increasing feeling of incapacity
to re-form either, he [Holden] attempts to escape
into a series of ideal worlds, fails, and is finally
brought to the realization of a higher and more
impersonal ideal, that man and the world, in spite
of all their imperfections, are to be loved."

783. Vail, Dennis. "Holden and Psychoanalysis." *PMLA*,
      91 (January 1976), 120-121.

      Vail responds to what he sees as James Bryan's
      "misreading of Holden's relationship with Phoebe"
      (see item 668).

784. Vanderbilt, Kermit. "Symbolic Resolution in *The
      Catcher in the Rye*: The Cap, the Carrousel, and
      the American West." *Western Humanities Review*,
      17 (Summer 1963), 271-277.

      Reacting to the "consistently slighted or mis-
      interpreted" final scene of *The Catcher*, Vander-
      bilt suggests that the symbols of the cap, the car-
      rousel, and the American West "reinforce each other
      and point the way to Holden's redemption into life
      rather than alienation and withdrawal from it.
      "His too-innocent idealism has begun to give way
      to the hopeful beginnings of maturity and a saner
      view of both himself and of the America in which
      he must live."

785. Walcutt, Charles Child. "Anatomy of Alienation."
      In *Man's Changing Mask: Modes and Methods of
      Characterization in Fiction*. Minneapolis: Uni-
      versity of Minnesota Press, 1966, pp. 302, 317-
      326, 341, 350, 354.

      Walcutt explains *The Catcher* as one novel "mis-
      understood by the most people": "it has fathered
      the Beat Generation, creating a role that has been
      played by increasing numbers since it appeared.
      Salinger's most fervent idolaters, whose number
      is a foreign legion in our midst, admiring him for
      everything he earnestly did *not* intend, have made
      a hero of his anti-hero and a carnival of what he
      wrote as almost a case study."

786. Weigel, John A. "Teaching the Modern Novel: From
      Finnegans Wake to *A Fable*." *College English*, 21
      (December 1959), 172-173.

      The Catcher "need not be taught" because it "has
      been read with pleasure and insight for several
      years by almost all undergraduates who have found
      a copy."

787. Widmer, Kingsley. "Poetic Naturalism in the Contem-
        porary Novel." *Partisan Review*, 26 (Summer 1959),
        467-472.

        In an analysis of Holden, Widmer writes that "as
        the whole child-cult of sensitivity suggests, none
        of the ordinary are really ordinary because naked
        awareness shows the ordinary as fantastically u-
        nique, though the un-naked pretend that it isn't
        so."

788. Williams, Raymond. "Realism and the Contemporary
        Novel." In *20th Century Literary Criticism: A
        Reader*. Ed. David Lodge. London: Longman, 1972,
        pp. 581-591.

        The Catcher has "a saving irony" but does have
        limitations.

789. Wilson, James R. *Responses of College Freshmen to
        Three Novels*. Champaign, Illinois: National
        Council of Teachers of English, 1966.

        One of a series of research reports, this study
        investigated the study of Salinger's *The Catcher*,
        Steinbeck's *The Grapes of Wrath*, and Hemingway's *A
        Farewell to Arms* by college freshmen in order "to
        determine how students perceive literature and what
        kind of change occurs" as a result of classroom
        study.

790. Witham, W. Tasker. *The Adolescent in the American
        Novel, 1920-1960*. New York: Ungar, 1964, pp. 18,
        19, 20, 23, 25, 98, 107, 115, 204, 241, 245,
        247-248, 252, 270, 277.

        Witham makes many references to *The Catcher* and
        Holden Caulfield, one of which is that this work
        is an example of a "completely frank" novel about
        male adolescence.

791. Woodman, Leonora. "Teaching Literature Thematically."
        English Journal, 55 (May 1966), 564-568.

        Calling *Walden*, "Civil Disobedience," *Adventures
        of Huckleberry Finn*, *Arrowsmith*, and *The Catcher*
        "literature of dissent," Woodman explains how she
        uses these works because they are "related to each
        other in their moral and intellectual assumptions
        and in their tacit or avowed solutions."

792. Workman, Brooke. "Parody: A Student's Response to
        J.D. Salinger." *English Journal*, 70 (January
        1981), 53-54.

After an intensive study of Salinger's works,
Workman, a teacher at West High School in Iowa City,
had his junior and senior students write "something
called 'The Summing Up.'" Most of them wrote parodies of Salinger; he includes a sample by Diane
Scott called "A Close Encounter of the Phony Kind."

793.   Workman, Molly F. *"The Catcher* in the Classroom."
        Virginia English Bulletin, 10 (December 1960),
        1-6.

        The Catcher "deserves to be read and studied"
        because it provides adolescents "the opportunity to
        study and reflect upon their own attitudes toward
        themselves and society, for the purpose of shaping
        and improving them."

(2.) Censorship, Controversy, Problems in the Classroom

The use of *The Catcher* in the classroom and the inclusion of it in school libraries have raised the issue
of censorship and caused controversy and problems in the
classroom and several communities. Listed alphabetically,
the entries in this category refer to material about these
various problems. For a detailed study of censorship and
The Catcher, see item 592 in the subsection above on dissertations and theses.

794.   Alvino, James. "Is It Book-Burning Time Again?" *New
        York Times,* 28 December 1980, Sec. 11, p. 18.

        In an article about censorship, Alvino recalls
        a 1977 incident in which *The Catcher* was attacked
        in Pittsgrove Township, Salem County, New Jersey.
        See item 854.

795.   Asheim, Lester. "Not Censorship But Selection."
        Wilson Library Bulletin, 28 (September 1953),
        63-67.

        Some find it difficult to believe "that there
        is stronger moral fibre in a book like *Catcher in
        the Rye"* than in books of milder language.

796.   Badeczewski, Dennis. "Censorship: A Difference in
        Kind, Not Degree." *Arizona English Bulletin,* 17
        (February 1975), 75-77.

        Badeczewski mentions that *The Catcher,* "written
        before some present English teachers were born,"
        still causes problems and is sometimes called a
        "subversive" novel.

797.   "Ban on Authors Is Urged Upstate: Salinger, Heming-
       way and Baldwin Are Attacked." *New York Times*, 7
       March 1965, p. 75.

       Report of the president of the Vestal (New York)
       School Board declaring that *The Catcher* is "'dirty'
       and shouldn't be allow [sic] in the doors of any
       secondary school in this country."

798.   "Banning Books: An Ancient Sport Makes a Rowdy Come-
       back Among School Boards." *American School Board
       Journal*, 160 (May 1973), 25-27, 37-38.

       The Catcher is mentioned as "the most widely cen-
       sored book in the U.S."

799.   Bartman, Robert I. "A Student's Right to Write."
       Arizona English Bulletin, 17 (February 1975),
       141-145.

       Bartman mentions a student in Michigan who "was
       expelled for having in his possession an *Argus* mag-
       azine which contained the offensive word," a viola-
       tion of school policy, but "the court noted that
       the same word appeared in *Catcher in the Rye* ...
       which was required or optional reading for ninth
       and tenth graders."

800.   Berninghausen, David K., and Richard W. Faunce.
       "An Exploratory Study of Juvenile Delinquency
       and the Reading of Sensational Books." *Journal
       of Experimental Education*, 33 (Winter 1964),
       161-168.

       Classifies *The Catcher* as an "adult book."

801.   Blough, Richard. "Censorship in Indiana." *Arizona
       English Bulletin*, 17 (February 1975), 63.

       Problems in English classes in Indiana have been
       lessened by teachers allowing students to select
       "another from a *suggested*, rather than a *required*
       reading list" if they object to a book like *The
       Catcher*.

802.   "Book Censorship Increasing in Schools." *New York
       Times*, 2 January 1979, p. 12C.

       Report that *The Catcher* was banned from class-
       rooms in Anaheim, California.

803.   Booth, Wayne C. "Censorship and the Values of Fic-
       tion." *English Journal*, 53 (March 1964), 155-164.

       Booth defends the use of *The Catcher* in the

classroom. The article suggests that teachers use
it along with *The Student's Right to Read* by NCTE
in order to deal with problems of censorship.

804. Burress, Lee. "A Brief Report of the 1977 NCTE Cen-
     sirship Survey." In *Dealing with Censorship*. Ed.
     James E. Davis. Urbana, Illinois: National Coun-
     cil of Teachers of English, 1979, pp. 14-17.

     The survey reports that *The Catcher* is often ob-
     jected to.

805. "Censors Hit Trade Books in School: Textbooks As-
     sessed." *Publisher's Weekly*, 16 May 1960, pp. 46-
     47.

     Summary of Beatrice Levin's problems with using
     The Catcher in the classroom in Tulsa, Oklahoma.

806. Church, Bud. "The Right to be a Reader ..." *The
     Leaflet*, 68 (May 1969), 37-40.

     Church calls for parents to consider objection-
     able passages in the context of the whole work.
     He provides examples from *The Catcher* that parents
     have objected to and says that in each case Salin-
     ger is making a "moral point," perhaps "the same
     point ... most parents would want made."

807. Clark, Susan H. "1975 Censorship Battleground: State
     Legislatures." *Arizona English Bulletin*, 17 (Feb-
     ruary 1975), 107-109.

     Some state laws "include extensive 'laundry
     lists' of prohibited sexual conduct, thus making
     it easier for over-zealous censors to find grounds
     for attack, as happened this year, with such works
     as" *The Catcher* and others.

808. *Combatting Undemocratic Pressures on Schools and
     Libraries: A Guide for Local Communities*. New
     York: American Civil Liberties Union, 1964, p. 8.

     The Catcher is included in a list of "works of
     literature which have been attacked as 'obscene.'"

809. Corbett, Edward P.J. "Raise High the Barriers, Cen-
     sors." *America*, 7 January 1961, pp. 441-443.

     Caling *The Catcher* "a subtle, sophisticated
     novel that requires an experienced, mature reader,"
     Corbett analyzes the major objections made to it:
     language, "scandalous" episodes, and Holden's hy-
     pocrisy about phoniness. Before readers condemn
     Salinger's novel, Corbett cautions, they need to

read it carefully and keep its merits in focus.
Rpt. in 400, 415, and 428.

810.   Crabb, Alfred L., Jr. "Censorship in Kentucky: Ken-
       tucky Council of Teachers of English Question-
       naire." *Arizona English Bulletin*, 17 (February
       1975), 152-157.

       In a Kentucky survey, *The Catcher* is the book
       listed most often as one "objected to."

811.   Davis, James E. "Censorship in Ohio." *Arizona Eng-
       lish Bulletin*, 17 (February 1975), 80.

       Davis includes *The Catcher* in a list of titles
       that "are still the most popular targets" for cen-
       sorship in Ohio.

812.   "The Debate: Whether and How to Censor 'Objection-
       able' School Books." *American School Board Jour-
       nal*, 160 (May 1973), 38-39.

       The Catcher is a good book, one not to be banned,
       "because of the accurate judgments young Holden
       makes on the adult world he sees."

813.   Dionne, E.J., Jr. "Ruling Sustains Entry by Police
       to Make Arrest." *New York Times*, 12 July 1978,
       pp. 1A, 20B.

       Report that a court "overturned the dismissal
       of a tenured teacher discharged for breaching an
       agreement not to use J.D. Salinger's 'Catcher in
       the Rye' in a sophomore English class in Mechanics-
       ville, N.Y." because the "dismissal was 'dispro-
       portionate to the offense' involved."

814.   Donart, Arthur C. "The Books They're Banning and
       Why: The List Has Something for Nearly Every-
       body." *American School Board Journal*, 160 (May
       1973), 42-43.

       The Catcher is listed as being banned for "ob-
       scenity."

815.   Donelson, Ken. "Censorship and Arizona English Teach-
       ing, 1971-1974." *Arizona English Bulletin*, 17
       (February 1975), 1-39.

       In a 1974 survey on censorship in Arizona, Donel-
       son reports that *The Catcher* is the work "most fre-
       quently attacked" and "most frequently *banned, re-
       moved, or placed on closed shelf*."

816.   ———. "Censorship in the 1970's: Some Ways to

Handle It When It Comes (And It Will)." *English Journal*, 63 (February 1974), 47-51; rpt. *Dealing with Censorship*. Ed. James E. Davis. Urbana, Illinois: National Council of Teachers of English, 1979, pp. 162-167.

In an article that gives advice to English departments for dealing with censorship, Donelson mentions that readers sometimes object to the language of *The Catcher*.

817.   ————. "Obscenity and the Chill Factor: Court Decisions about Obscenity and Their Relationships to School Censorship." In *Dealing with Censorship*. Ed. James E. Davis. Urbana, Illinois: National Council of Teachers of English, 1979, pp. 63-75.

Donelson indicates that when communities are unable to rid themselves of hardcore pornography, they often turn their attention to easier targets like *The Catcher*.

818.   ————. "White Walls and High Windows: Some Contemporary Censorship Problems." *English Journal*, 61 (November 1972), 1191-1198; condensed as "Some Contemporary Censorship Problems." *Education Digest*, 38 (April 1973), 51-54.

Donelson mentions that *The Catcher* is often censored.

819.   "East Side School Superintendent May Organize Book 'Reviewers.'" [San Jose] *News*, 26 April 1960, p. 13.

Report on problems caused by the inclusion of *The Catcher* and other books on a reading list for United States history. Rpt. in 428.

820.   "Embattled City Teacher Assured She'll Keep Job." [Tulsa] *Daily World*, 26 April 1960, p. 5.

Report on problems Beatrice Levin had when she used *The Catcher* in junior English. See items 824, 837, 842, 843, and 851. Rpt. in 428.

821.   Fagan, Edward R. "Censorship in Pennsylvania." *Arizona English Bulletin*, 17 (February 1975), 48.

Fagan mentions that in 1974 a school board in one city in Pennsylvania voted unanimously against banning *The Catcher*.

822.   Fiene, Donald M. "From a Study of Salinger: Controversy in *The Catcher*." *The Realist*, 1 (December

1961), 23-25.

Fiene summarizes incidents of trouble, including
his own, with *The Catcher* in the classroom. Rpt.
in 428.

823. ———. "Rye on the Rocks." *Time*, 30 May 1960, p.
      2.

Fiene reports that he was fired for trying to
teach *The Catcher* in a Kentucky high school and for
"the unheard-of defiance" of the banning of the
book.

824. Foresman, Bob. "Edison Parents Protest 'Smutty'
      Book in Class." [Tulsa] *Tribune*, 19 April 1960,
      pp. 1, 10.

Report of the parents' objections to Beatrice
Levin's use of *The Catcher*. See item 820, 837,
842, 843, and 851. Rpt. in 428.

825. Gard, Robert R. "Censorship and Public Understand-
      ing." *English Journal*, 60 (February 1971), 255-
      259.

Gard calls *The Catcher* a "moderate" book that
has lost to the argument "that any hint of profan-
ity, obscenity, or immoral behavior, in a book or
elsewhere, is wrong."

826. Gardiner, Harold C., S.J. "Words and Conscience."
      America, 7 January 1961, p. 444.

Gardiner considers teachers' problems in dealing
with the language in a work like *The Catcher*: teachers should "point out to students that Salinger or
Chaucer or Shakespeare did have valid reasons for
employing such terms ... [and] indicate that such
terms are not in the active vocabulary of cultured
people, let alone in the conversation of Christians
and Catholics."

827. Gordon, Edward J. "Censorship Is Disrupting Our
      Schools." *The Leaflet*, 68 (May 1969), 3-8.

Gordon mentions the trouble caused by *The Catcher* in Tulsa and concludes that it should not be
banned because it "is calling for a good world in
which people can *connect*--a key word in twentieth
century writing."

828. Greenburg, Paul. "An Unmindful Society Ignores Real
      Goals of Education." *Chicago Tribune*, 9 April
      1981, Sec. 3, p. 2, col. 3.

Greenburg refutes the statement made by Terrel
H. Bell, Secretary of Education, that Salinger's
The Catcher and Golding's *Lord of the Flies* "should-
n't be made available in public schools."

829. Greenlaw, M. Jean. "Children's Books That Have Met
      the Censor." *Arizona English Bulletin*, 17 (Feb-
      ruary 1975), 181-183.

      Because "the content seems so mild in comparison
      with more recent publications," Greenlaw finds it
      "strange that *Catcher in the Rye* ... is still a fo-
      cus for contention."

830. H[arvey], J[ames] A. "'Catcher' Catches It--Again."
      Newsletter on Intellectual Freedom, 21 (May
      1972), 88.

      Harvey reports on trouble with *The Catcher* in
      the Shawnee Mission School in Kansas.

831. "Hill High Parents Air Some Views." [San Jose] *Mer-
      cury*, 5 April 1960, p. 21.

      Report on parents' objections to *The Catcher*.
      Rpt. in 428.

832. Hogan, Robert F. "Censorship Cases May Increase."
      Arizona English Bulletin, 17 (February 1975),
      193-195.

      Reprinted from the "For the Members" insert in
      all January 1974 NCTE publications, Hogan writes,
      "The strongest community I belong to--which is to
      say my family--agrees that the younger members of
      that community ought to have access in school to
      Spoon River, *Catcher in the Rye*, and--I guess--
      virtually everything in print that the school can
      afford to purchase."

833. ————. "Some Thoughts on Censorship in the Schools."
      In *Dealing with Censorship*. Ed. James E. Davis.
      Urbana, Illinois: National Council of Teachers
      of English, 1979, pp. 86-95.

      Commenting that parents see "the language of
      The Catcher in the Rye, the visual content of *Deep
      Throat*, and the window displays of the typical 'a-
      dult' bookstore" as all the same, Hogan argues that
      there are distinctions and that *The Catcher* "is
      defensible not despite its language, but because of
      its language."

834. Janson, Donald. "Help of Fundamentalist Minister
      Sought to Ban 'Catcher in the Rye.'" *New York*

Times, 9 November 1977, p. 25B.

Janson provides a detailed report on the school board meeting in Pittsgrove Township, New Jersey, in which no action was taken against *The Catcher*. See item 854.

835.   ————. "Use of Salinger's 'Catcher in the Rye' in Salem County School Stirs a Dispute." *New York Times*, 31 October 1977, p. 67.

Report of the furor caused over *The Catcher* in Pittsgrove Township High School, New Jersey, which quotes the defense of the novel from English teachers and statements both for and against it from ministers. See items 834 and 854.

836.   Jenkinson, Edward B. "Dirty Dictionaries, Obscene Nursery Rhymes, and Burned Books." In *Dealing with Censorship*. Ed. James E. Davis. Urbana, Illinois: National Council of Teachers of English, 1979, pp. 2-13.

In a list of books often censored, Jenkinson lists *The Catcher* as a book "frequently labeled 'trash.'"

837.   Kane, George. "'Catcher in the Rye' Teacher Resigns." [Tulsa] *Daily World*, 22 May 1960, p. 1.

Report of Beatrice Levin's resignation after parents objected to her teaching *The Catcher*. See items 820, 824, 842, 843, and 851. Rpt. in 428.

838.   Kvaraceus, William C. "Can Reading Affect Delinquency?" *ALA Bulletin*, 59 (June 1965), 516-522.

Kvaraceus discusses five principles related to the "factors [that] should be considered before we let out on loan or before we remove from the juvenile shelves books such as *The Catcher in the Rye*."

839.   LaConte, Ronald T. "The English Department Chairmen--Selector or Censor?" *The Leaflet*, 68 (May 1969), 40-47; rpt. "Who Are the Real Censors?" *English Education*, 1 (Spring 1970), 166-170; condensed in *Education Digest*, 36 (October 1970), 44-46.

Of high school English department chairmen in New Jersey responding to a survey on censorship, "70% said they considered *The Catcher in the Rye* unsuitable for use in the twelfth grade because of its 'indecent language.'"

840. Lacy, Dan. "Freedom and Books." *Nieman Reports*, 8
        (January 1954), 28-31.

        Lacy reports that *The Catcher* "so long as it re-
        mained in hard covers encouraged little adverse pub-
        lic attention," but "its inexpensive reprint ... is
        banned from sale in more than one city."

841. Lawson, Ray H. "Censorship: The English Teacher's
        Nemesis." *Arizona English Bulletin*, 17 (February
        1975), 196-199.

        Lawson reports on a "case of unexpected censor-
        ship" involving *The Catcher* in a literature course
        entitled 'Quest for Identity'" in Rochester, Mich-
        igan.

842. Levin, Beatrice. "J.D. Salinger in Oklahoma." *Chi-
        cago Jewish Forum*, 19 (Spring 1961), 231-233.

        Recounting the troubles that she had in using
        The Catcher in a high school in Tulsa, Levin writes
        that she used the book in hopes that her students
        "would, under mature guidance, read a book, identi-
        fy with the character, and do some reflective think-
        ing about what makes young people 'tick.'" See items
        820, 824, 837, 843, and 851.

843. ———. *Time*, 30 May 1960, pp. 2, 4.

        Levin responds (see item 851) that many parents
        "went on record endorsing me as a teacher and my
        wisdom to choose suitable literature for their
        youngsters. See items 820, 824, 837, and 842.

844. Mathis, Jim. "'The Catcher in the Rye': Controversy
        on Novel in Texas Is Just One in Long List of
        Episodes." *Houston Post*, 4 May 1961, Sec. 7,
        p. 6.

        This article mentions various schools and librar-
        ies where *The Catcher* has been banned, but concen-
        trates on Donald Fiene's troubles in Louisville,
        Kentucky, and quotes part of Salinger's letter to
        Fiene. See item 341.

845. McAllaster, Elva. *Time*, 30 May 1960, p. 4.

        Reports that "at the instigation of student pro-
        test against the stench of its vocabulary, *Catcher*
        has recently been removed from circulation" by Green-
        ville (Illinois) College library.

846. McIntosh, Harriet. "Freedom for Readers and Other
        Endangered Species." *Arizona English Bulletin*,

17 (February 1975), 40-44.

McIntosh assumes that *The Catcher* "may be one of the all time targets for censorship."

847. McLaughlin, Frank. "Selecting and Defending Contro-
      versial Books." *School Paperback Journal*, 1
      (September 1965), 8-11.

Teachers have lost their jobs for teaching *The Catcher*, and parents who complain about the novel "refuse to listen to reasons why teachers want to use books like *The Catcher*."

848. Moore, Everett T. "Catcher and Mice." *ALA Bulletin*,
      55 (March 1961), 229-230.

In a review of censorship problems with *The Catcher* in the classroom, Moore praises "the kind of strong community support that was demonstrated by the school board in Marin County." Rpt. in 413.

849. *New York Times*, 20 March 1960, p. 85.

Announcement of Donald Fiene's release as high school English teacher in Louisville, Kentucky, for "proposed use of 'The Catcher in the Rye' for male high school tenth graders." Rpt. in 428.

850. Rigsby, Ruth. "Raise High the Book Ban, Librarian."
      Saturday Review, 15 August 1959, p. 21.

The Catcher was banned from Grayslake High School in Illinois.

851. "Rye on the Rocks." *Time*, 9 May 1960, p. 67.

Beatrice Levin almost loses her job for trying to teach *The Catcher*. See items 820, 824, 837, 842, and 843.

852. "School Board Head Is Ignored Upstate on Banning
      Books." *New York Times*, 28 March 1965, p. 76.

Despite the objections of the president of the school board (see item 797), the students of Vestal (New York) put *The Catcher* on sale "at the Student Book Fair."

853. "School Board Shuns Reply to Book Banning Charges."
      [San Jose] *Mercury*, 22 April 1960, p. 21.

The superintendent indicates that "the answers to charges [of book banning] would be made in the form of a report to the board." Rpt. in 428.

854.   "School Refuses to Ban 'Catcher in the Rye.'" *New York Times*, 8 November 1977, p. 72.

      After the parents of a high school junior had called *The Catcher* "totally obscene and totally depraved," the school board of Pittsgrove, New Jersey, failed to take any action on removing the novel from the classroom. See item 794.

855.   Schramm, Wilbur. *Responsibility in Mass Communications*. New York: Harper and Row, 1957, pp. 285-286.

      Referring to Dan Lacy's comments (see item 840), Schramm points out that "the shocked reaction of censors and objectors to a book like *Catcher in the Rye* in its paper-back edition ... was due in large measure to the book's exposure to 'large masses of people previously habituated only to carefully industry-censored magazines, movies, and radio programs, and unaccustomed to the greater latitude always enjoyed by books.'"

856.   Severy, Bruce. "Scenario of Bookburning." *Arizona English Bulletin*, 17 (February 1975), 68-74.

      Severy includes a reference to a teacher who "was hounded out of a teaching job ten years ago because he assigned *Catcher in the Rye* to one of his high school classes."

857.   Shugert, Diane P. "A Body of Well-Instructed Men and Women: Organizations Active for Intellectual Freedom." In *Dealing with Censorship*. Ed. James E. Davis. Urbana, Illinois: National Council of Teachers of English, 1979, pp. 215-221.

      Mentions *The Catcher* as an example of a book that one might defend to a school board.

858.   ————. "How to Write a Rationale in Defense of a Book." In *Dealing with Censorship*. Ed. James E. Davis. Urbana, Illinois: National Council of Teachers of English, 1979, pp. 187-201.

      Shugert includes two statements of rationale for *The Catcher*—one by Mary McLaughlin and one by Patricia Nero.

859.   Stewart, Donald C. "Censorship in Kansas." *Arizona English Bulletin*, 17 (February 1975), 145.

      A high school principal in Kansas makes "objection ... to certain books, such as *Catcher in the Rye*, which are more notoriously pornographic than others."

860.   Tovatt, Anthony, and Ted DeVries. "This World of
         English." *English Journal*, 60 (February 1971),
         271.

         Report on Ronald LaConte's survey of high school
         English department chairmen (see item 839), the
         majority of whom find *The Catcher* "unsuitable."

861.   Veix, Donald B. "Teaching a Censored Novel: *Slaugh-
         terhouse-Five*." *English Journal*, 64 (October
         1975), 25-34.

         Veix refers to James Symula's comments on cen-
         sorship (see item 592) and mentions an incident
         where *The Catcher* was taken from the classroom after
         the superintendent saw "*The Word*" written by a
         teacher on the blackboard.

(3.) Relationship with Other Literary Works and Authors

         Salinger's style of writing and the themes in his
fiction have been compared to those of several other writers, and *The Catcher* has been compared to many other literary works, most notably Mark Twain's *The Adventures of
Huckleberry Finn*. The following listings refer to any
comparison of *The Catcher* and other works. The entries
are arranged alphabetically. For other comparative studies, see items 581, 584, 585, 589, and 593 in the subsection above on dissertations and theses and the reviews of
The Catcher, items 594-636.

862.   Alcantara-Dimalanta, O. "Christian Dimensions in
         Contemporary Literature." *Unitas*, 46 (June 1973),
         213-223.

         Discussing four novels, *The Catcher*, Golding's
         Lord of the Flies, Camus' *The Plague*, and Greene's
         The Power and the Glory, the author finds that "Sal-
         inger, not avowedly a Christian writer, shows sin
         as hardly in the attractive form of shocks and temp-
         tations an adolescent is confronted with."

863.   Aldridge, John W. *In Search of Heresy: American Lit-
         erature in an Age of Conformity*. New York: McGraw-
         Hill, 1956, pp. 117, 128-131, 133, 144, 148.

         In a chapter entitled "The Society of Three Nov-
         els" (*The Catcher*, *The Adventures of Augie March*,
         and *Lie Down in Darkness*), Aldridge, in comparing
         The Catcher and *Huckleberry Finn*, comments that
         Holden does not change but remains "cynical, de-
         fiant, and blind." Rpt. in 413, 415, and 428.

864. Allen, Walter. *The Modern Novel: In Britain and
        the United States*. New York: E.P. Dutton, 1964,
        pp. 309-312.

        In an analysis of *The Catcher* and comparison of
        it with *Huckleberry Finn*, Allen calls Salinger's
        novel "*the* American novel of its generation," in
        which "Salinger has created a myth-figure with which
        millions of young and youngish Americans have iden-
        tified themselves." Rpt. in 400.

865. ————. *The Urgent West: The American Dream and
        Modern Man*. New York: E.P. Dutton, 1969, p. 59.

        Brief comparison of Salinger's *The Catcher* and
        Steinbeck's *The Grapes of Wrath*: "These two novels
        in their different ways are seemingly criticism of
        the American dream in that they show its inadequacy
        in the face of the brute facts of American life."

866. Beaver, Harold. "A Figure in the Carpet: Irony and
        the American Novel." *Essays and Studies*, 15
        (1962), 101-114.

        Salinger, among other writers, uses what Beaver
        calls "a chunkier prose, handled flatly and imper-
        sonally." Even though Holden is "a modern Huck
        Finn," Holden's escape contrasts with Huck's: "Huck
        was still happily at the centre of his world: Holden
        Caulfield, nervous, depressed, lonesome, is modern
        maladjusted man."

867. Bellman, Samuel I. "Peripheral in *Huckleberry Finn*
        and *Catcher in the Rye*." *Mark Twain Journal*, 19
        (Winter 1977-1978), 4-6.

        Both *Huck Finn* and *The Catcher* evoke similar
        kinds "of tragic children's world."

868. Bier, Jesse. *The Rise and Fall of American Humor*.
        New York: Holt, Rinehart, Winston, 1968, pp. xi,
        340-341, 347, 354, 355.

        Mentioning elements of pure comedy and satire
        in *The Catcher*, Bier writes that "Salinger's tech-
        nical use of anticlimax and inversion of phrase are
        often consummate"; Bier finds *The Catcher* less ef-
        fective in humor than *Huckleberry Finn* but more ef-
        fective than Salinger's Glass works.

869. Bowden, Edwin T. *The Dungeon of the Heart*. New York:
        Macmillan, 1961, pp. 54-65.

        In a comparison and contrast of Holden Caulfield
        and Huck Finn, Bowden finds that "the victory that

he [Holden] finally wins, the answer that he dis-
covers for himself through the love of old Phoebe,
is the answer that Bradford on his frontier had
given Americans three hundred years before: a man
cannot live within himself in contempt of the world;
he must be a part of that human race to which he is
by nature morally committed; a decent regard, even
a potential love for others, is the unavoidable re-
quirement for life in America--or anywhere else--
if a man is to avoid the torture of isolation that
American life can bring." Rpt. in 428.

870.   Boyle, Robert, S.J. "Teaching 'Dirty Books' in Col-
        lege." *America*, 13 December 1958, pp. 337-339.

        "J.D. Salinger's *Catcher in the Rye*, a study of
        an idealistic boy in a confused, pharisaical, im-
        pure civilization, ... expresses a vision which
        American boys cannot fail to find more profoundly
        familiar, revealing and deeply moving than they can
        ever again find that of *Tom Sawyer* to be."

871.   Boyle, Ted E., and Terence Brown. "The Serious Side
        of Kingsley Amis' *Lucky Jim*." *Critique*, 9, No. 1
        (1966), 100-107.

        Jim Dixon is similar to Holden and Huck.

872.   Branch, Edgar. "Mark Twain and J.D. Salinger: A
        Study in Literary Continuity." *American Quarterly*,
        9 (Summer 1958), 144-158.

        The Catcher and *Huckleberry Finn* have three dis-
        tinct similarities: "narrative pattern and style,
        characterization of the hero and critical import."
        Branch's purpose is "to bare one nerve of cultural
        continuity in America." Rpt. in 400, 404, 413,
        415, and 428.

873.   Brouse, Albert J. "What Really Happened to Holden
        Caulfield." *College Composition and Communication*,
        23 (December 1972), 410-411.

        Brouse writes that Holden lives on in Lenny
        "Bruce's autobiography, 'How to Talk Dirty and In-
        fluence People.'"

874.   Brown, Rosellen. "On Willa Cather and 'Paul's Case.'"
        In *The American Short Story*. Ed. Calvin Skaggs.
        New York: Dell, 1980, II, 188-194.

        Brown contrasts Holden and Paul: "hungry and sen-
        sitive, *he* [Holden] had the defenses of 'cool' and
        a mouthy honesty that protected him not only from
        others but also from himself. Holden would never

be caught taking himself too seriously, while Paul--
Paul had a case of walking desperation, of adolescent willingness-to-die-for-it that, perversely,
offended me because it was so open."

875. Bryan, James. "Sherwood Anderson and *The Catcher in
      the Rye*: A Possible Influence." *Notes on Contem-
      porary Literature*, 1 (November 1971), 2-6.

      Bryan finds Salinger's story "I'm Crazy" similar
      to Anderson's "I'm a Fool" and "I Want to Know Why";
      ultimately, the influence of Anderson on Salinger
      shows in *The Catcher* in the "effortless colloquial
      surface."

876. Bryer, Jackson R. *Sixteen Modern American Authors*.
      Durham, North Carolina: Duke University Press,
      1974, p. 301.

      In the discussion of F. Scott Fitzgerald, there
      is a reference to Mario D'Avango's comparisons of
      Holden Caulfield and Gatsby (see item 883).

877. Bungert, Hans. "Salinger's *The Catcher in the Rye*:
      The Isolated Youth and His Struggle to Communi-
      cate." Trans. Wulf Griessbach. In *Studies in J.D.
      Salinger: Reviews, Essays, and Critiques of "The
      Catcher in the Rye" and Other Fiction*. Eds. Mar-
      vin Laser and Norman Fruman. New York: Odyssey
      Press, 1963, pp. 177-185.

      In a translation of a portion of Bungert's essay,
      Holden Caulfield is shown to be "an outsider like
      Gatsby, Joe Christmas, Thomas Sutpen" but also dif-
      ferent from them. See item 413.

878. Carpenter, Frederic I. "The Adolescent in American
      Fiction." *English Journal*, 46 (September 1957),
      313-319.

      With comparisons to Mark Twain's *Huckleberry
      Finn*, Carpenter uses Salinger's *The Catcher*, Car-
      son McCullers' *The Heart Is a Lonely Hunter*, and
      Jessamyn West's *Cress Delahanty* to demonstrate that
      "at his best the modern American novelist of adoles-
      cence describes the problems of his protagonists so
      that they become also the problems of our adolescent
      civilization, with both its mixed-up confusion and
      its splendid potentiality." Rpt. in 428.

879. Coard, Robert L. "Tom Sawyer, Sturdy Centenarian."
      Midwest Quarterly, 17 (Summer 1976), 329-349.

      In making comparison between Holden Caulfield
      and Tom Sawyer, Coard is assured that Twain's work
      is superior.

880. Connelly, Wayne C. "Optimism in Burgess's *A Clock-
       work Orange.*" *Extrapolation: A Science-Fiction
       Newsletter*, 14 (December 1972), 25-29.

       Huckleberry Finn, The Catcher, and *A Clockwork
       Orange,* "presented ostensibly as first person ver-
       nacular narratives--or naive autobiographies," are
       similar in humor.

881. Conrad, Robert C. "Two Novels About Outsiders: The
       Kinship of J.D. Salinger's *The Catcher in the
       Rye* with Heinrich Böll's *Ansichten eines Clowns.*"
       University of Dayton Review, 5 (Winter 1968-69),
       23-27.

       Böll translated *The Catcher* at about the same
       time that his own novel *Ansichten eines Clowns* ap-
       peared; in both works, the "outsiders, at great
       cost, remain true to themselves. Hans Schnier is
       the German Holden Caulfield."

882. Cox, James M. "Toward Vernacular Humor." *Virginia
       Quarterly Review*, 46 (Spring 1970), 311-330.

       In a study of "vernacular forms of Mark Twain,
       Ring Lardner, and J.D. Salinger," Cox finds that
       "Salinger's vernacular is vastly different from
       Mark Twain's or Lardner's."

883. D'Avanzo, Mario L. "Gatsby and Holden Caulfield."
       Fitzgerald Newsletter, No. 38 (Summer 1967),
       270-271.

       "As the model character of innocence and illusion
       in American literature, Gatsby has a successor in
       Holden Caulfield. Salinger acknowledges that debt
       in the text of the novel." See item 876.

884. DeSchweinitz, George W. "Huck and Holden." *Proceed-
       ings of Conference of College Teachers of Eng-
       lish of Texas*, 31 (September 1966), 27-28.

       The author places *Huckleberry Finn* and *The Catch-
       er* in "the dramatic tradition of the novel that be-
       gins with *Don Quixote* and goes through *Joseph An-
       drews.*" The two novels by Twain and Salinger are
       similar in subject and method: "the central sub-
       ject is the discovery of sham in society, or the
       old philosophical problem of appearance and reali-
       ty" and "both abjure and reject the lyric mode as
       out of reach of their respectively pre-adolescent
       and adolescent protagonists."

885. Drake, Robert Y., Jr. "Two Old Juveniles." *Georgia
       Review*, 13 (Winter 1959), 443-453.

"J.D. Salinger's *The Catcher in the Rye*, with
its burden of adolescent revolt, has been rashly
hailed by many as a twentieth-century *Huckleberry
Finn*."

886. Eckber, Kathy. "So What's Dirty?" *The Leaflet*, 68
      (May 1969), 27-28, 30.

      Brief reference to Philip Roth's *Portnoy's Com-
      plaint* being "hailed as an equal to Salinger's *Catch-
      er in the Rye* even before it was published."

887. Ely, Sister M. Amanda, O.P. "The Adult Image in
      Three Novels of Adolescent Life." *English Jour-
      nal*, 56 (November 1967), 1127-1131.

      In a study of *Lord of the Flies*, *Separate Peace*,
      and *The Catcher*, Sister Amanda finds that these
      "novels seem to state communication and real under-
      standing between the generations are not easily
      achieved."

888. Faulkner, William. "A Word to Young Writers." In
      *Faulkner in the University: Class Conferences at
      the University of Virginia 1957-1958*. Eds. Fred-
      erick L. Gwynn and Joseph L. Blotner. Charlottes-
      ville, Virginia: University of Virginia Press,
      1959, pp. 244-245, 246-248.

      Faulkner calls *The Catcher* "the best one" from
      "this present generation of writing," compares
      Holden and Huck Finn and Wall Street Panic Snopes
      and Holden, and comments on Holden's not falling
      and his lack of human contact.

889. French, Warren. "Steinbeck and J.D. Salinger: Mes-
      siah-Moulders for a Sick Society." In *Steinbeck's
      Literary Dimension: A Guide to Comparative Stud-
      ies*. Ed. Tetsumaro Hayashi. Metuchen, New Jer-
      sey: Scarecrow Press, 1973, pp. 105-115.

      French provides comparison between *The Catcher*
      and Steinbeck's *The Grapes of Wrath* and between the
      writings of Salinger and Steinbeck in general.

890. ─────. "Steinbeck's Winter Tale." *Modern Fiction
      Studies*, 11 (Spring 1965), 66-74.

      French suggests that Hawley in *The Winter of Our
      Discontent* and Holden in *The Catcher*, "despite a
      difference in age," are similar.

891. French, Warren, and Marc Rosenberg. "The Beast That
      Devours Its Young." *College Composition and Com-
      munication*, 13 (May 1962), 4-8.

In a discussion of James Purdy's *Malcolm* between instructor (French) and student (Rosenberg), the student makes comparisons between Malcolm and Holden.

892.   Furst, Lilian R. "Dostoyevsky's *Notes from the Underground* and Salinger's *The Catcher in the Rye*." *Canadian Review of Comparative Literature*, 5 (Winter 1978), 72-85.

Furst writes that Holden has "a wider literary lineage" than is usually seen; he "represents not merely the American adolescent but also a prime example of the anti-hero as he has evolved on both sides of the Atlantic from Dostoyevsky's seminal portrait."

893.   Gale, Robert L.   "Redburn and Holden--Half-Brothers One Century Removed." [Houston] *Forum*, 3 (Winter 1963), 32-36.

Herman Melville and J.D. Salinger, born a century apart, wrote, Gale asserts, similar books, *Redburn* and *The Catcher*--similar "in structure, style, incident, and characterization" and in theme.

894.   Goldberg, M.A. "Chronology, Character, and the Human Condition: A Reappraisal of the Modern Novel." *Criticism*, 5 (Winter 1963), 1-12.

Goldberg compares *The Catcher* to *David Copperfield*, *Tristram Shandy*, and several other novels.

895.   Green, Martin. "Amis and Salinger: The Latitude of Private Conscience." *Chicago Review*, 11 (Winter 1958), 20-25.

"The Welsh world in *Lucky Jim*, the Gruffydd-Williams world in *That Uncertain Feeling*, the prep school and New York world in *The Catcher in the Rye* are all dominated by phonies; the main work of all of the novels is the presentation and exploration of different kinds of phoniness."

896.   Hertzel, Leo J. "Rabbit in the Great North Woods." *University Review*, 33 (Winter 1966), 143-147.

Hertzel used John Updike's *Rabbit, Run*, Salinger's *The Catcher*, Ken Kesey's *One Flew Over the Cuckoo's Nest*, Bernard Malamud's *The Assistant*, and J.F. Powers' *Morte D'Urban* to "present a cross section of the alienation and the revolt that seem to lie at the bottom of much of the prose of our time."   Students reacted negatively to Holden Caulfield.

897. Howell, John M. "Salinger in the Waste Land." *Modern Fiction Studies*, 12 (Autumn 1966), 367-375.

In both theme and structure, Howell illustrates that "Salinger ... found in T.S. Eliot's *The Waste Land* a controlling metaphor for" *The Catcher*.

898. Johnson, James William. "The Adolescent Hero: A Trend in Modern Fiction." *Twentieth Century Literature*, 5 (April 1959), 3-11.

In a brief comparison of *The Catcher* and *Huckleberry Finn*, Johnson calls Salinger's novel "an archetype of an increasingly important literary genre--that which treats the adolescent as the embodiment of modern man and the turbulent atmosphere of adolescence as a microcosmic twentieth-century world."

899. Kaplan, Charles. "Holden and Huck: The Odysseys of Youth." *College English*, 18 (November 1956), 76-80.

"Huck Finn and Holden Caulfield are true blood brothers, speaking to us in terms that kept their wanderings from the level of the merely picaresque to that of a sensitive and insightful criticism of American life." Rpt. in 413 and 415.

900. Kearns, Francis E. "Salinger and Golding: Conflict on Campus." *America*, 26 January 1963, pp. 136-139.

Kearns contrasts *The Catcher* and *Lord of the Flies*, two books popular on college campuses: "Salinger demonstrates the liberal's healthy acceptance of the challenge of freedom and possibility"; "Golding manifests the conservative's profound insight into the limitations of human nature."

901. Kegel, Charles H. "Incommunicability in Salinger's *The Catcher in the Rye*." *Western Humanities Review*, 11 (Spring 1957), 188-190.

Kegel reads *The Catcher* "as Holden Caulfield's quest for communicability with his fellow man" and claims that "the hero's first person after-the-fact narration indicates ... that he has been successful in his quest." Rpt. in 400, 413, 415, and 428.

902. Lewis, R.W.B. "Recent Fiction: Pícaro and Pilgrim." In *A Time of Harvest: American Fiction 1910-1960*. Ed. Robert E. Spiller. New York: Hill and Wang, 1962, pp. 144-153.

Salinger has been influenced by "the slippery heroism and the colloquial rhythms of *Huckleberry Finn*" as he creates Holden Caulfield, "a latter-day Huck, an urbanized and upper-class Huck with money in his pocket--but still, like Huck, an adolescent on the run, confronting again the shocks and temptations of life with the same mixture of naiveté and shrewdness and profound, ineradicable faith."

903.   Little, Gail B. "Three Novels for Comparative Study in the Twelfth Grade." *English Journal*, 52 (October 1963), 501-505.

Little suggests using *Huckleberry Finn*, *The Catcher*, and *Intruder in the Dust* for comparative study.

904.   Ludwig, Jack. *Recent American Novelists*. Minneapolis, Minnesota: University of Minnesota Press, 1962, pp. 28-30, 33-34, 35.

For Ludwig, *The Catcher* "is an interesting departure from its model, *The Adventures of Huckleberry Finn*."

905.   Luedtke, Luther S. "J.D. Salinger and Robert Burns: *The Catcher in the Rye*." *Modern Fiction Studies*, 16 (Summer 1970), 198-201.

Luedtke uses Burns' poem to show "that Holden will emerge from his immersion, from his adult baptism, no longer self-consciously innocent and consigned to eternal childhood, like his dead brother Allie, but rather, like Phoebe, free to express and to receive the multitudes of love."

906.   Lydenberg, John. "American Novelists in Search for a Lost World." *Revue des Langues Vivantes*, 27 (1961), 306-321.

With comparisons between *The Catcher* and *The Adventures of Huckleberry Finn*, Lydenberg uses *The Catcher* as an example of "a literature characterized not by optimism but by pessimism, expressing hope less often than despair, emphasizing not success but failure, remarkable not for its firm gaze into the future, but for its bittersweet note of nostalgia."

907.   Martin, Hansford. "The American Problem of Direct Address." *Western Review*, 16 (Winter 1952), 101-114.

Martin "hope[s] to demonstrate here through three current novels--Irwin Shaw's *The Troubled Air*, J.D.

Salinger's *The Catcher in the Rye*, Norman Mailer's
Barbary Shore--examples of the way in which such
pressures ["the material itself, and especially the
milieu which is supplying that material"] can affect or distort the formal achievement of a work."

908.   Martin, John S. "Copperfield and Caulfield: Dickens
       in the Rye." *Notes on Modern American Literature*,
       4 (1980), Item 29.

       Noting the other commentaries on similarities
       between the writings of Salinger and Dickens (see
       items 645, 711, 771), Martin develops this idea:
       "The Dickensian frame of reference in *Catcher*, dis-
       cernible throughout the novel's background, struc-
       ture, theme, and particularly in the name of its
       protagonists, defines and clarifies an important
       part of the inimitable world of Holden Caulfield."

909.   Mathewson, Joseph. "The Hobbit Habit." *Esquire*, 66
       (September 1966), 130-131, 221-222.

       "Tolkien has taken the place of Salinger and
       Golding. *The Catcher in the Rye* and *Lord of the Flies*
       both touched a responsive chord deep in the breasts
       of their readers, and it follows that *The Lord of
       the Rings* has somehow done the same."

910.   Noon, William T. "Three Young Men in Rebellion."
       Thought, 38 (Winter 1963), 559-577.

       In an article about Samuel Butler's *The Way of
       All Flesh*, James Joyce's *A Portrait of the Artist
       as a Young Man*, and J.D. Salinger's *The Catcher*,
       Noon contrasts *The Catcher* and the other two. Those
       by Butler and Joyce are autobiographical and of
       social protest. *The Catcher* presents "a vision of
       personal evil that is heartbreaking for the young
       person of the novel, and a vision that transfixes
       the reader forever and ever."

911.   Olan, Levi A. "The Voice of the Lonesome: Alienation
       from Huck Finn to Holden Caulfield." *Southwest
       Review*, 48 (Spring 1963), 143-150.

       Both Holden Caulfield, "the modern version of
       Huck Finn," and Huck find "adaptation to the world
       is worse than hell, a condition they unhappily pre-
       fer."

912.   Peavy, Charles D. "'Did You Ever Have a Sister?'
       Holden, Quentin, and Sexual Innocence." *Florida
       Quarterly*, 1 (Winter 1968), 82-95.

       Taking a cue from what William Faulkner says

about Salinger's work (see item 888), Peavy compares
Holden and Quentin, both of whom "are desperately
afraid of life and the changes it can bring."

913.   Perloff, Marjorie G. "'A Ritual for Being Born
       Twice': Sylvia Plath's *The Bell Jar*." *Contemporary Literature*, 13 (Autumn 1972), 507-522.

       "*The Bell Jar* has become for the young of the
       early seventies what *Catcher in the Rye* was to their
       counterparts of the fifties."

914.   Pilkington, John. "About This Madman Stuff." *University of Mississippi Studies in English*, OS 7
       (1966), 67-75.

       In this study of Holden and Huck, Pilkington
       finds the two similar "in their idealism, their individualism, their compassion, and most of all their
       sanity," but different in that Holden decides "not
       to 'light out for the territory.'"

915.   Pinsker, Sanford. "Heller's *Catch-22*: The Protest
       of a *Puer Eternis*." *Critique: Studies in Modern
       Fiction*, 7 (Winter 1964-65), 150-162.

       Pinsker compares Holden and Yossarian.

916.   Rees, Richard. *Brave Men: A Study of D.H. Lawrence
       and Simone Weil*. Carbondale, Illinois: Southern
       Illinois University Press, 1959, pp. 9, 178-187.

       As "a sort of Odyssey of a young, unsatisfied,
       hungry human soul in the megalopolitan jungle,"
       The Catcher, Rees writes, "is relevant to a study
       of Lawrence and Simone Weil ... [in] the way Mr.
       Salinger can convey the purity of taste and the
       generous instincts of a baffled and unhappy but unspoilt boy."

917.   Riggan, William. *Pícaros, Madmen, Naïfs, and Clowns:
       The Unreliable First Person Narrator*. Norman:
       University of Oklahoma Press, 1981, pp. 159-170
       et passim.

       With both comparisons and contrasts between Holden and Huck Finn, Riggan categorizes Holden as a
       naif, whose "narrative thus resembles that of both
       the *picaro* and the madman in one respect: namely,
       in that the unreliable nature of the narrative is
       used to convey the implied author's vilification or
       at least his serious critique of given social norms
       and practices."

918.   Roberts, Preston Thomas, Jr. "*The Catcher in the*

Rye Revisited." *Cresset*, 40 (November/December 1976), 6-10.

Roberts' interpretation of *The Catcher* is that it is an example of the contemporary Christian story, similar to the contemporary "neo-Stoic" story like Hemingway's *The Old Man and the Sea*, in which "a profoundly humanistic kind of courage transcends despair by accepting or denying it" and in which "that despair itself can be and often is a means of judgment and grace."

919. Rose, Alan Henry. "Sin and the City: The Uses of Disorder in the Urban Novel." *Centennial Review*, 16 (Summer 1972), 203-220.

"In Charles Brockden Brown's *Arthur Mervyn* (1800), Bayard Taylor's *John Godfrey's Fortunes* (1864), Theodore Dreiser's *Sister Carrie* (1900), F. Scott Fitzgerald's *The Great Gatsby* (1925), and J.D. Salinger's *The Catcher in the Rye* (1951), the protagonist repeats the same journey toward crime and degradation."

920. Rubin, Louis D., Jr. "Dox Quixote and Selected Progeny: Or, the Journeyman as Outsider." *Southern Review*, 10 January 1974, pp. 31-58.

Brief reference to *The Catcher*: "Holden Caulfield ... knows what it is to tilt with windmills."

921. Severin-Lounsberry, Barbara. "Holden and Alex: A Clockwork from the Rye?" *Four Quarters*, 22 (Summer 1973), 27-38.

Thinking that perhaps Burgess was influenced by Salinger's *The Catcher*, Severin-Lounsberry writes that "in characterization, narrative style, symbolism, structure, and even thematically, *A Clockwork Orange* has much in common with *The Catcher*."

922. Simpson, Lewis P. "Southern Fiction." In *Harvard Guide to Contemporary American Writing*. Ed. Daniel Hoffman. Cambridge, Massachusetts: The Belknap Press, 1979, p. 166.

Simpson mentions William Faulkner's contrast between Holden Caulfield and Huck Finn: Holden "has no society and thus no human race to be accepted into"; "Huck is kicked around a good deal but he knows he is growing up in the human race."

923. Sisk, John P. "Mass in the Catacombs." *America*, 17 December 1960, pp. 404-406.

Sisk praises the presence of characters like Huck
Finn and Holden Caulfield in American literature because they represent "a hero who stands for a sacral
view of the cosmos."

924. Sklar, Robert. "Tolkien and Hesse: Top of Pops."
      Nation, 8 May 1967, pp. 598-601.

      Mentions that *The Catcher* "and *Lord of the Flies*
      reflected the fear young people felt in that era of
      McCarthy and the bomb, their helplessness, their
      hopelessness."

925. Stafford, William T. *Books Speaking to Books: A
      Contextual Approach to American Fiction*. Chapel
      Hill: The University of North Carolina Press,
      1981, p. 14.

      "J.D. Salinger's Holden Caulfield ... is no less
      the all-American boy than is Huck Finn--or Horatio
      Alger" is Stafford's complete statement about Sal-
      inger.

926. Starinshak, Melanne. "Personal Testimonial." *Ameri-
      ca*, 23 February 1963, p. 244.

      In a letter to the editor, Starinshak praises
      Francis Kearns' analyses of William Golding's *Lord
      of the Flies* and Salinger's *The Catcher* (see item
      900).

927. Stone, Edward. "Salinger's Carrousel." *Modern Fic-
      tion Studies*, 13 (Winter 1967-68), 520-523.

      Stone compares Salinger's carrousel in *The Catch-
      er* to the one in Rainer Maria Rilke's poem *"Das
      Karussell."*

928. Sundell, Carl. "The Architecture of Walter Mitty's
      Secret Life." *English Journal*, 56 (December 1967),
      1284-1287.

      Sundell sees similarities in the reasons young
      readers identify with Walter Mitty and Holden Caul-
      field: "Walter, like most adolescents, is a chronic
      daydreamer, just as Holden provides for every ado-
      lescent the catharsis of a series of crises typical
      of young people." Mitty and Caulfield are differ-
      ent in that Holden "is recovering from a mental
      breakdown. Walter Mitty is headed for one."

929. Tick, Stanley. "Initiation In and Out: The American
      Novel and the American Dream." *Quadrant*, June
      1961, pp. 63-74.

      Huck Finn, the Deerslayer, Christopher Newman,

and Holden Caulfield "are rootless children, alone
and innocent. They represent in some incarnate but
pristine form the dream figures of a nation. Their
vitality as well as their recurrence attests to the
enduring strength of that dream."

930. Trilling, Lionel. *"Lord of the Flies."* *Midcentury*,
       No. 45 (October 1962), 10-12.

       In a review of William Golding's *Lord of the
       Flies*, Trilling mentions that Golding's novel is
       the first to have "charmed the young to the same
       extent" *The Catcher* did even though the two books
       are very much "unlike each other in moral import."

931. Trowbridge, Clinton W. "Hamlet and Holden." *English
       Journal*, 57 (January 1968), 26-29.

       Trowbridge suggests that an understanding of the
       similarities between Hamlet and Holden "helps clari-
       fy Salinger's attitude toward" Holden and explain
       our fascination with Holden.

932. Tucker, Martin. "Clinton Williams Is a Wonderful
       Kid." *New York Herald Tribune Book Review*, 7
       August 1960, p. 4.

       In a review of James Herlihy's *All Fall Down*,
       Tucker compares Herlihy's hero, Clinton Williams,
       to Holden Caulfield.

933. Warner, Deane M. "Huck and Holden." *CEA Critic*, 27
       (March 1965), 4a-4b.

       Warner writes that in *The Catcher* "the American
       novel continues to attempt its delineation of the
       discovery of self in a nation where the individual
       is supposed to count." See items 670 and 755.

934. Weber, Ronald. "Narrative Method in *A Separate
       Peace.*" *Studies in Short Fiction*, 3 (Fall 1965),
       63-72.

       A Separate Peace and *The Catcher* "illustrate ...
       the close functional relation of meaning and method
       of telling in carefully-wrought fiction."

935. Wells, Arvin R. "Huck Finn and Holden Caulfield:
       The Situation of the Hero." *Ohio University Re-
       view*, 2 (1960), 31-42.

       In contrast to Edgar Branch (see item 872), Ar-
       thur Heiserman and James Miller (see item 708), and
       Charles Kaplan (see item 859), Wells explores con-
       trasts between *The Catcher* and *Huckleberry Finn*:
       the two books "rest upon very different assumptions

about what might be called the situation of the he-
ro--about the relationship of the individual to society." Rpt. in 415.

936.   Widmer, Kingsley. "The American Road: The Contempo-
       rary Novel." *University of Kansas City Review*,
       26 (Summer 1960), 309-317.

       In comparing *The Catcher* and Jack Kerouac's *On
       the Road*, Widmer writes that Salinger's novel, which
       he calls a "slick novel of sensitivity," is "not
       life but a psychiatric confession that adolescent
       therapy may take care of--he may even learn to love
       the pervasive phoniness of modern life that he was
       fleeing--and the road and revolt won't be necessary."

937.   Wiener, Gary A. "From Huck to Holden to Bromden:
       The Nonconformist in *One Flew Over the Cuckoo's
       Nest*." *Studies in the Humanities*, 7 (September
       1979), 21-26.

       Noting that readers have seen similarities be-
       tween *Huckleberry Finn* and *The Catcher*, Wiener il-
       lustrates that Ken Kesey's "*One Flew Over the Cuck-
       oo's Nest* makes similar comments on society, using
       similar techniques to those found in" Twain and Sal-
       inger.

938.   Wilcox, Earl. "Right On! *All the King's Men* in the
       Classroom." *Four Quarters*, 21 (May 1972), 69-78.

       Jack Burden, the narrator in *All the King's Men*,
       "is [like] Huck Finn or Holden Caulfield or Telema-
       chus in search of a father."

                       3. Nine Stories

       In this part of the bibliography under "Secondary
Sources," each of the sections for Salinger's four books
has similar subsections on initial reviews of the book and
on references, articles, and chapters. For *The Catcher*,
there is an additional subsection on study and teaching
aids. For *Nine Stories*, a third subsection is included to
list reviews of the movie *My Foolish Heart*, based on one
of the stories contained in *Nine Stories*. For other references to *Nine Stories*, see the subsections above on reference works (items 336-397), on book-length studies (items
398-429), on miscellaneous references, articles, and chapters (items 430-572), and on dissertations and theses (i-
tems 579-593).

                       a. Reviews

Listed alphabetically below are the initial reviews

of *Nine Stories*. A few of the reviews are not annotated.
For later and more detailed studies of this collection of
stories and of stories within the collection, see items
970-998 below.

939. *The Age*, 17 October 1953, p. 14.

940. Allen, Thomas J. "Books." *Saturday Night*, 9 May
      1953, pp. 21-22.

      These stories "read together between the covers
      of a book ... make one gag."

941. Baro, Gene. "Some Suave and Impressive Slices of
      Life." *New York Herald Tribune Book Review*, 12
      April 1953, p. 6.

      After noting that "the special quality of Mr.
      Salinger's stories is humaneness," Baro writes that
      "Salinger's vision tempers an all-embracing senti-
      mentality with a personal sophistication, so that
      these stories run to a kind of intellectual and e-
      motional chic." Rpt. in 378.

942. Blackshear, Orrilla. "Recent Adult Books." *Wiscon-
      sin Library Bulletin*, 49 (July-August 1953),
      175-176.

      Comparing Salinger to Katherine Anne Porter and
      Eudora Welty, the reviewer finds *Nine Stories* "pene-
      trating in insight, moving in their quiet indirect-
      ness, and polished in their craft."

943. *Booklist*, 1 May 1953, p. 286.

      The reviewer compares the stories to *The Catch-
      er*.

944. Butcher, Franny. *Chicago Sunday Tribune*, 26 April
      1953, p. 2.

      "The publication of these 'Nine Stories' will
      give the reader further assurance of the author's
      literary gift ... [but] his serious, shiny intent
      as an artist is not necessarily burnished by all of
      them."

945. "Early Excursions into Glass Country." *Times Liter-
      ary Supplement*, 8 April 1960, p. 228.

      In a review of a British reissue of *Nine Stories*,
      the reviewer finds "emptiness ... a writer trapped
      by his own cleverness and increasingly cut off from
      his true subject-matter."

946. Highet, Gilbert. "New Books: Always Roaming with a
     Hungry Heart." *Harper's*, 206 (June 1953), 100-
     109.

     "There is not a failure in the book: I would
     rather read a collection like this than many a nov-
     el which is issued with more fanfare."

947. Hough, Graham. *The Listener*, 24 September 1953,
     p. 517.

948. Hughes, Riley. *Catholic World*, 178 (June 1953),
     233.

     These stories "are, however great their insight,
     little more than specialized reporting. It is to
     be hoped that Mr. Salinger will next attempt sub-
     jects and characters more universal and profound."

949. *Kirkus*, 1 February 1953, p. 80.

     Calling the collection "appealing and effective,"
     the reviewer writes that the stories contain "the
     burnish over the heartache, juveniles' acceptance,
     on their own terms, of the unexperienced adult
     world, the matter-of-factness that covers hysteria
     and the imaginative escapes from an inability to
     adjust."

950. Krim, Seymour. "Surface and Substance in a Major
     Talent." *Commonweal*, 24 April 1953, p. 78.

     Krim "believe[s] that Salinger is not quite clear
     about the meaning of his material; he is extremely
     deft, sometimes over-sophisticated in his surface
     technique, and for the most part it is a pure pleas-
     ure to follow his artistic strokes," but Krim "sus-
     pects a dodging of issues." Rpt. in 378 and 404.

951. Larrabee, C.X. "Nine Short Stories by a Writer with
     an Extraordinary Talent." *San Francisco Chroni-
     cle*, 3 May 1953, p. 13.

     Even though these stories are "not 'major,'"
     Larrabee finds them "intense and gripping without
     being feverish ... alive with the elements of force
     and climax without indulging the pat gimmicks that
     cheapen so much current fiction," and he praises
     Salinger's talent for "an astonishing, almost per-
     fectly disciplined capacity for dialogue."

952. Martin, Hansford. "Four Volumes of Short Stories:
     An Irreverant [sic] Review." *Western Review*, 18
     (Winter 1954), 172-174.

     "Almost all these stories are 'rich' stories,

with snappers in the place of endings; the method
of O. Henry overlaid by a manner the late Conde
Nast would have envied."

953.   Mizener, Arthur. "In Genteel Traditions." *New Re-
       public*, 25 May 1953, pp. 19-20.

       These stories "have, as the novel [*The Catcher*]
       did not, a controlling intention which is at once
       complex enough for Mr. Salinger's awareness and
       firm enough to give it a purpose."

954.   Monas, Sidney. "Fiction Chronicle: 'No Mommy and
       No Daddy.'" *Hudson Review*, 6 (Autumn 1953), 466-
       470.

       In a mixed review of *Nine Stories*, Monas com-
       ments that the stories contain "a peculiar concep-
       tual separation of the child from the adult, as
       though they were of different species, not merely
       different ages."

955.   "Nine by Salinger." *Newsweek*, 6 April 1953, p. 98.

       Comparing these stories to "the art of Saki or
       John Collier," the reviewer finds that Salinger has
       "a flair for necromancy ... to make them credible."

956.   Peden, William. "Esthetics of the Story." *Saturday
       Review*, 11 April 1953, pp. 43-44.

       The best of these stories are "humorous, warm-
       hearted, even frivolous in tone"; the others "have
       a tendency toward being chi-chi, cute, or even coy."
       Rpt. in 378.

957.   Phelps, Robert. "The Difference IS Qualitative."
       The Freeman, 24 August 1953, p. 857.

       In contrast to John Cheever who "just writes,"
       Salinger "has a vision, a deep compelling one which
       selects and orders everything he writes, and gives
       it a memorable unity." Phelps calls "For Esme--
       with Love and Squalor" the best story in the col-
       lection.

958.   Pickrel, Paul. "Outstanding Novels." *Yale Review*,
       NS 42 (Summer 1953), vi-xvi.

       "It could be argued that the nine (as well as
       Mr. Salinger's novel, *Catcher in the Rye*) are all
       one story, written in various ways--the story of
       an almost pathologically sensitive male shut up in
       the little room of his own misery, with only three
       ways out: a temporary exit into the innocence of

childhood, or a long exile in the land of love and
squalor, or suicide."

959.   Poore, Charles. "Books of The Times." *New York
       Times*, 9 April 1953, p. 25.

       Poore praises *Nine Stories* but complains because
       the collection of stories, even though better than
       what others write, is not better than *The Catcher*.

960.   Price, R.G.G. *Punch*, 15 July 1953, p. 101.

961.   Sadleir, Michael. *The Sunday Times*, 28 June 1953,
       p. 4.

962.   *Springfield* [Massachusetts] *Republican*, 19 April
       1953, p. 8C.

963.   *The Sydney Morning Herald*, 16 August 1953, p. 13.

964.   Townsend, Sally. "Short Stories." *Globe and Mail*,
       16 May 1953, p. 8.

       Salinger "writes with a splendidly disciplined
       technique that is warmed and supported by a keen
       perception and deep compassion."

965.   Toynbee, Philip. "Voice of America." *The Observer*,
       14 June 1953, p. 9.

966.   *United States Quarterly Book Review*, 9 (June 1953),
       166.

       In these stories, Salinger treats "the theme of
       nightmare with surface lightness if not downright
       flippancy"; the stories contain "pictures of over-
       wrought humanity [that] are sharp and even import-
       ant as they make telling use of frighteningly human
       irrelevant details."

967.   Welty, Eudora. "Threads of Innocence." *New York
       Times*, 5 April 1953, Sec. 7, p. 4.

       With lavish praise for this volume of Salinger's
       stories, Welty likes Salinger's ability to "honor
       what is unique and precious in each person on earth"
       with "a loving heart."   Rpt. in 378.

968.   Wilson, Angus. *New Statesman and Nation*, 15 August
       1953, p. 187.

969.   "Youthful Horrors." *Nation*, 18 April 1953, p. 332.

       "Mr. Salinger is a fiction writer of great bril-
       liance; the danger is that he will become one of
       definite and ultimately disappointing limitations."

b. References, Articles, Chapters

The entries listed alphabetically below refer both to
references to and studies of individual stories contained
in *Nine Stories* and to studies of more than one of the stories in this collection.

970. Browne, Robert M. "In Defense of Esmé." *College
      English*, 22 (May 1961), 584-585.

      Rebutting John Hermann's interpretation (see i-
      tem 985) of Charles in "For Esmé--with Love and
      Squalor," Browne claims that Hermann "read the sto-
      ry in the light of a rather romantic preconception"
      and "neglect[ed] the role of the narrator." Rpt.
      in 385, 400, and 413.

971. Bryan, James. "The Admiral and Her Sailor in Sal-
      inger's 'Down at the Dinghy.'" *Studies in Short
      Fiction*, 17 (Spring 1980), 174-178.

      Bryan examines the relationship between Lionel
      and his mother, Boo Boo Tannenbaum, in "Down at
      the Dinghy," and concludes that "one finishes the
      story with the conviction that--piloted by Boo Boo--
      he [Lionel] will surely manage."

972. ————. "A Reading of Salinger's 'For Esmé--with
      Love and Squalor.'" *Criticism*, 9 (Summer 1967),
      275-288.

      In contrast to the emotional reactions to Sal-
      inger's "For Esmé--with Love and Squalor," Bryan
      believes that the story has "an unsentimental and
      even philosophical attitude toward love and squalor,
      as the young protagonist comes to recognize their
      complexities--and interdependency--in his life."

973. ————. "A Reading of Salinger's 'Teddy.'" *American
      Literature*, 40 (November 1968), 352-369.

      Commenting on Salinger's use of oriental philos-
      ophy and his symbolism, Bryan concludes that "read-
      ers who cannot accept the mysticism and Oriental
      ideas will find a coherent and tenable artistic
      vision of the world."

974. Burke, Brother Fidelian, F.S.C. "Salinger's 'Esmé':
      Some Matters of Balance." *Modern Fiction Studies*,
      12 (Autumn 1966), 341-347.

      After a detailed analysis of the story as a basic
      two-part structure with each part having four simi-
      lar subsections, Burke judges the story "successful"

because Salinger consistently and effectively integrates the major sections and sub-sections in order to "display the consonance which can be achieved only when the developing possibilities of a unique context are realized and capitalized upon."

975.   Davison, Richard Allan. "Salinger Criticism and 'The Laughing Man': A Case of Arrested Development." *Studies in Short Fiction*, 18 (Winter 1981), 1-15.

Davison summarizes the history of Salinger criticism, cites three Salinger studies in progress, and notes "a relative moratorium on Salinger commentary for about a decade." In contrast to those who examine Salinger's portrayal of children, Davison studies "The Laughing Man,' which shows that Salinger's "preoccupation ... is largely with adult considerations and adult struggles in which all of the actions of children are judged against a norm that, when not of Christ, is of an adult world with its flaws and imperfections, its phoniness and cruelty, but a world also peopled with D.B.'s and the Mr. Antolinis, whose hearts may have lost some of the purity but none of the love." Gedsudski lives in a world "where values are not so much childlike as childish."

976.   Elmen, Paul. "Twice-Blessed Enamel Flowers: Reality in Contemporary Fiction." In *The Climate of Faith in Modern Literature*. Ed. Nathan A. Scott, Jr. New York: Seabury Press, 1964, pp. 84-101.

Elmen interprets "De Daumier-Smith's Blue Period" as a "story of the rejection of a fanciful romance with a nun, and ... glad acceptance of the enameled flowers."

977.   Fiedler, Leslie A. "From Redemption to Initiation." *New Leader*, 26 May 1958, pp. 20-23.

Fiedler refers to Salinger's use of "the redemption theme" in "A Perfect Day for Bananafish" and mentions that Lionel in "Down at the Dinghy" is an example of "the child as Peeping Tom" established by Henry James. See item 466.

978.   ————. "The Profanation of the Child." *New Leader*, 23 June 1958, pp. 26-29.

Fiedler asserts that in "A Perfect Day for Bananafish" Salinger "demands that we accept this ambiguous love-making [Seymour and Sybil] as a moment of sanity before suicide, that we read the child as the embodiment of all that is clean and life-giving

as opposed to the vulgar, destructive (*i.e.*, fully
sexual) wife." See item 466.

979. Freeman, Fred B., Jr. "Who Was Salinger's Sergeant
        X?" *American Notes & Queries*, 11 (September 1972),
        6.

        Refuting Dan Wakefield's identification (see i-
tem 564) of Sergeant X as Buddy Glass and Tom Davis'
identification (see item 462) as Seymour Glass, Freeman decides that Sergeant X "is not a member of the
Glass family at all" and that "he cannot be concrete-
ly identified."

980. French, Warren. *The Social Novel at the End of an
        Era.* Carbondale, Illinois: Southern Illinois
        University Press, 1966, p. 120.

        French contrasts Ernest Hemingway's not having
Robert Jordan commit suicide with Salinger's treatment of Seymour Glass.

981. Genthe, Charles V. "Six, Sex, Sick: Seymour, Some
        Comments." *Twentieth Century Literature*, 10 (Jan-
        uary 1965), 170-171.

        Genthe explains the significance of the number
six in "A Perfect Day for Bananafish."

982. Goldstein, Bernice, and Sanford Goldstein. "Zen and
        Nine Stories." *Renascence*, 22 (Summer 1970),
        171-182.

        The Goldsteins consider the *Nine Stories* "through
... two extreme of the *koan* experience[:] ... the
struggle with a particular insoluable problem that
is beyond the realm of the rational [which] may lead
to mental breakdown; ... the struggle with a problem beyond the guidelines of reason [which] may lead
to enlightenment, satori."

983. Hagopian, John V. "'Pretty Mouth and Green My Eyes':
        Salinger's Paolo and Francesca in New York." *Mod-
        ern Fiction Studies*, 12 (Autumn 1966), 349-354.

        Disagreeing at length with Stevenson's unfavor-
able comparison of "Pretty Mouth and Green My Eyes"
with Ernest Hemingway's "The Short, Happy Life of
Francis Macomber" (see item 555), Hagopian finds
this unappreciated and misunderstood story a "mag-
nificently wrought purely adult story, with its
profoundly religious overtones ... one of the best
of the lot" of "the finest American short stories
by Salinger."

984.   Hamilton, Kenneth. "Hell in New York: J.D. Salinger's
       'Pretty Mouth and Green My Eyes.'" *Dalhousie Re-
       view*, 47 (Autumn 1967), 394-399.

       Hamilton focuses on one of the seldom discussed
       stories in *Nine Stories* in order to illustrate that
       "Salinger unfolds for us the map of a universe
       ruled by the anti-virtues of faithlessness, fear,
       and lust."

985.   Hermann, John. "J.D. Salinger: Hello Hello Hello."
       College English, 22 (January 1961), 262-264.

       In agreement with several critics who see "For
       Esmé--with Love and Squalor" as Salinger's best
       story, Hermann, in contrast with other interpre-
       tations, finds Esmé's brother Charles, not Esmé
       herself, as the central character. Esmé has "in-
       telligence, poise, and breath-taking levelheaded-
       ness"; "Charles, with the orange eyes and the arch-
       ing back and the smacking kiss, who knows without
       counting the house, with 3:45 and 4:15 P.M.'s, the
       riddles of the heart," is able to restore Sergeant
       X's faculties. See item 970. Rpt. in 385, 400,
       and 413.

986.   Kirschner, Paul. "Salinger and His Society: The
       Pattern of *Nine Stories*." *London Review*, 6 (Win-
       ter 1969-70), 34-54; rpt. in two parts in *Liter-
       ary Half-Yearly*, 12 (1971), 51-60; 14 (1973),
       63-78.

       With "the suicide in the first story ... trans-
       muted in the last, for death has been stripped of
       its conventional meanings," Kirschner finds that "a
       completed pattern emerges from the sequence of sto-
       ries: despair within a glossy, ego-bemused society;
       provisional rescue through intuitive love; ultimate
       passage through the boundaries of personality."

987.   LaHood, Martin J. "A Note on Salinger's 'Uncle Wig-
       gily in Connecticut.'" *Revue des Langues Vivan-
       tes*, 33 (1967), 597-598.

       LaHood demonstrates that Eloise "has become an
       unhappy and cynical human being" because her vision
       of an idealistic, "make-believe" world has been re-
       placed by the harsh reality of "blind fate."

988.   Lane, Gary. "Seymour's Suicide Again: A New Reading
       of J.D. Salinger's 'A Perfect Day for Banana-
       fish.'" *Studies in Short Fiction*, 10 (Winter
       1973), 27-33.

       Lane suggests that the "German poems" referred

to in this story are Rainer Rilke's *Duino Elegies*,
which are "reflections about precisely the problems
that ... oppress Seymour."

989. Lewis, Roger. "Textual Variants in J.D. Salinger's
      Nine Stories." *Resources for American Literary
      Study*, 10 (Spring 1980), 79-83.

      For the eight of the stories included in *Nine
      Stories* that had appeared in print prior to the
      publication of this collection, Lewis lists the
      textual "variants between the magazine printing and"
      the collected volume in order to "show us the crafts-
      man at work."

990. Metcalf, Frank. "The Suicide of Salinger's Seymour
      Glass." *Studies in Short Fiction*, 9 (Summer
      1972), 243-246.

      Metcalf thinks that "one can make an interesting
      case for Salinger's being consciously concerned with
      ... heterosexual pedophilia," which will explain why
      Seymour commits suicide.

991. Perrine, Laurence. "Teddy? Booper? Or Blooper?"
      Studies in Short Fiction, 4 (Spring 1967), 217-
      224.

      Perrine is critical of Salinger's story "Teddy"
      because of its ambiguous ending: "If we only knew
      what happened, we might be clear as to *why* it hap-
      pened."

992. Russell, John. "Salinger, From Daumier to Smith."
      Wisconsin Studies in Contemporary Literature, 4
      (Winter 1963), 70-87.

      Russell looks at "De Daumier-Smith's Blue Period"
      as a story "of enormous pivotal significance," which
      "looks two ways at once ... back at the successful
      dramatic designs of Salinger's early work ... [and]
      forward to the pluralism that has held Salinger in
      all subsequent stories."

993. Stein, William Bysshe. "Salinger's 'Teddy': *Tat Tvam
      Asi* or That Thou Art." *Arizona Quarterly*, 29
      (Autumn 1973), 253-265.

      Stein provides an explanation of "Teddy" based
      on "Salinger's familiarity with the Vedantic (and
      traditional Indian) concept of *lila.*"

994. Stone, Edward. *A Certain Morbidness: A View of Amer-
      ican Literature.* Carbondale, Illinois: Southern
      Illinois University Press, 1969, pp. 121-139.

A story packed with allusions to and echoes of
"Picasso, St. Paul, Rilke, Mann, and very possibly,
Shakespeare," "De Daumier-Smith's Blue Period" de-
picts a character who "can given an account of his
earlier condition ... by the implicit judgment of
echo and allusion put to the uses of comedy."

995.   Takenaka, Toyoko. "Synopsis: 'On Seymour's Suicide.'"
       Kyushu American Literature, No. 12 (January 1970),
       59-60.

Takenaka provides a synopsis in English of her
essay in Japanese, in which she sees the bananafish
as symbolic of "Seymour himself," who commits suicide as "a kind of escape" because he "has been
mentally deranged by the war ... [and] he is too
sensitive and too self-conscious." See item 1443.

996.   VandeKieft, Ruth M. *Eudora Welty*. New York: Twayne
       Publishers, 1962, p. 153.

Mentions Seymour Glass' suicide as an example
of "the excess of joy [being] a 'problem.'"

997.   Wenke, John. "Sergeant X, Esmé, and the Meaning of
       Words." *Studies in Short Fiction*, 18 (Summer
       1981), 251-259.

"For Esmé--with Love and Squalor" is a story about
"the problem of finding valid forms of communication"
and one which shows "how individuals might pass
through squalor to love, achieving meaningful, re-
demptive expression, even though the successful uses
of language are a constant reminder of its general
failure."

998.   Wiebe, Dallas E. "Salinger's 'A Perfect Day for
       Bananafish.'" *Explicator*, 23 (September 1964),
       Item 3.

"The description of a bananafish is actually the
description of a foot in the sand with the toes pro-
truding."

c. Reviews of *My Foolish Heart*

In 1950, the movie *My Foolish Heart*, starring Susan
Hayward and Dana Andrews, appeared. Based on Salinger's
story "Uncle Wiggily in Connecticut," this movie was a
great disappointment to Salinger. He has not allowed any
of his other works to be filmed. Donald Fiene (see items
341 and 342) lists the following reviews of *My Foolish
Heart*. Because they are reviews of a work not directly
Salinger's, the reviews are not annotated.

999. Brog[den, William]. "My Foolish Heart." *Variety*,
      19 October 1949.

1000. "Cinema." *Time*, 6 February 1950, p. 83.

1001. Crowther, Bosley. "The Screen in Review." *New York
      Times*, 20 January 1950, p. 29; rpt. *The New York
      Times Film Reviews, 1913-1968*. New York: New
      York Times and Arno Press, 1970, p. 2394.

1002. ————. "Heart Trouble." *New York Times*, 22 January
      1950, Sec. II, p. 1.

1003. "Current Feature Films." *Christian Century*, 15 Feb-
      ruary 1950, p. 223.

1004. Daugherty, A.A. "Bob Keith as Lovable Papa Brightens
      Up Muggy Romance." *Louisville Times*, 22 June
      1950, Sec. I, p. 19.

1005. Freeman, Marilla Waite. "Current Feature Films."
      Library Journal, 1 March 1950, p. 411.

1006. Hartung, Philip T. "The Screen." *Commonweal*, 20
      January 1951, p. 415.

1007. Hill, Gladwyn. "On the Theory That Practice Makes
      Perfect." *New York Times*, 3 July 1949, Sec. II,
      p. 3.

1008. Lockhart, Jane. "Looking at Movies." *The Rotarian*,
      75 (April 1950), 39.

1009. Martin, Boyd. "'My Foolish Heart' ... Is an Appeal-
      ing Story of Girl's Grave Mistakes." [Louisville]
      Courier-Journal, 22 June 1950, p. 4.

1010. McCarten, John. "The Current Cinema." *New Yorker*,
      28 January 1950, p. 75.

1011. "New Films." *Newsweek*, 23 January 1950, p. 80.

4. Franny and Zooey

    This section of "Secondary Sources" on Salinger's
third book contains two subsections: initial reviews and
references, articles, and chapters. For other references
to and studies of *Franny and Zooey*, see the subsections
above on reference works (items 336-397), on book-length
studies (items 398-429), on miscellaneous references, articles, and chapters (items 430-572), and on dissertations
and theses (items 579-593).

a. Reviews

The initial reviews of *Franny and Zooey* are listed below alphabetically. Some of the reviews are not annotated. For later and more detailed studies of this volume and of either of the two stories in the collection, see items 1061-1075 below.

1012. Allsop, Kenneth. "Salinger, old buddy, it hurts to say this." *The Daily Mail*, 7 June 1962, p. 12.

1013. Bode, Carl. *Wisconsin Studies in Contemporary Literature*, 3 (Winter 1962), 65-71; rpt. "1961: *Mr. Salinger's* Franny and Zooey." In *The Half-World of American Culture*. Carbondale, Illinois: Southern Illinois University Press, 1965, pp. 212-220.

Bode reads "Franny" as "a Dialogue between Body and Soul in terms not much changed since the Middle Ages. And 'Zooey' is a theological tract."

1014. *Booklist*, 15 September 1961, p. 64.

"Lifelike dialog and discerning character portrayal mark both of these pieces by the author of *The Catcher*."

1015. Bradbury, Malcolm. "Other New Novels." *Punch*, 27 June 1962, pp. 989-990.

Salinger, a remarkable craftsman, tends to become more and more arch as he nears the centre of his story and as he deals with the Glasses, who are very close to him indeed. One can't really say that he is completely successful, that his search for truth isn't taking him close to silence."

1016. Bryden, Ronald. "Living Dolls." *Spectator*, 8 June 1962, pp. 755-756.

In a review of Salinger's *Franny and Zooey* and Iris Murdoch's *An Unofficial*, Bryden asks if "Salinger [is] going to be the American Isherwood: the sharpest eye and ear of his generation, the ... [one] who blazed trails for other rebels to follow, but himself subsided into the warm clutch of quietism and cosmic cosiness?"

1017. *The Bulletin*, 13 October 1962, pp. 37-38.

1018. Daniels, Sally. *Minnesota Review*, 11 (Summer 1962), 553-557.

"Salinger looks most like a 'major writer' in

those moments when he creates, as he surely does,
an almost unbearable pressure between the dark up-
surgings of his characters' despair, and the tight
lid of humor, wit, whimsy, yes and sentimentality,
which is, through tremendous efforts, just held
down."

1019. Derrick, C. *The Tablet*, 23 June 1962, p. 595.

1020. Didion, Joan. "Finally (Fashionably) Spurious."
       National Review, 18 November 1961, pp. 341-342.

       Even though appealing to many readers, *"Franny
       and Zooey* is finally spurious," Didion writes, be-
       cause of "Salinger's tendency to flatter the essen-
       tial triviality within each of his readers, his
       prediliction for giving instructions for living."
       Rpt. in 385 and 404.

1021. Dolbier, Maurice. "'Franny and Zooey.'" *New York
       Herald Tribune*, 14 September 1961, p. 19.

       "Love is the key to Salinger's Glass house--even
       the contents of a cluttered medicine cabinet, and
       of a crowded living room, are lovingly described,
       in a way that brings a family's past and present
       together."

1022. Engle, Paul. "Brilliantly Detailed Glimpses of the
       Glass Family." *Chicago Tribune*, 24 September
       1961, p. 3.

       Engle finds that this volume contains "incompar-
       ably lively and witty" writing, "diverting reading,"
       and "no true resolution at all."

1023. Fiedler, Leslie A. "Up from Adolescence." *Partisan
       Review*, 29 (Winter 1962), 127-131.

       In a negative review, Fiedler sees Salinger's
       major theme as the "presentation of madness as the
       chief temptation of modern life, especially for the
       intelligent young ... [and] the chief heroism pos-
       sible to us now is the rejection of madness, the de-
       cision to be sane." Rpt. in 379, 385, and 404.

1024. Fremont-Smith, Eliot. "Franny and Zooey." *The Vil-
       lage Voice*, 8 March 1962, pp. 5-6.

       "One of the fascinations of 'Franny and Zooey'--
       and I submit that is also at the core of the book's
       artistic failure--is the inseparableness of the
       author from his work, the deliberate confusion of
       who is who, and who is real."

1025. Gallagher, Patricia. *Tamarack Review*, No. 21 (Au-
       tumn 1961), 88-89.

1026.   Green, Martin. *Guardian*, 8 June 1962, p. 6.

1027.   Hartt, J.N. "The Return of Moral Passion." *Yale Re-
        view*, 51 (December 1961), 300-308.

        "*Franny and Zooey* is less of a novel than *Catch-
        er in the Rye*, but it is an advance in psychological
        and stylistic sophistication. I have the feeling
        that we have fragments of a novel in *Franny* etc.,--
        long meticulously-developed case-book studies that
        require the discipline of a plot, or at least an
        idea, before they can become a novel."

1028.   Hicks, Granville. "Another Look at the Deserving."
        Saturday Review, 23 December 1961, p. 18.

        Of the American books of 1961, Hicks puts Sal-
        inger's *Franny and Zooey* "at the top of any list":
        this book "has something to say about the human
        predicament, and it makes its point with humor and
        the shrewdness that are Salinger's great assets."

1029.   ————. "Sisters, Sons, and Lovers." *Saturday Re-
        view*, 16 September 1961, p. 26.

        Hicks finds Salinger in *Franny and Zooey* "at
        the top of his form."

1030.   Hogan, William. *San Francisco Chroncile*, 5 Septem-
        ber 1961, p. 33; 19 September 1961, p. 33.

1031.   Holloway, David. "Salinger's Glass Menagerie." *The
        Daily Telegraph and Morning Post*, 8 June 1962,
        p. 19.

1032.   Hugh-Jones, Siriol. "The Salinger Puzzle." *The Tat-
        ler and Bystander*, 20 June 1962, p. 748.

1033.   Jackson, Robert B. *Library Journal*, 1 October 1961,
        p. 3303.

        "This significant work, especially pertinent for
        the young, must be included in all collections of
        important American writing."

1034.   Kapp, Isa. "Salinger's Easy Victory." *New Leader*,
        8 January 1962, pp. 27-28.

        Generally critical of this Salinger volume, Kapp
        does allow Salinger a few "well-handled" scenes:
        "small in scope and safely outside the responsibil-
        ities of philosophy, a reader may be impressed by
        the Salinger touch." Rpt. in 404.

*   Kazin, Alfred. "Everybody's Favorite." *Atlantic*,

208 (August 1961), 27-31.

Cited above as item 241.

1035.   Kennedy, Sighle. "New Books: *Franny and Zooey*."
        Catholic World, 194 (February 1962), 312-313.

        Kennedy praises Salinger for his "virtuoso per-
        formance in mid-twentieth-century, middle-class
        New York lingo," but hopes that before he writes
        the "promised additional episodes on the Glass fam-
        ily ... Salinger will have time to polish up a bit
        on his Glass-family lenses."

1036.   Kermode, Frank. "J.D. Salinger: One Hand Clapping."
        New Statesman, 8 June 1962, p. 831; rpt. *Conti-
        nuities*. New York: Random House, 1969, pp. 194-
        199.

        In a negative review, Kermode considers Salin-
        ger and his audience: Salinger "very carefully
        writes for an audience he deplores, an audience
        that disposes of a certain amount of smart cultur-
        al information and reacts correctly to fairly com-
        plex literary stimuli: an audience that is familiar
        with Creative Writing, and has a strong stiffening
        of people who have turned in pretty good papers on
        Flaubert or Faulkner. Or Salinger."

1037.   *Kirkus*, 15 June 1961, p. 512.

        "Without, really, any beginning--middle or end--
        these fragments,--of a situation, of an issue, of
        an attitude, of life in a family,--build, but not
        to the affecting pitch of *Catcher*, which may be a
        disappointment to lesser adherents but a seminar
        course for the serious analysts."

1038.   Kirkwood, Hilda. *Canadian Forum*, 41 (November 1961),
        189-190.

        "In essence, Salinger's message seems to be the
        same as E.M. Forster's so differently delivered
        'only connect.' In all the miles of Glass family
        prose, no one ever does."

1039.   Lerman, Leo. "It Takes 4." *Mademoiselle*, 53 (Octo-
        ber 1961), 108-111.

        With a big picture of Salinger, Lerman announces
        that Salinger's "four important children [Franny,
        Zooey, Seymour, and Buddy Glass] ... cry out in one
        self-examining voice the anguish of today's campus-
        age intellectuals."

1040.   "The Making of a Saga." *Times Literary Supplement*,

8 June 1962, p. 425.

"Most important is the rediscovery of Mr. Salinger's ability to handle the tragic on a comic level
and yet make it no less tragic," but the "occasional
intrusion of the author in the second of these two
stories ... alters the flavour--and not for the better."

1041.   Marple, Anne. "Salinger's Oasis of Innocence." *New
        Republic*, 18 September 1961, pp. 22-23.

        Marple questions Salinger's avoiding the sexual,
"so obvious a part of human life." Rpt. in 413.

1042.   Mayhew, Alice Ellen. "Salinger's Fabulous Glass Fam-
        ily." *Commonweal*, 6 October 1961, pp. 48-50.

        For Mayhew, "reviewing *Franny and Zooey* is like
reading and reviewing only a small part of a larger,
more conclusive work. It's interesting and hope-
ful, artful and brimming with vitality and the need
to proceed, but necessarily inconclusive."

1043.   McCarthy, Mary. "*Franny and Zooey*." [London] *Ob-
        server*, 3 June 1962, p. 21; rpt. *Harper's*, 225
        (October 1962), 46-48.

        In *Franny and Zooey*, "the theme is the good people
against the stupid phonies, and the good is still all
in the family, like a family-owned 'closed' corpor-
ation," but "Seymour's suicide suggests that Salinger
guesses intermittently or fears intermittently that
there may be something wrong, somewhere."

1044.   McIntyre, John R., S.J. "A Preface for 'Franny and
        Zooey.'" *Critic*, 20 (February-March 1962), 25-
        28.

        McIntyre praises *Franny and Zooey* because "in a
literary way, Mr. Salinger makes us conscious not
only of his religious sensibility, but more particularly of the tension which exists between 'the
Kingdom of God is here!' and 'the day of the Lord
approaches.' In doing this, he defines the very
purpose of society."

1045.   Mizener, Arthur. "Defining 'the Good American.'"
        Listener, 16 August 1962, pp. 241-242.

        "This publication of the Glass story in bits
and pieces lost at least two important effects,
both of them unfortunate. It concedes the serious
purpose of the work as a whole, and it makes it
difficult for any but the most devoted readers to

straighten out a story that Salinger, as a matter
of imaginative principle, has filled with compli-
cated details."

1046.   Murray, James G. "Books." *Critic*, 20 (October-Novem-
        ber 1961), 72-73.

        With just two complaints--"the writing is a bit
        too precious" and "Paul and Zen, Jesus and the gurus
        are too closely linked," Murray praises *Franny and
        Zooey* for being "genuine and original": Salinger's
        "people are interesting; his talk is stimulating;
        and his craftsmanship is impeccable."

1047.   Nordell, Rod. "The Salinger Phenomenon." *Christian
        Science Monitor*, 14 September 1961, p. 7.

        Nordell ends a generally positive review by
        quoting Holden Caulfield from *The Catcher*: "'If you
        do something too good, then, after a while, if you
        don't watch it, you start showing off.'"

1048.   "Notes on Current Books." *Virginia Quarterly*, 38
        (Winter 1962), viii.

        "As a writer whose inconsiderable output is
        matched by his obvious passion for perfection, Mr.
        Salinger easily attracts zealots ready to attribute
        to him modern literary miracles on what is mani-
        festly slender evidence and not altogether realized
        promise, for all the coruscations of style and con-
        tent."

1049.   Nye, Robert. "The Trouble with Franny." *The Scots-
        man*, 2 June 1962, p. 6.

1050.   Phelps, Robert. "A Writer Who Talks to and of the
        Young." *New York Herald Tribune Books*, 17 Sep-
        tember 1961, pp. 3, 14.

        The major concern of *Franny and Zooey* is "with
        the nature of religious experience--with its uncon-
        ditional innerness; with the anomaly of its inci-
        dence in the everyday life of human beings; with
        what Auden has called 'depravity'--'the constant
        tendency of the spiritual life to degenerate into
        an aesthetic performance'; and above all, with the
        trust that a man's life is ultimately measured not
        by what he does, but by the pureness-in-heart with
        which he does it."

1051.   Poore, Charles. "Books of The Times." *New York Times*,
        14 September 1961, p. 29.

        Franny and Zooey, "better than anything Mr.

Salinger has done before," contains "a miraculous
vitality [that] rides with their [the Glasses']
ritual-riddled despair."

1052. Pugh, Griffith T. "From Recent Books." *English Jour-
       nal*, 51 (May 1962), 374-377.

       Calling *Franny and Zooey* "as fine a work as any
       since" *The Catcher*, Pugh writes, "the inner con-
       sciousness, the sensitivity to the vicissitudes of
       life, the neurotic reaction to obtuseness and to
       even the suggestion of coarseness, are vividly and
       convincingly presented."

1053. Raymond, John. "The Salinger Situation." *The Sunday
       Times*, 3 June 1962, p. 33.

1054. Rowland, Stanley J., Jr. "Love Parable." *Christian
       Century*, 6 December 1961, pp. 1464-1465.

       Rowland summarizes "some of Salinger's central
       insights": "moral sensitivity and integrity can
       lead easily to isolation and meaninglessness";
       "this happens because sin ... is acutely recognized";
       "a person must honestly know and learn to accept
       himself and others as creatures immensely valuable
       to God and dwelt in by his love."

1055. *Saturday Night*, 14 October 1961, pp. 36-37.

*   [Skow, Jack.] "Sonny: An Introduction." *Time*, 15
       September 1961, pp. 84-90.

       Cited above as item 288.

1056. Sullivan, Walter. "Truth in Fiction." *Modern Age*,
       6 (September 1962), 211-212.

       In a review which is mostly plot summary, Sul-
       livan praises Salinger for "his skill" and "his
       perception."

1057. Swenson, Ruth P. "Books for Adults." *Wisconsin Li-
       brary Bulletin*, 57 (September-October 1961),
       307-308.

       "Salinger's efforts are compounded of much more
       than inspiration--uncanny understanding, wit, humor,
       satire, compassion mingle with art, craft, and un-
       erring use of language."

1058. *The Sydney Morning Herald*, 9 September 1962, p. 14.

1059. Updike, John. "Anxious Days for the Glass Family."
       New York Times, 17 September 1961, Sec. 7, pp. 1,

52; rpt. *Assorted Prose*. New York: Alfred A.
Knopf, 1965, pp. 234-239; rpt. Greenwich, Connecticut: Fawcett, 1966, pp. 181-184.

For Updike, Salinger's "Glass saga ... potential-
ly contains great fiction," and Salinger's "refusal
to rest content, the willingness to risk excess on
behalf of one's obsessions, is what distinguishes
artists from entertainers, and what makes some artists adventurers on behalf of us all." Rpt. in
385, 404, and 413.

1060. Walker, Gerald. "Salinger and the Purity of Spirit."
       Cosmopolitan, 151 (September 1961), 36.

       "J.D. Salinger is offering what appears to be the
       Ivy League alternative to the Beat rebellion against
       the conforming, 'phony' materialism to be seen in
       America today. He's worth listening to even though
       he doesn't have the final answer, yet."

              b. References, Articles, Chapters

       The entries listed alphabetically below refer both
to references to and studies of either "Franny" or "Zooey"
and to studies of the two stories as a single work.

1061. Balke, Betty Tevis. "Some Judeo-Christian Themes
       Seen Through the Eyes of J.D. Salinger and Na-
       thanael West." *Cresset*, 31 (May 1968), 14-18.

       After a brief comparison of the personal and
       religious lives of Salinger and West, Balke con-
       cludes that *Miss Lonelyhearts* and *Franny and Zooey*,
       "written by Jews in dazzling style about Christian
       themes, are very different in total effect because
       they differ in depth, and ... in sincerity": West
       treated his Christian themes "with fidelity and re-
       spect"; Salinger did not.

1062. Dembo, L.S. "Salinger's Pilgrim Finds His Way."
       Uclan, 8 (Summer 1962), 19-24.

       For Dembo, *Franny and Zooey* is a novel, "the
       point of ... [which] does not lie only in what the
       characters talk about ... [but] in the fact that
       what is being said is, ultimately, listened to."

1063. Fleischmann, Wolfgang Bernhard. "The Contemporary
       'Jewish Novel' in America." *Jahrbuch für Ameri-
       kastudien*, No. 12 (1967), 159-166.

       Including Salinger as a Jewish writer, Fleischmann

uses *Franny and Zooey*, *Herzog*, *The Assistant*, and
Goodbye, Columbus to illustrate that "any attempt
to create a thematic uniqueness for the American
Jewish novel is doomed to failure."

1064. Goldstein, Bernice, and Sanford Goldstein. "Bunnies
       and Cobras: Zen Enlightenment in Salinger." *Dis-
       course*, 13 (Winter 1970), 98-106.

       With his interest in Zen Buddhism, Salinger "of-
       fers us a ... way out of the major dilemma of dual-
       ity that has beset the West for more than two thou-
       sand years"; "the dissolution of supposed opposites
       results in an experience that is immediate, deci-
       sive, and total. The capacity for enlightenment
       lies within each person."

1065. Nichols, Lewis. "In and Out of Books." *New York
       Times*, 19 November 1961, Sec. 7, p. 8.

       Nichols reports that as the result of alleged
       problems over a publisher "at the moment there's
       no English edition" of *Franny and Zooey*.

1066. Ogata, Mayumi. "The Pilgrimage in Salinger's *Franny
       and Zooey*." *Kyushu American Literature*, 21 (June
       1980), 62-65.

       Written by a senior at Fukuoka Women's Univer-
       sity, this essay suggests that *Franny and Zooey*
       must be considered as the story of both Franny and
       Zooey, not just Franny's.

1067. Panichas, George A. "J.D. Salinger and the Russian
       Pilgrim." *Greek Orthodox Theological Review*, 8
       (Summer 1962--Winter 1962-1963), 111-126; rpt.
       *The Reverent Discipline: Essays in Literary Crit-
       icism and Culture*. Knoxville: University of Ten-
       nessee Press, 1974, pp. 292-305.

       Salinger's use of *The Way of a Pilgrim* in *Franny
       and Zooey* shows "how modern fiction can affirm the
       divinity of all men."

1068. Phillips, Paul. "Salinger's *Franny and Zooey*." *Main-
       stream*, 15 (January 1962), 32-39.

       After detailed summaries of the two stories con-
       tained in this volume, Phillips concludes that Sal-
       inger is "best understood as a satirist, a satirist
       whose vision has distinct limitations." Because Sal-
       inger "is generally unconcerned with world issues,"
       his characters, "cut off from the world in which
       they live, ... will inevitably be as 'phony' as the
       ecstasy of those same television commercials they so
       passionately repudiate."

1069.   Ranly, Ernest W. "Journey to the East." *Commonweal*,
        23 February 1973, pp. 465-469.

        Ranly comments on his personal experience as af-
        afected by Salinger's *Franny and Zooey*.

1070.   Razdan, Brij M. "From Unreality to Reality: *Franny
        and Zooey*--A Reinterpretation." *Panjab University
        Research Bulletin*, 9 (April-October 1978), 3-15.

        With "the Upanishadic frame of reference," Razdan
        shows that "Franny journeys from the state of un-
        reality when Zooey (the Guru figure) jolts her in-
        to awareness that she could realize herself only
        through *others via* love and disinterested action."

1071.   Seitzman, Daniel. "Salinger's 'Franny': Homoerotic
        Imagery." *American Imago*, 22 (Spring-Summer
        1965), 57-76.

        In a later article (see item 1072), Seitzman ex-
        plains that his purpose in this essay is "to explain
        the psycho-dynamics of an encounter between Franny
        ... and her 'boy friend' and first 'therapist,'
        Lee--an encounter that culminates in her breakdown
        on a Saturday morning in November."

1072.   ———. "Therapy and Antitherapy in Salinger's
        'Zooey.'" *American Imago*, 25 (Summer 1968), 140-
        162.

        In a companion article for his essay about "Fran-
        ny" (see item 1071), Seitzman now explains "how the
        cure [for Franny's breakdown] took place."

1073.   Stuart, Robert Lee. "The Writer-in-Waiting." *Chris-
        tian Century*, 19 May 1965, pp. 647-649.

        Comments that "Salinger's *Franny and Zooey* is
        almost all 'talk'" and that Salinger does "make a
        gesture toward affirmation."

1074.   Weales, Gerald. "The Not So Modern Temper." *Antioch
        Review*, 17 (Winter 1957-58), 510-515.

        In a review of Joseph Wood Krutch's *The Measure
        of Man*, Weales reports Krutch's claim that modern
        writers are "determinists." "J.D. Salinger's
        Zooey," Weales writes, "taught his sister the sig-
        nificance of Seymour's fat lady."

1075.   Young, Philip. "Ernest Hemingway." In *Seven Modern
        American Novelists: An Introduction*. Ed. William
        Van O'Connor. Minneapolis: University of Minne-
        sota Press, 1959, pp. 153-188.

Brief mention of and quotation from "Zooey."

5. *Raise High the Roof Beam, Carpenters and*
Seymour: An Introduction

Like the sections under "Secondary Sources" for Salinger's other three books, this section on *Raise High the
Roof Beam, Carpenters and Seymour: An Introduction* contains a subsection for initial reviews and one for later
references and studies. For more studies of this volume,
see the subsections above on reference works (items 336-
397), on book-length studies (items 398-429), on miscellaneous references, articles, and chapters (items 430-
572), and on dissertations and theses (items 579-593).

a. Reviews

This subsection alphabetically lists the initial reviews of *Raise High the Roof Beam, Carpenters and Seymour:
An Introduction*. One of the reviews is not annotated.
See the following subsection (items 1099-1105) for later
references to and studies of either of the two stories in
this volume and of the two stories as a single work.

1076.   Adams, Robert M. "Fashions in Fiction." *Partisan Re-
        view*, 30 (Spring 1963), 128-133.

        In a negative review, Adams suggests that "if
        Mr. Salinger can't forget about Seymour Glass al-
        together, he'd be well advised to hold back indef-
        initely his further appearance in fiction." Rpt.
        in 379.

1077.   Barrett, William. "Reader's Choice." *Atlantic*, 211
        (February 1963), 128, 129.

        Barrett sees "Salinger's persistent theme ...
        [as] the contrast between the wonderful and magi-
        cal world of children and the crass materialism of
        adults."

1078.   Fry, John R. "Skill Is the Word." *Christian Century*,
        6 February 1963, pp. 175-176.

        Salinger "is the world heavyweight champion for
        tour de force, long sentences and long paragraphs,
        involved narrative, use of italics and parentheses,
        use of the Upper Case for Fun, exact phonetic rep-
        resentation of the overemphasizing speech patterns
        of the upper middle class American."

1079.   "The Glass House Gang." *Time*, 8 February 1963, p.
        86.

A rather negative review, which concludes that "increasingly the grown reader is beginning to wonder whether the sphinxlike Seymour had a secret worth sharing. And if so, when Salinger is going to reveal it."

1080. Gold, Arthur R. "J.D. Salinger: Through a Glass Darkly." *New York Herald Tribune Books*, 7 April 1963, p. 8.

Gold finds Salinger's style obscure: his style "has become so infernally clever, so precious and inwrought that it gives you the sense of being toyed with--toyed with by a mind girlishly shy of coming clear about its commitment to the subject matter at hand."

1081. Hassan, Ihab. "The Casino of Silence." *Saturday Review*, 26 January 1963, p. 38.

Salinger's efforts represent something that "has [not] occurred in American literature since Whitman," Hassan writes, and "the comic battle man fights with eternity. No one in recent fiction has accepted more difficult terms for that battle than Salinger. It is to our honor that he persists in it with love and grace."

1082. Hicks, Granville. *Saturday Review*, 26 January 1963, pp. 37-38.

Even though the book may not be well received, "Salinger remains a remarkably interesting and gifted and serious writer."

1083. Hill, William B. *America*, 11 May 1963, p. 678.

"*Raise High the Roof Beam, Carpenters* is vintage Salinger, with the banalities of most people contrasted to Seymour's brilliant perceptions into the almost unbearable beauty of life," but the volume "would not suffer terribly by the excision of the second story."

1084. Holzhauer, Jean. *Commonweal*, 22 February 1963, p. 575.

"Discursive, partisan, 'closed-circuit' and special as ever; also full of magical ideas and therefore enchanting."

1085. Howe, Irving. "More Reflections in the Glass Mirror." *New York Times Book Review*, 7 April 1963, pp. 4-5, 34.

Salinger's two stories in this volume "represent

an ambitious effort to unite a narrative mode with
contemplative matter, the dynamism of the short
story with prolonged moments of quiet in which the
narrator keeps staring, to the point of mystical
intuition or neurotic crack-up, at the character of
Seymour Glass." Howe criticizes Salinger for "a
loss of creative discipline, a surrender to cher-
ished mannerisms."

1086. "In Place of the New, A Reissue of the Old." *News-
        week*, 28 January 1963, pp. 90, 92.

        Critical of Salinger's volume from the beginning,
        the review closes negatively: "it ceases to matter
        whether one accepts literally or rejects wholly the
        notion of Buddy as Salinger's alter ego. Buddy is
        a fool and a fake in either case, and Seymour still
        awaits a proper Introduction."

1087. Jackson, Robert B. *Library Journal*, 15 January 1963,
        p. 237.

        "Significant work by an important writer and es-
        sential ... to all fiction collections."

1088. Kermode, Frank. "The Glass Menagerie." *New States-
        man*, 15 March 1963, p. 388; rpt. "J.D. Salinger:
        The Glass Menagerie." In *Continuities*. New York:
        Random House, 1969, pp. 199-201.

        The first of these two stories is good enough to
        put "in a book with good Salinger-Glass, such as
        'A Perfect Day for Bananafish,' without doing much
        harm," but "Seymour: An Introduction" "is ... close
        enough to mere rubbish for someone who enjoys exag-
        geration to call it that."

1089. Kirkwood, Hilda. "The Shape of His Nose." *Canadian
        Forum*, 43 (April 1963), 19-20.

        "There is such a thing as too much of the peren-
        nial victim, the living sacrifice, the bleeding
        heart"; "this book is a much less important and com-
        plete achievement than its predecessors."

1090. *Library Journal*, 15 April 1963, p. 81.

        Recommended as a book "for young adults," "this
        book will be of interest to ... serious students of
        modern literature."

1091. McGovern, Hugh. *America*, 2 February 1963, pp. 174-
        175.

        These "two stories are really nothing much";
        "not even a writer of Salinger's stature--and he is

our only authentic living literary giant--can make
a god out of a suicide. And he'd better not try."

1092.   Nott, Kathleen. "Novels." *Encounter*, 20 (June 1963),
        80-82.

        Calling this "a bad book" and "a wicked one,"
        Nott writes that her "own theory about this book is
        that it is a *Koan*, one of those cock-eyed Zen rid-
        dles which provide the formula for the anti-ration-
        al."

1093.   Plotnick, Harvey. "The House of Glass." *Modern Age*,
        7 (Fall 1963), 429-431.

        While Plotnick thinks that Salinger's previous
        work has proved his talent, he hopes that "*Raise
        High the Roof Beam, Carpenters and Seymour--An In-
        troduction* ... [is] only a temporary aberration in
        the creative output of a superb writer."

1094.   Quinn, J.J. *Best Sellers*, 1 February 1963, p. 408.

        After a brief summary of each piece in this vol-
        ume, Quinn writes, "Mature readers will marvel at
        the brilliant performance that marks the unmistak-
        able Salinger style in presenting his remarkable
        Glass Family."

1095.   "Saint or Slob?" *Times Literary Supplement*, 8 March
        1963, p. 165.

        "Raise High the Roof Beam, Carpenters," the re-
        viewer says, "is a delightful story," and "Seymour:
        An Introduction" has a "self-conscious manner";
        "Seymour the saint emerges."

1096.   Sheed, Wilfred. *Jubilee*, 10 (April 1963), 48-54.

1097.   Smith, Laurence. *Critic*, 21 (February-March 1963),
        73-74.

        Despite the fact that this volume will probably
        not be well received, Smith feels that no matter
        "what one might think of the eclectic religious
        views in the Glass stories, with all their gallop-
        ing mysticism, it should be kept in mind that this
        pre-occupation with love and reconciliation keeps
        Salinger from being backed into a corner, in Holden
        Caulfield fashion, where refreshing humor is re-
        placed by blinding hate."

1098.   Wain, John. "Go Home, Buddy Glass." *New Republic*,
        16 February 1963, pp. 21-22.

        Salinger unsuccessfully tackles "the two most

difficult objectives known to man, to describe good-
ness and to make happiness credible."

b. References, Articles, Chapters

    The alphabetical entries below refer both to refer-
ences to and studies of each of the two stories in this
collection and to the collection as a whole.

1099. Alsen, Eberhard. "'Raise High the Roof Beam, Car-
         penters' and the Amateur Reader." *Studies in
         Short Fiction*, 17 (Winter 1980), 39-47.

         Admitting that there are other interpretations
         of this story, Alsen demonstrates that this story
         is for the "amateur reader" in that "its form does
         not pose any problems that require a specialist's
         knowledge of narrative technique and because the
         core of its meaning can be understood without the
         help of outside information from other Seymour sto-
         ries and from Eastern philosophy."

1100. Bruccoli, Matthew. "States of Salinger Book." *Amer-
         ican Notes & Queries*, 2 (October 1963), 21-22.

         "There are at least three states of the first
         printing of J.D. Salinger's latest book," *Raise
         High the Roof Beam, Carpenters and Seymour: An In-
         troduction*.

1101. Goldstein, Bernice, and Sanford Goldstein. "Sey-
         mour's Poems." *Literature East and West*, 17
         (June, September, and December 1973), 335-348.

         Seeing "interesting parallels between the lives
         of "the major haiku poet Matsuo Bashō (1644-1690)"
         and Seymour, the Goldsteins demonstrate that "Sey-
         mour was either a haiku poet or was strongly in-
         fluenced by Japanese poetry" and that his "poems
         achieve ... synthesis" in the visual, "in which all
         contradictions are erased."

1102. ————. "'Seymour: An Introduction'--Writing as Dis-
         covery." *Studies in Short Fiction*, 7 (Spring
         1970), 248-256.

         The Goldsteins read this "ambitious" Salinger
         story as "an 'Introduction' to Seymour, but most
         importantly it is the process of Buddy's changing
         view and style that is the main subject."

1103. Johannson, Ernest J. "Salinger's Seymour." *Carolina
         Quarterly*, 12 (Winter 1959), 51-54.

Although at the time he writes Johannson thinks
that it is too early to judge "the character of Seymour," he wonders "if Salinger has forgotten that
the path from experience to literary expression involves more than memory and translation."

1104. Lyons, John O. "The Romantic Style of Salinger's
       'Seymour: An Introduction.'" *Wisconsin Studies
       in Contemporary Literature*, 4 (Winter 1963),
       62-69.

       In "Seymour: An Introduction," Salinger "returns
       to the style of the early Romantics" to a celebra-
       tion of "joy ... in life" even though he does attack
       "formalism and symbolism in literature, psychiatry
       and togetherness in the home, and pompousness and
       do-goodism in public life. All of these targets
       deny the essential mystery (and joy in the mystery)
       in spontaneous creation and life."

1105. Walters, Raymond, Jr. "In and Out of Books." *New
       York Times*, 23 September 1962, Sec. 7, p. 8.

       Announcement that Salinger's two stories "Raise
       High the Roof Beam, Carpenters" and "Seymour: An
       Introduction" would be published as a book.

C. TRANSLATIONS

Many of Salinger's works have been translated into
several languages and published in many countries. The
following translations have been taken from *Index Translationum* and Donald Fiene's two bibliographies (see items
341 and 342). The translations are arranged alphabetically
by the name of the country in which they were published.
Under each country, translations of each of Salinger's four
books are listed in the chronological order in which they
were published originally in the United States: *The Catcher*,
Nine Stories (British title, *For Esmé--with Love and Squal-
or*), *Franny and Zooey*, and *Raise High the Roof Beam, Carpenters and Seymour: An Introduction*. Unique translations of
works that did not appear as books in the United States appear in chronological order after the above four works.

1. Argentina

The Catcher in the Rye

1106. Mendez de Andes, Manuel, trans. *El cazador oculto*.
       Buenos Aires: Compania General Fabril Editora,
       1961.

Nine Stories

1107.   Berri, Marcelo, trans. *Nueve cuentos*. 3rd ed. Bue-
        nos Aires: Sudamericana, 1975.

*Raise High the Roof Beam, Carpenters and Seymour: An
Introduction*

1108.   Bernardez, Aurora, trans. *Levantad Carpinteros la
        viga del Tejado. Seymour, una introduccion*. Bue-
        nos Aires: Sudamericana, 1973.

2. Belgium

The Catcher in the Rye

1109.   Rossi, Jean-Baptiste, trans. *L'Homme hilare*. Thuin:
        Editione de la Grippelotte, 1970.

3. Brazil

The Catcher in the Rye

1110.   Alencar, Alvaro, Antonio Rocha, and Jorio Dauster,
        trans. *O apanhador no campo de centeio*. Rio de
        Janeiro: Editora do Autor, 1969.

Nine Stories

1111.   Magalhaes, Jorio Dauster, and Silva A. Gurgel de
        Alencar, trans. *Nove estorias*. Rio de Janeiro:
        Editora do Autor, 1969.

4. Bulgaria

The Catcher in the Rye

1112.   Sotirova, Nadja, trans. *Spasiteljat v Razta*. Sofi-
        ja: Narodna Kultura, 1973.

        In Romanian.

Pretty Mouth and Green My Eyes

1113.   Valcev, Todor, trans. *Ustata mi hubava, ocite mi
        zeleni*. Plovdiv: Darzhavno Izdatelstvo Khristo
        G. Danov, 1967.

5. China

The Catcher in the Rye

1114. Shik, Wu Yu, and Liu Shou Shih, trans. *Mai t'ien pu shou*. Taipei: Buffalo Book Company, 1968.

Stories of New York

1115. O'Hara, John, J.D. Salinger, Dorothy Parker, et al. *Niu yueh ta tu hui ch'uan ch'i weichih*. Kaohsiung: Shih Sui Public Service, 1963.

6. *Czechoslovakia*

The Catcher in the Rye

1116. Pellar, Luba, and Rudolf Pellar, trans. *Kdo chytá v zite*. In *Svetová Literatura*, Nos. 3, 4 (1960), 159-201, 113-175.

1117. ———. *Kdo chytá v zite*. Praha: Státni Nakladatelstvi Krásné Literatury, Hudby a Umeni, 1960; Odeon, 1967.

1118. Marusiaková, Viera, trans. *Kto chytá v zite*. Bratislava: Smena, 1964.

Nine Stories

1119. Pellarová, Luba, and Rudolf Pellar, trans. *Devet Povídek*. Praha: Odeon, 1971.

Franny and Zooey

1120. Janos, Elbert, and Dezsö Tandori, trans. *Franny és Zooey*. Bratislavia: Madách Konyvkiadó, 1970.

In Hungarian.

Raise High the Roof Beam, Carpenters and Seymour: An Introduction

1121. Lenygel, Peter, and Dezsö Tandori, trans. *Magasabbra a tetöt, ácsok. Seymour: Bemutatás*. Bratislava: Madách Konyvkiadó, 1970.

In Hungarian.

"A Perfect Day for Bananafish"

1122. Ruxová, Eva, trans. "Den jako styovený na banánové rybicky." In *Deset Novel*. Eds. Eva Ruxová and Vitezslav Kocourek. Praha: Ceskoslovensky Spisovatel, 1958, pp. 331-346.

"The Laughing Man"

1123. Urbánek, Zdenek, trans. "Smejíci se muz." *Svetová*

Literatura, No. 6 (November–December 1959), 68–
76.

7. *Denmark*

The Catcher in the Rye

1124. Cerri, Vibeke, trans. *Forbandede ungdom*. København:
       J.H. Schultz Forlag, 1953; Gyldendal, 1960.

Nine Stories

1125. Schram, Vibeke, trans. *Tilegnet Esme og andre novel-
       ler*. København: J.H. Schultz Forlag, 1954.

       Donald Fiene (see items 341 and 342) notes that
       Vibeke Schram is the married name of Vibeke Cerri,
       translator of other works by Salinger published in
       Denmark. This publication contains the same stories
       as Salinger's *Nine Stories*.

1126. Cerri, Vibeke, trans. *Ni Noveller*. København: Gyl-
       dendal, 1965.

Franny and Zooey

1127. ———. *Franny og Zooey*. København: Gyldendal, 1962.

*Raise High the Roof Beam, Carpenters and Seymour: An
Introduction*

1128. ———. *Der skal vaere højt til Loftet, Tømrer,
       og Seymour--En Introduktion*. København: Gylden-
       dal, 1964.

8. *Finland*

The Catcher in the Rye

1129. Saarikoski, Pentti, trans. *Sieppari ruispellossa*.
       Helsinki: Kustannusosakeyhtiö Tammi, 1961–1977.

Nine Stories

1130. Kapari, Marjatta, and Kristiina Kivivuori, trans.
       Yhdeksan Kertomusta. Helsinki: Tammi, 1966.

Franny and Zooey

1131. Saarikoski, Pentti, trans. *Franny ja Zooey*. Hel-
       sinki: Tammi, 1962.

9. *France*

The Catcher in the Rye

1132. Rossi, Jean-Baptiste, trans. *L'attrape-Coeurs*. Paris:
        Editions Robert Laffont, 1953, 1961; le Livre de
        poche, 1967.

Nine Stories

1133. ————. *Nouvelles*. Paris: Robert Laffont, 1961.

1134. ————. *Neuf Nouvelles*. Paris: Club des libraires
        de France, 1962.

1135. ————. *Nouvelles*. Paris: le Livre de poche, 1966.

Franny and Zooey

1136. Willerval, Bernard, trans. *Franny et Zooey*. Paris:
        Robert Laffont, 1962.

1137. ————. *Franny et Zooey*. Paris: le Livre de poche,
        1971.

Raise High the Roof Beam, Carpenters and Seymour: An
Introduction

1138. ————. *Dressez haut la poutre maîtresse, charpen-*
        tiers. Seymour, une introduction. Paris: le Livre
        de poche, 1964, 1971.

"A Perfect Day for Bananafish"

1139. Rossi, Jean-Baptiste, trans. "Un Jour reve pour le
        poisson banane." *L'Express*, No. 527 (20 July
        1961), 28-30.

"The Laughing Man"

1140. ————. "L'Homme hilare." *Candide*, 26 October-2 Nov-
        ember 1961, pp. 17-18.

10. *Germany*

The Catcher in the Rye

1141. Muelhon, Irene, trans. *Der Mann im Roggen*. Stutt-
        gart: Diana Verlag, 1954.

1142. ————. *Der Fänger im Roggen*. Berlin: Verlag Volk
        und Welt, 1965.

1143. Böll, Heinrich, trans. *Der Fänger im Roggen*. Köln:

Kiepenheuer und Witsch, 1962, 1965, 1975.

1144. ————. *Der Fänger im Roggen*. Reinbek bei Hamburg:
Rowohlt, 1966, 1967, 1968, 1969, 1970, 1971,
1974, 1977.

1145. ————. *Der Fänger im Roggen*. Berlin: Verlag Volk
und Welt, 1969, 1975.

1146. ————. *Der Fänger im Roggen*. Leipzig: Reclam Verlag, 1974.

Nine Stories

1147. Schnack, Elisabeth, et al., trans. *Neun Erzählungen*.
Köln and Berlin: Kiepenheuer ut Witsch, 1966.

1148. ————. *Neun Erzählungen*. Reinbek bei Hamburg: Rowohlt, 1968, 1969, 1971, 1974, 1975, 1976, 1977.

Franny and Zooey

1149. Böll, Annemarie, and Heinrich Böll, trans. *Franny
und Zooey*. Köln and Berlin: Kiepenheuer und
Witsch, 1963.

1150. ————. *Franny und Zooey*. Reinbek bei Hamburg: Rowohlt, 1967, 1968, 1970, 1971, 1974, 1975, 1976,
1977.

*Raise High the Roof Beam, Carpenters and Seymour: An
Introduction*

1151. Böll, Annemarie, and Heinrich Böll, trans. *Hebt den
Dachbalken Hoch, Zimmerleute. Seymour wird vor-
gestellt*. Köln and Berlin: Kiepenheuer and
Witsch, 1965.

1152. ————. *Hebt den Dachbalken Hoch, Zimmerleute. Seymour wird vorgestellt*. Reinbek bei Hamburg: Rowohlt, 1968, 1970, 1971, 1974, 1975, 1976.

For Esmé

1153. Schnack, Elisabeth, trans. *Für Esmé*. München: Nym-
phenburger Verlagshandlung, 1959, 1963.

This collection contains five stories: "For Es-
mé--with Love and Squalor," "A Perfect Day for Bananafish," "Pretty Mouth and Green My Eyes," "Down
at the Dinghy," and "Teddy."

"Uncle Wiggily in Connecticut"

1154. Schnack, Elisabeth, trans. "Onkel Wackelpeter in

Connecticut." In *Junge amerikanishe Literatur*.
Ed. Walter Hasenclever. Frankfurt am Main: Ull-
stain Taschenbucher Verlag, 1959, pp. 42-57.

Just Before the War with the Eskimos and Other Stories

1155. Böll, Annemarie, et al., trans. *Kurz dem Krieg
       gegen die Eskimos. Und andere Kurzgeschichten*.
       Köln-Marienburg: Verlag Kiepenheuer und Witsch,
       1961.

       This collection contains four stories: "Uncle
       Wiggily in Connecticut," "Just Before the War with
       the Eskimos," "The Laughing Man," and "De Daumier-
       Smith's Blue Period."

1156. ————. *Kurz vor dem Krieg gegen die Eskimos. Und
       andere Kurzgeschichten*. Berlin: Deutsche Buch-
       Gemeinschaft, 1968.

       See annotation for item 1155.

11. Hungary

The Catcher in the Rye

1157. Gyepes, Judit, trans. *Zabhegyezo*. Budapest: Európa
       Kiadó, 1964, 1965, 1974.

Nine Stories

1158. Bartos, Tibor, et al., trans. *Kilenc Történet*. Buda-
       pest: Európa Kiadó, 1966, 1967.

Franny and Zooey

1159. János, Elbert, and Dezsö Tandori, trans. *Franny és
       Zooey*. Budapest: Európa Kiadó, 1970.

*Raise High the Roof Beam, Carpenters and Seymour: An
Introduction*

1160. Lengyel, Péter, and Dezsö Tandori, trans. *Magasab-
       bra a Tetöt, Acsok! Seymour; bamutatas*. Budapest:
       Európa Kiadó, 1970.

12. Iceland

The Catcher in the Rye

1161. Olafsson, Flosi, trans. *Bjargvaetturinn í grasinu*.
       Reykjavik: Almenna Bókafelagid, 1975.

13. Israel

The Catcher in the Rye

1162.   Damieli, Avraham, trans. *Ani-New York, w-khol ha-shear*. Tel Aviv: Dafna, 1954.

1163.   Doron, Daniel, and Avraham Yavin, trans. *ha-Tafsan bisede ha-shippon*. Tel Aviv: Am Oved, 1975.

14. Italy

The Catcher in the Rye

1164.   Darca, Jacopo, trans. *Vita da uomo*. Roma: Gherardo Casini Editore, 1952.

1165.   Motti, Adriana, trans. *Il Giovane Holden*. Torino: Einaudi, 1961, 1970.

Nine Stories

1166.   Fruttero, Carlo, trans. *Nove Racconti*. Torino: Einaudi, 1962, 1970.

Franny and Zooey

1167.   Cerrone, Romano Carolo, and Ruggero Bianchi, trans. *Franny e Zooey*. Torino: Einaudi, 1963.

Raise High the Roof Beam, Carpenters and Seymour: An Introduction

1168.   Cerrone, Romano Carlo, trans. *Alzate L'Architrave, Carpentieri. Seymour. Introduzione*. Torino: Einaudi, 1965.

15. Japan

The Catcher in the Rye

1169.   Hashimoto, Fukuo, trans. *Kiken na nenrei*. Tokyo: David-sha, 1952.

1170.   Yamada, Toshinari, trans. *Kokonotsu no monogatari*. Tokyo: Shieho-sha, 1963.

1171.   Takashi, Nozaki, trans. *Rye-mugibatake de Tsukamaete*. Tokyo: Hakusuisha, 1964.

1172.   Takeju, Suzuki, trans. *Kokonotsu no monogatari*. Tokyo: Kadokawa shoten, 1969.

1173. Sutoshi, Nakagawa, trans. *Kokonotsu no monogatari*.
      Tokyo: Shueisha, 1977.

Nine Stories

1174. Shigeo, Hisashi, and Takeda Katsuhiko, trans. *Sa-
      kuhinshu*. Tokyo: Bunken shubo, 1964.

1175. Koji, Numasawa, trans. *Bananauo biyori*. Tokyo: Ko
      dansha, 1973.

1176. Takashi, Nozaki, trans. *Nain sutorizu*. Tokyo: Shin-
      cho-sha, 1974.

Franny and Zooey

1177. Keiichi, Harada, trans. *Franny. Zooey*. Tokyo:
      Arechi shuppansha, 1968.

1178. Takashi, Nozaki, trans. *Franny to zoi*. Tokyo: Shin-
      chosha, 1968, 1976.

1179. Takeju, Suzuki, trans. *Franny Zooey*. Tokyo: Kadoka-
      wa shoten, 1969.

*Raise High the Roof Beam, Carpenters and Seymour: An
Introduction*

1180. Takashi, Nozaki, and Inoue Kenji, trans. *Daiku yo,
      Yane no hari o takaku Ageyo*. Tokyo: Kamade sho-
      bo shinchan, 1970.

1181. Takeki, Suzuki, trans. *Daikurayo, Yane no hari o
      takaku Ageyo*. Tokyo: Kadokawa shoten, 1972.

The Inverted Forest and Other Stories

1182. Motoj, Karita, and Akio Atsumi, trans. *Tosaku no
      mori Tampensha*. Tokyo: Arechi shuppansha, 1968.

The Young Folks and Other Stories

1183. ————. *Wakamono tachi*. Tokyo: Arechi shuppansha,
      1968.

1184. Takeju, Suzuki, trans. *Wakamono tachi*. Tokyo: Kado-
      kawa shoten, 1971.

The Inverted Forest

1185. ————. *Tosaku no mori*. Tokyo: Kadokawa shoten, 1970.

*The Catcher in the Rye and Raise High the Roof Beam,
Carpenters*

1186. Shigeo, Hisashi, Takeda Katsuhiko, and Takizawa

Juzo, trans. *Kokonotsu no monogatari. Daiki
tashi yo, yane no hari o takaku ageoyo.* Tokyo:
Arechi shuppansha, 1969.

Hapworth 16, 1924

1187.   Keiichi, Harada, trans. *Hapworth 16, 1924.* Tokyo:
        Arechi shuppansha, 1977.

16. Korea

The Catcher in the Rye

1188.   Lee, Chang-dae, trans. *Danae.* Seoul: Namhunsa,
        1961.

1189.   Yu, Gyeong-hwan, and Bing Ro, trans. *Homilbut-eui
        Pasuggan.* Seoul: Pyeonghwachulpansa, 1963.

"For Esmé--with Love and Squalor"

1190.   Ra, Yong-kyun, trans. "Esmé egge: sarang kwa huchu
        wa doburo." *Sasangge Monthly*, 10 (February 1962),
        347-361.

17. Netherlands

The Catcher in the Rye

1191.   Graaf, Henk de, trans. *Eenzame zwerftocht.* 's-Graven-
        hage: Uitgeverij Oisterwijk, 1954.

1192.   ———. *Puber.* Rotterdam: Ad Donker, 1958, 1963.

1193.   Schuchart, Max, trans. *De Kinderredder van New York.*
        Utrecht: Bruna, 1967.

Franny and Zooey

1194.   Schuur, Koos, trans. *Franny and Zooey.* Amsterdam:
        Bezige Bij, 1963, 1968.

*Raise High the Roof Beam, Carpenters and Seymour: An
Introduction*

1195.   Toonder, Jan Gerhard, trans. *Heft hoog de nokbalk,
        timmerlieden. Seymour, een introduktie.* Amster-
        dam: Bezige Bij Meulenhoff, 1970.

18. Norway

The Catcher in the Rye

1196. Fen, Åke, trans. *Hver tar sin--så far vi andre ingen.* Oslo: J.W. Cappelens Forlag, 1952, 1974.

Franny and Zooey

1197. Gabrielsen, Thor, trans. *Franny og Zooey.* Oslo: Cappelens, 1962.

19. Poland

The Catcher in the Rye

1198. Skibniewska, Maria, trans. *Buszujacy w zboozu.* Warszawa: Państwowe Wydawnictwo Iskry, 1961, 1964, 1967.

Nine Stories

1199. Glinczanka, Agnieszka, and Krzysztof Zarzecki, trans. *Dziewiei Opowidan.* Warszawa: Państwowy Instytut Wydawniczy, 1964, 1967.

Franny and Zooey

1200. Skibniewska, Maria, trans. *Franny i Zooey.* Warszawa: Spóldzielnia Wydawnicza Czytelnik, 1966.

Raise High the Roof Beam, Carpenters and Seymour: An Introduction

1201. ————. *Wyżej Podnieście Strop, Cieśle i Seymour-- Introdukcja.* Warszawa: Spóldzielnia Wydawnicza Czytelnik, 1966.

"Pretty Mouth and Green My Eyes"

1202. Klinger, Krzysztof, trans. "Ladne usta i zielone oczy." *Ty I Ja* (February 1962).

"A Perfect Day for Bananafish"

1203. Oledzka, Jadwiga, trans. "Goraczka bananowa." *Panorama*, No. 16 (23 April 1962).

1204. Welczar, Franciszek, trans. "Wymarzony dzien na bananowa rybe." *Prezekroj*, No. 908 (2 September 1962), 9-11.

"Uncle Wiggily in Connecticut"

1205. Zarecki, Krzystof, trans. "Pan Kostek w Connecticut." *26 Wspolczesnych opwiadan amerykańskich.* Warszawa: Państwowe wydawnictwo, 1963.

20. *Portugal*

The Catcher in the Rye

1206. Ferreira, João Palma, trans. *Uma Agulha no Palheiro.*
       Lisboa: Livros do Brasil, 1961.

Nine Stories

1207. Monteiro, Luis de Sttau, and Vasuo Pulido Valente,
       trans. *Nove Contos.* Lisboa: Bertrand, 1966.

Franny and Zooey

1208. Mendes, Berta, trans. *Franny e Zooey.* Lisboa: Ber-
       trand, 1963.

*Raise High the Roof Beam, Carpenters and Seymour: An
Introduction*

1209. ————. *Carpinteiros, Levantem alto o pan de fileira
       e Seymour--Introdução.* Lisboa: Bertrand, 1965.

21. *Romania*

The Catcher in the Rye

1210. Ralea, Catinca, and Lucian Bratu, trans. *De Veghe
       in Lanul de secara.* Bucuresti: Editura Pentru
       Literatura Universala, 1964.

1211. Gyepes, Judit, trans. *Zabhegyezö.* Bukarest: Irodalmi
       Könyukiadó, 1968.

       Published in Romania, this translation is in
       Hungarian.

Nine Stories

1212. Cornis- Pop, Marcel, trans. *Noua povestiri.* Bucu-
       resti: Editura Univers, 1971.

22. *Spain*

Nine Stories

1213. Berri, Marcelo, trans. *Nueve Cuentos.* Barcelona:
       Bruquera, 1977.

Franny and Zooey

1214. Pardo, Jesús, trans. *Franny y Zooey.* Barcelona:
       Plaza y Janes, 1963.

1215.   Sarsanedas, Jordi, trans. *Franny i Zooey*. Barcelona:
        Edicions Proa, 1970.

*Raise High the Roof Beam, Carpenters and Seymour: An
Introduction*

1216.   Bernández, Aurora, trans. *Levantad carpinteros la
        viga maestra*. Barcelona: Bruquera, 1977.

23. *Sweden*

The Catcher in the Rye

1217.   Birgitta, Hammar, trans. *Räddaren i Nöden*. Stock-
        holm: Albert Bonnier, 1953.

1218.   ————. *Räddaren i Nöden*. 2nd ed. Stockholm: Borför-
        laget Aldus/Bonnier, 1960, 1961, 1964, 1966,
        1968, 1969, 1971.

Nine Stories

1219.   ————. *Till Esmé--Karleksfullt och Solkigt*. Stock-
        holm: Aldus/Bonnier, 1963, 1966.

*Raise High the Roof Beam, Carpenters and Seymour: An
Introduction*

1220.   Alfons, Harriet, trans. *Res Takbjälken högt, Timmer-
        män och Seymour, en Presentation*. Stockholm:
        Bonnier, 1964.

"For Esmé--with Love and Squalor"

1221.   Hammar, Birgitta, trans. "Till Esmé--kärleksfullt
        och solkigt." *Bonniers Litterära Magasin*, No. 4
        (April 1952), 247-259.

1222.   ————. "Till Esmé--Kärleksfullt och Solkigt." In
        En Silverantologoi. Eds. Georg Svensson and Ake
        Runnquist. Stockholm: Albert Bonnier, 1956, pp.
        418-436.

"Uncle Wiggily in Connecticut"

1223.   Alfons, Harriet, trans. "Stackars onkel Ankel."
        All Världens Berättare, No. 5 (May 1954), 418-
        427.

"A Perfect Day for Bananafish"

1224.   Eriksson, Lill-Inger, trans. "En utmärkt dag för
        bananfiskar." In *Rysare fran när och fjärran*.
        Ed. Mårten Edlund. Stockholm: Folket i Bild,

1961, pp. 124-138.

Donald Fiene (see items 341 and 342) notes that this is an "anthology of horror stories."

1225.   ———. "En utmärkt dag för banafiskar." *All Värl-dens Berättare*, No. 5 (May 1966), 18-26.

24. *Switzerland*

The Catcher in the Rye

1226.   Muehlon, Irene, trans. *Der Mann im Roggen*. Zurich: Diana Verlag Zurich, 1954.

"Pretty Mouth and Green My Eyes"

1227.   Schnack, Elisabeth, trans. "Hübscher Mund, grün meine Augen." In *Amerikanische Erzählen von F. Scott Fitzgerald bis William Goyen*. Ed. Elisabeth Schnack. Zürich: Manesse Bibliothek der Weltliteratur, 1957, pp. 340-362.

25. *Turkey*

The Catcher in the Rye

1228.   Benk, Adnan, trans. *Gönül-Çelen*. Istanbul: Cem Yayinevi, 1967.

26. *Union of Soviet Socialist Republics*

In the Russian translations, the entries for *The Catcher* come first in chronological order; the other Russian translations follow in the chronological order of their publication.

1229.   Rait-Kovaleva, Rita, trans. *Nad propsatyu vo rzhi*. In *Inostrannaya Literatura*, No. 11 (November 1960), 28-137.

1230.   Raud, V., trans. *Kuristik Rukkis*. Tallin: Ajalehtede-Ajakirjade Kirjastus, 1961.

1231.   ———. *Kuristik Rukkis*. Tallin: Gaz.-zurn, 1961.

1232.   Rait-Kovaleva, Rita, trans. *Nad propastyu vo rzhi*. Moskva: Izdatelstvo Inostrannaya Literatury, 1961.

1233.   Celidze, V., trans. *Nad propast'ju vo rzi*. Tbilisi:

Nakaduli, 1963.

In Georgian.

1234. Gasiulus, Rovlias, trans. *Rugiuose Prie Bedugnes.*
Vil'njus: Vaga, 1966, 1970.

In Lithuanian.

"A Perfect Day for Bananafish"

1235. Golysheva, V., and E. Nappelbaum, trans. "Luchshi
den bananovoi ryby." *Voskresnoe Pridozhenie Izvestia: Nedelya*, No. 8 (19-25 February 1961),
8-9.

1236. Raud, Valda, trans. *Parim paev banaanikala puugiks.*
Tallin: Periodika, 1966.

In Esthonian.

"For Esmé--with Love and Squalor"

1237. Mitina, S., trans. "Posviashchaetsia Esmé." *Noviy
Mir*, No. 3 (March 1961), 63-78.

"Pretty Mouth and Green My Eyes"

1238. Gail, Nora, trans. "I eti guby i glaza zelenye."
Voskresnoe Pridozhenie Izvestia: Nedelya, No. 19
(6-12 May 1962), 8-9.

1239. Simonian, K.N., trans. *I eti guby, I glaza zelenye.*
Erevan: Ajpetrat, 1962.

In Armenian.

Grustnyj Motiv

1240. Bernstejn, I., et al., trans. *Grustnyj motiv.* Moskva: Pravda, 1964.

This title translates "sad (gloomy, mournful,
dreary) motif." This collection of stories, which
I have not seen, perhaps includes "De Daumier-Smith's
Blue Period."

1241. Celidze, V., trans. *Grustny Motiv.* Tbilisi: Nakaduli, 1967.

In Georgian. See annotation for item 1240.

*The Catcher in the Rye, Raise High the Roof Beam, Carpen-
ters, and Other Stories*

1242. Rajy-Kovaleva, I., trans. *Nad propast'ju vo rzi.*

Vyse stropila, plotniki. Rasskazy. Moskva: Molodaya Gvardiya, 1965.

The Catcher in the Rye and Other Stories

1243.   Bauga, Anna, and Dzesija Dzerve, trans. *Uz kraujas rudzu Lauka.* Riga: Liesma, 1969.

        In Latvian.

The Catcher in the Rye, Raise High the Roof Beam, Carpenters, A Perfect Day for Bananafish, For Esmé--with Love and Squalor, The Laughing Man, Pretty Mouth and Green My Eyes, and Grustnyj Motiv

1244.   Celidze, V., trans. *Nad propast'ju vo rzi. Vyse stropila, plotniki. Horoso lovitsja rybka-bananka. Posvjascaetsja Esme. Lapa-rastjapa. I eti guby, i glaza zelenye. Grustnyj motiv.* Tbilisi: Nakaduli, 1961.

        In Georgian. See annotation for item 1240 for a note on the last item in this translation.

The Catcher in the Rye, Nine Stories, Raise High the Roof Beam, Carpenters, and Franny and Zooey

1245.   Raud, Valda, trans. *Kuristik Rukkie. Novellid. Puusepad, tostke korgele sarikad! Franny ja Zooey.* Tallin: Eesti raamat, 1973.

27.   Viet Nam

The Catcher in the Rye

1246.   Shaw, Irwin, and J.D. Salinger. *Anh hùng thâm mêt Trân-Phong-Gia.* Saigon: Giao-Diem, 1965.

28.   Yugoslavia

The Catcher in the Rye

1247.   Krsic, Nikola, trans. *Lovac u zitu.* Sarajevo: Svjetlost, 1958, 1963.

1248.   Cvetanovski, Save, trans. *Igra vo rzta.* Skopje: Makedsonska Kniga, 1966.

1249.   Mirtic-Saje, Milka, trans. *Igra v rzi.* Ljugljana: Mladinska Knijiga, 1966.

Nine Stories

1250.   Krsic, Nikola, trans. *Za Esme.* Beograd: Jugoslavija

Izdavacki Zavod, 1969.

Franny and Zooey

1251. Stefanovic-Cicanovic, Nevena, trans. *Freni i Zui*.
        Beograd: Prosveta, 1965.

*Raise High the Roof Beam, Carpenters and Seymour: An
Introduction*

1252. Pecnik-Kroflin, Blanka, trans. *Podignite visoko
        Krovnu gredu, Tesari. Seymour--Uvod*. Zagreb:
        Zora, 1971.

"A Perfect Day for Bananafish"

1253. Soljan, Nada, trans. "Savrsen dan za ribu bananu."
        In *Izabrane Novels*. Ed. Slobodan Novak. Zagreb:
        Lykos, 1959, pp. 22-32.

1254. Segedin, T., trans. "Sanjani dan za ribu bananu."
        Telegram, 1 September 1961, p. 12.

D. *FOREIGN CRITICISM*

        The following foreign criticism includes both reviews
of translations of Salinger's works and later and more detailed studies. Most of the entries in this section refer
to criticism published in languages other than English;
however, a few of the items refer to criticism that I have
not seen but which was published in foreign countries and
which may be in English. In Donald Fiene's two bibliographies (see items 341 and 342), he includes many pieces of
foreign criticism, particularly reviews of translations,
for which he does not include page numbers. I omit those
entries for which I have not been able to document page
numbers. The order throughout the section is alphabetical.

1255. Adrianne, René. "Lettres Americaines: J.D. Salin-
        ger." *Revue Nouvelle*, 35 (February 1962), 101-
        104.

1256. Amoruso, Vito. "La visione e il caos: Il decadentis-
        mo di Salinger." *Studi Americani*, 10 (1964), 317-
        342.

1257. Ando, Shoei. *America Bungaku to Zen--Salinger no
        Sekai* [*American Literature and Zen--Salinger's
        World*]. Tokyo: Eihosha, 1970.

1258. Antonini, Giacomo. "Il successo di Salinger."

Fiera Letteraria, 28 October 1962, pp. 1, 4.

1259.   Arbasino, Alberto. "Il Talemaco Moderno." *Il Mondo*,
        12 August 1958, p. 8.

1260.   Aronson, Harry. "J.D. Salinger--ungdomens vän." *Vår
        lösen*, 58 (1967), 41-46.

1261.   Atsami, Akio, and Kenju Inoue, eds. *Sarinja no Se-
        kai [Salinger's World]*. Tokyo: Arechi Shuppansha
        and Kochishuppansha, 1959.

1262.   B., L.M. "Wrazenia i oceny: Rozmowa z Bronislawem
        Zielinskim." *Nowa Kultura*, 31 May 1959, p. 8.

1263.   Balota, Nicolae. "Salinger şi umanismul infantil
        ["Salinger and Infantile Humanism"]." In *Umani-
        tati [Humanities]*. Bucharest: Editura Eminescu,
        1973, pp. 298-300.

1264.   Bandić, Milos I. *Knjizevnost*, No. 12 (December 1959),
        586-591.

1265.   Barbulescu, Simion. "Un scriitor de notorietate
        mondicla: J.D. Salinger ["A World-Wide Notorious
        Writer"]." In *Comentarii critics [Critical Com-
        mentaries]*. Bucarest: Editura pentru literatura,
        1969, pp. 355-362.

1266.   Baruch, Gertrud. *Bücherei und Bildung*, 6 (July-
        August 1954), 728-729.

1267.   Bien, Günter. "Das Bild des Jugendlichen in der
        modernen Literatur." *Deutsche Rundschau*, 9 (March
        1964), 4045.

1268.   Blöcker, Günther. "Jerome D. Salinger." *Literatur
        als Teilhabe*. Berlin: Kritische Orientierungen
        zur literarische Gegenwart, 1966, pp. 22-23,
        145-155.

1269.   Bonosky, Phillip. "J.D. Salinger: *Kdo chytá v zite*."
        Svetová Literatura, No. 3 (May-June 1960), 156-
        158.

1270.   Bory, Jean-Louis. "Jeune Amérique." *Samedi-Soir*, 7-
        13 May 1953, p. 7.

1271.   Brix, Hans. "En amerikansk stud. art." *Berlingske
        Aftenavis*, 7 October 1953, p. 4.

1272.   ————. "En mestersvend." *Berlingske Aftenavis*, 16
        October 1954, p. 8.

1273.   Brodin, Pierre. *Présences contemporaines: Écrivains americains d'aujourd'hui.* Paris: Nouvelles Editions Debrisse, 1964.

1274. Brüning, Eberhard. "Tendenzen der Persönlichkeitsgestaltugn im amerikanischen Gegenwartsroman." *Zeitschrift für Anglistik und Amerikanistik*, 16 (1968), 390-401.

1275. Camerino, Aldo. "Adolescente Americano." *Fiera Letteraria*, 16 November 1958, p. 5.

1276. Coy, Juan José. *Jerome David Salinger.* Barcelona: Fontanella, 1968.

1277. Curtis, Jean-Louis. "Préface." *Nouvelles.* Trans. Jean-Baptiste Rossi. Paris: Editions Robert Laffont, 1961, pp. 9-22.

1278. Delpech, Jeanine. "Un Kennedyste s'explique." *Nouvelles Littéraires*, 16 (February 1967), 3.

1279. *Deutsche Zeitung*, 5 October 1961, p. 10.

1280. *Die Kiepe*, 9 (1961), 4.

1281. Dixsaut, J., trans. *L'Ouvre romanesque de J.D. Salinger.* Frederick L. Gwynn and Joseph L. Blotner. Paris: Minard, 1962.

1282. Dolecki, Zbigniew. "Chlopiec w Babilonie." *Kierunki*, 29 October 1961, p. 8.

1283. Drawicz, Andrzej. "Zbuntowani maloletni." *Sztandar Mlodych*, 5 December 1961, p. 2.

1284. Elektorowicz, Leszek. "Purytanizm w fazie buntu." *Zycie Literackie*, 11 February 1962, p. 5.

1285. Erdmenger, Manfred. "*How to catch a phony* oder warum auch *Love Story* in den Lehrplan kommen kann." *Die neueren Sprachen*, 21 (June 1972), 324-327.

1286. Fink, Guido. "Salinger, o la magia del nome propria." *Studi Americani*, 12 (1966), 259-276.

1287. Flaker, Aleksandar. *Modelle der Jeans Prosa: Zur literarischen Opposition bei Pelnzdorf im osteuropaischen Romankontext.* Kronberg/Ts.: Scriptor Verlag, 1975; *Prozu u trapericama.* Zagreb: Liber, 1976.

1288. Fleisher, Frederic. "J.D. Salinger och hans familj." *Bonniers Litterära Magasin*, 30 (December 1961), 846-848.

1289.   Fluck, Winfred. "*Citizen Kane* als 'filmischer'
        Text und als Text der amerikanischen Kultur."
        Literatur in Wissenschaft und Unterricht, 13
        (December 1980), 296-321.

1290.   Franconeri, Franceso. "Jerome David Salinger: Un
        americano in cerca d'amore." *Vita e Pensiero*,
        45 (1962), 394-411.

1291.   Freese, Peter. "*Adventures of Huckleberry Finn* and
        The Catcher in the Rye: Zur exemplarischen Deu-
        tung der Romananfänge ["On Exemplary Interpre-
        tations of the Beginnings of These Novels."]."
        Die neueren Sprachen, 22 (1973), 658-688.

1292.   ————. "J.D. Salinger *Nine Stories*: Eine Deutung
        der frühen Glass-Geschicten." *Kieler Beiträge
        zur Anglistik und Amerikanistik*, 6 (December
        1968), 242-283; rpt. *Amerikanische Erzählungen
        von Hawthorne bis Salinger: Interpretation*. Ed.
        Paul G. Buchloh. Neumünster, 1968, pp. 242-283.

1293.   ————. "Jerome David Salinger." In *Amerikanische
        Literatur der Gegenwart*. Ed. Martin Christadler.
        Stuttgart: Alfred Kröner, 1973, pp. 43-68.

1294.   ————. "Jerome David Salinger: *The Catcher in the
        Rye*." *Literature in Wissenschaft und Unterricht*,
        1 (1968), 123-152; rpt. *Der amerikanische Roman
        im 19. und 20. Jahrhundert: Interpretationen*.
        Ed. Edgar Lohner. Berlin: Erich Schmidt, 1974,
        pp. 320-336.

1295.   ————. "Zwei unbekannte Verweise in J.D. Salingers
        The Catcher in the Rye: Charles Dickens und Ring
        Lardner." *Archiv für das Studium der neueren
        Sprachen und Literaturen*, 211 (1974), 68-72.

1296.   Fusini, Nadia. "Holden, il feticcio abbandonato."
        Studi Americani, 15 (1969), 465-478.

1297.   Gail, Nora. *Komsomolskaya Pravda*, 13 December 1960,
        p. 3.

1298.   Galinskaia, Irina L'vovna. *Filosofskie i estetich-
        eskie osnovy poetiki Dzh. D. Selindzhera [The
        Philosophical and Aesthetic Basis of the Poetics
        of J.D. Salinger]*. Moscow: Namka, 1975.

1299.   ————. "Divnii svet geroiv Selindzhera ["The Mi-
        raculous World of Salinger's Heroes"]." *Vsevit,
        Kiev*, 8 (1967), 62-68.

1300.   Geraths, Armin. "Salinger: 'The Laughing Man.'" In
        Die amerikanische Kurzgeschicte. Eds. Karl Heinz

Göller and Gerhard Hoffman. Düsseldorf: Bagel,
1972, pp. 326-336.

1301. Groene, Horst. "Jerome David Salinger, 'Uncle Wig-
       gily in Connecticut' (1948)." In *Die amerikanische
       Short Story der Gegenwart: Interpretationen*. Ed.
       Peter Freese. Berlin: Schmidt, 1976, pp. 110-118.

1302. Grzeniewski, Ludwik B. "Histeria z dystansem."
       Przeglad Kulturalny, 5 October 1961, p. 6.

1303. Günter, Bernd. "Holden Caulfield: Sentimentaler
       oder sentimentalischer Idealist?" *Die neueren
       Sprachen*, 21 (December 1972), 728-738.

1304. ————. "J.D. Salinger: *The Catcher in the Rye*."
       In *Der Roman im Englischunterricht der Sekundar-
       stufe, II: Theorie und Praxis*. Eds. Peter Freese
       and Fresel Hermes. Paderborn: Shoningh, 1977,
       pp. 207-222.

1305. H., R. *Paivan Sanomat*, 10 March 1961, p. 2.

1306. den Haan, Jacques. "Ein Keurige Uitgave." *Critisch
       Bulletin*, 22 (June 1955), 278-282.

1307. ————. "Glass Saga." *Litterair Passport*, No. 157
       (June-July 1962), 125-217.

1308. ————. *De Lagere Hartstochten: Meditaties over
       Pornografie*. Den Haag: Bert Bakker, 1962, pp.
       87-88, 152-153, 156-159.

1309. ————. "Talking Shop." *Litterair Passport*, No.
       157 (June-July 1962), 134.

1310. Hájek, Igor. "Hríbe mezi mrakodrapy." *Kdo chytá v
       zite*. Praha: SNKLHU, 1960, pp. 223-230.

1311. Hamada, Seijiro. "'The Laughing Man' ni tsuite ["On
       'The Laughing Mas'"]." *Eigo Seinen [The Rising
       Generation]*, 114 (1968), 578-579.

1312. Hardy, John Edward. "J.D. Salinger: 'Down at the
       Dinghy.'" In *Commentaries on Five Modern Ameri-
       can Short Stories*. Frankfurt am Main, Germany:
       Verlag Moritz Diesterweg, 1962, pp. 7-10.

1313. Harpprecht, Klaus. "Zwei Erfolgreiche." *Der Monat*,
       No. 207 (December 1965), 77-80.

1314. Hashimoto, Fukuo. "Atogaki." *Kiken na nenrei*.
       Tokyo: David-sha, 1952, pp. 252-256.

1315. Häusermann, H.W. *Moderne amerikanische Literatur*.
       Bern and München, 1965.

1316. Hesse, Herman. [Review of *The Catcher*]. *Die Welt-woche*, 24 December 1953.

1317. Hüllen, W., W. Rossi, and W. Christopeit, eds. *Zeitgenössische amerikanische Dichtung*. 2nd ed. Frankfurt, 1964.

1318. Iwamato, Iwao, and Katsuji Takamura. *America Shoset-su no Tenkai* [*The Development of the American Novel*]. Tokyo: Shohakusha, 1977.

1319. Johansen, Niels Kaas. *Information*, 21 September 1953, p. 2.

1320. Joop, Gerhard. *Westermanns Monatshefte*, 96 (February 1955), 84-85.

1321. Jovic, Zvezdan. *Knjizevne Novine*, 21 November 1958, p. 9.

1322. Joysmith, Toby. "Some Notes on J.D. Salinger." *The News*, 3 September 1961, Sec. 1, p. 8A.

1323. Jung, C.G., and K. Kerenyi. *Einführung in das Wesen der Mythologie: Das göttliche Kind/Das göttliche Madchen*. 4th ed. Zürich, 1951.

1324. Kanesaki, Hisao. "J.D. Salinger." *Jinbun Kenkyu*, 12 (June 1961), 123-124.

1325. Kanters, Robert. "Salinger, la gross dame et le bouddha." *Figaro Littéraire*, 29 December 1962, p. 2.

1326. ————. "Le mystère Salinger--Un Alain Fournier américain?" *Figaro Littéraire*, 11 November 1961, p. 2.

1327. Karanfilov, Efrem. "Mezdu zaledenoto ezero i caf-nalata niva." In *Dzerom Dejvid Selindzar. Spasi-teljat v razta*. Sofia: Narodna Kultura, 1973, pp. 189-202.

1328. Keiichi, Haraka. "After *Franny and Zooey*." In *Ameri-can Literature in the 1950's*. Tokyo: Tokyo Chapter of the American Literature Society of Japan, 1977, pp. 90-95.

1329. Khomyakov, V.A. "Selindzher--novellist." *Uchenye zapiska: Leningradskii pedagogicheskii institut imeni A.I. Gertsena*, Leningrad, 106 (1967), 240-250.

1330. ————. "O dekadentskikh tendentsiyakh v tvorchestve

Sèlindzhera ["On Decadent Trends in Salinger's
Works"]." *Uchenye zapiski: Vologodskii pedagogicheskii institut, Vologda*, 30 (1967), 96-108.

1331. Khvitaria, Lia. *Dzherom Devid Sèlindzher*. Tbilisi:
Ganatleba, 1970.

1332. Kim, Chong-Un. "The Novels of J.D. Salinger." *English Language and Literature*, No. 8 (June 1960),
107-119.

1333. Kipphoff, Petra. "Zwischen Trauer und Zorn." *Die
Zeit*, 23 November 1962, p. 19.

1334. "Kirja nuorisosta nuorisolle--ja vanhemmillekin."
Kansan Voima, 4 March 1961, p. 4.

1335. Kistrup, Jens. "Raffineret Mesternovellist." *Berlinske Tidende*, 19 December 1954, p. 23.

1336. ———. "Sytten Aar--alene i New York." *Berlinske
Tidende*, 17 November 1953, p. 10.

1337. Kivimies, Yrjö. "Teos ja vää rennys." *Suomalainen
Suomi*, No. 3 (1961), 179.

1338. Knipovich, Yevgenia. "Lyudi nad propastyu." *Znamya*,
31 (June 1961), 215-224.

1339. Konsulova, Violeta. "S ljubov kam coveka." *Teatar*,
9 (1967), 45-46.

1340. Kopperi, Paul A. *Virkamieslehti*, 43 (March 1961),
26.

1341. Korjust, Jaakko. "Ihanteet korkealla." *Nuori Oikes-
to*, No. 4 (April 1961), 11.

1342. Kraul, Fritz. "Jerome D. Salingers Roman *Der Fänger
im Roggen* als Pflichtlektüre im Deutschunterricht
der Oberstufe." *Der Deutschunterricht*, 20, No. 1
(1968), 79-86.

1343. Krsić, Nikola. "Biljesca o piscu." *Lovac u zitu*.
Sarajevo: Svjetlost, 1958, pp. 285-286.

1344. Kustova, L.S. "Roman Sèlindzera *Nad propast'ju vo
rzi* i ego perevod na russkij jazyk." *Vestnik Mos-
kovskogo Universiteta*. Serija VII, Filologija
Zurnalistika, 19 (1964), 68-81.

1345. Ladan, Tomislav. "Pathetica Americana." *Izraz*, 3
(January 1959), 63-67.

1346. Laffont, Robert. "Lettre aux lecteur." *Vient de*

Paraitre Laffont, December 1961, p. 8.

1347.   Laitinen, Kai. "Sieppari." *Parnasso*, 11 (1961),
        208-211.

1348.   Lembourn, Hans Jørgen. "Bag den Gyldne Facade."
        Berlingske Tidende, 23 October 1962, p. 4.

1349.   Levidova, Inna. "Neprikayannye dushi: Geroi knig J.
        Kerouac, J. Salinger, T. Capote i E. Connell."
        Voprosy literatury, No. 10 (October 1960), 108-
        131.

1350.   Levine, Paul. "Fiction of the Fifties: Alienation
        and Beyond." In *America in the Fifties*. Ed. Anne
        R. Clauss. Copenhagen: University of Copenhagen,
        1979.

1351.   Ligeza, Lukasz. "Antykonformista." *Wiez*, Nos. 11-
        12 (November-December 1961), 235-239.

1352.   "Los libros que viven; Sintesis." *Vea y Lea*, 26
        April 1962, pp. 65-69.

1353.   Lydenberg, John. "Romanciers Americains ... A la
        Recherche d'un Monde Perdu." *Travaux du Centre
        D'Etudes Anglaises et Americaines*, 1 (1962),
        24-46.

1354.   Maksimovik, Miodrag. *Illustrovana Politika*, 11 No-
        vember 1958, p. 39.

1355.   Mannoni, O. "Le masque et la parole." *Temps Moder-
        nes*, 20 (1964), 930-942.

1356.   Manson, Eleonore. "Bemerkungen zu der deutschen
        Übersetzung von J.D. Salingers *The Catcher in
        the Rye Acta Germanica: Jahrbuch des Sudafri-
        kanischen Germanistenverbandes*, 11 (1979), 181-
        190.

1357.   Masuda, Takahiro. "J.D. Salinger's *The Catcher in
        the Rye*: An Analysis of Time, Space, and Love."
        Chu-Shikoku Studies in American Literature, 14
        (1978), 35-47.

1358.   Mattson, Margaretta. "Amerikansk favorit." *Dagens
        Nyheter*, 28 August 1961, p. 5.

1359.   Mauriac, Claude. "La Vie des Lettres: J.D. Salinger:
        revelation d'un chef-d'oeuvre." *Le Figaro*, 1
        November 1961, p. 10.

1360.   Michalski, Hieronim. "O starszym bracie 'beatnikow.'"
        Nowa Kultura, 8 October 1962, p. 2.

Foreign Criticism   233

1361. Miedszyrzecki, Artur. "Pisarzdziecko." *Swiat*, 18
       February 1962, p. 8.

1362. Miyamoto, Yokichi. *America Bungaku o Yomu [American
       Authors and Japanese Readers]*. Tokyo: Shueisha,
       1977.

1363. ————. "J.D. Salinger o megutte, No. 2: 'Franny
       and Zooey' Sambun." *Eigo Seinen [The Rising Gen-
       eration]*, 1 March 1962, pp. 142-143.

1364. Moule, Fox. "Skrap syttenaarig." *B.T.*, 15 September
       1953, p. 21.

1365. Müller, Christopher. "Der Nonkomformist J.D. Salin-
       ger und seine Versöhnung mit der Welt des Kapi-
       talismus." *Wissenschaftliche Zeitschrift der
       Humboldt-Universität zu Berlin*, 25 (1976), 261-
       264.

1366. Mutka, Pertti Aulis. "Taiteen tarjotin." *Savonmaa*,
       30 April 1961, p. 6.

1367. Nakamura, Yasuo. "Amerikano sengo sakka: Gendai
       shosetsu no ichijyokyo, No. 7." *Waseda daigaku
       shinbun*, 24 May 1961, No. 836.

1368. ————. "Amerikano sengo sakka: Gendai shosetsu no
       ichijyokyo, Nc. 8." *Waseda daigaku shinbun*, 7
       June 1961, No. 838.

1369. Namba, Tatsuo. "Adverbs Peculiar to American Eng-
       lish in J.D. Salinger's *The Catcher in the Rye*."
       Chu-Shikoku Studies in American Literature, 13
       (1977), 65-76.

1370. ————. "Some Notes on Articles in J.D. Salinger's
       The Catcher in the Rye." *Chu-Shikoku Studies in
       American Literature*, 16 (1980), 11-18.

1371. ————. "Some Notes on the Use of Conjunctions and
       Conjunctional Phrases in J.D. Salinger's *The
       Catcher in the Rye   Chu-Shikoku Studies in Amer-
       ican Literature*, 14 (1978), 49-60.

1372. Narita, Shigetoshi. "Shineibei bungaku." *Eigo Kyoi-
       ku: The English Teachers' Magazine*, 11 (May
       1962), 20-21.

1373. Nathan, Monique. "J.D. Salinger et le rêve améri-
       cain." *Critique*, 18, No. 179 (April 1962), 299-
       305.

1374. Nemoianu, Virgil. "J.D. Salinger si înnobilarea
       divertismentului ["J.D. Salinger and the Elevating

of Division"]." In *Calmul volorilor* [*The Calm of Values*]. Cluj: Dacia, 1971, pp. 227-235.

1375. Nistor, Cornelia. "J.D. Salinger si solutia inocent ei in literatura ["J.D. Salinger and Solution to Innocence in Literature"]." *Analele Universitatü din Timisoara*, 7 (1969), 205-217.

1376. "O autorze: (prosimy koniecznie przeczytać)." *Przekrój*, 12 September 1962, pp. 10-11.

1377. Ohff, Heinz. *Die Bücher-Kommentare*, 15 September 1961, p. 15.

1378. Oleneva, Valentina I. *Sotsialnye motivy v amerikanskoi novelistike* [*Social Motives in the American Short Story*]. Kiev: Naukova Dumka, 1978.

1379. *Opettajain lehti*, 6 May 1961, p. 1.

1380. Orlova, R. "malchishka bezhit iz Ameriki." *Literaturnaya gazeta*, 26 November 1960, p. 5.

1381. Ortseifen, Karl. "J.D. Salinger: 'De Daumier-Smith's Blue Period.'" In *Amerikanische Erzählliteratur 1950-1970*. Eds. Frieder Bush and Renate Schmidt-von Bardeleben. Munich: Fink, 1975, pp. 186-196.

1382. ————. *Kritische Rezeption und stilistische Interpretation von J.D. Salingers Erzählprosa: Studien zum Stil der fruhen Kurzgeschichten und zu seinem Fortwirken im späteren Werk*. Frankfurt, Germany: Peter Lang, 1979.

1383. Paetel, Karl O. "J.D. Salinger." *Neue Sammlung: Zeitschrift für Erziehung und Gesellschaft*, 4 (1964), 567-574.

1384. Palm, Göran. "Fenomenet Salinger." *Bonniers Litterära Magazin*, No. 9 (September 1953), 706-707.

1385. Panova, Vera. "O romane J.D. Salinger." *Inostrannaya Literatura*, No. 11 (November 1960), 138-141.

1386. Pardi, Francesca. *Nuova Antologia*, No. 1964 (August 1964), 554-556.

1387. Parkinson de Saz, Sara M. "*The Catcher in the Rye*: ¿Un pícaro en Nueva York?" In *La picaresca: Origenes, textos y estructuros*. Ed. Manuel Criado de Val. Madrid: Fundación Univer. Espanola, 1979, pp. 1185-1192.

1388. Persson, Ola. "'Räddaren i nöden'" J.D. Salinger's märkliga roman." *Studiekamraten*, 54 (1972), 14-16.

1389.   Peterson, Lennart. "J.D. Salingers 'Räddaren i
        nöden' (1951): Amerikanska efterkrigsromaner
        lästa pa nytt, 2." *Horisont*, 15 (1968), 53-57.

1390.   Petrov, Nikola. "'Spasiteljat v razta' v Narodnija
        teatar na mladezta ["'The Catcher in the Rye' at
        the National Youth Theatre"]." *Literaturen front*,
        No. 41 (October 1967), 5.

1391.   Petrovskii, Yu A. "Tvorchestvo vo Selindzhera i trad-
        itsii mirovoi literatury ["Salinger's Works and
        the Tradition of World Literature"]." *Uchenye
        zapiski: Novgorodskogo pedagogicheskogo instituta
        Novgorad*, 20 (1970), 96-108.

1392.   Phylax. "Jerome David Salinger domina, con su per-
        sonalidad desconcertante, el panorama de las
        letras norteamericanas." *Leoplan*, 6 June 1962,
        p. 60.

1393.   "Portrait: L'homme pâle de Cornish: 'L'Express'
        présente ici le seul 'profil' connu de l'ecrivain
        celebre le plus mysterieux des États-Unis." *L'Ex-
        press*, 9 November 1961, pp. 32-34.

        Translated sections of item 288.

1394.   "Portret van een 16-jarige." *Vrij Nederland*, 18
        September 1954.

1395.   Rait-Kovaleva, R. ["Introduction."] *Povesti [Sto-
        ries]*. Moscow: Molodaya gvardiya, 1967, pp. 3-
        10.

1396.   Ramamurthy, V. "J.D. Salinger: The Tragi-Comic
        Vision." *The Banasthali Patriak* (Rajasthan),
        No. 11 (July 1968), 37-42.

1397.   Raud, V. "Afterword to Estonian Translation of 'The
        Catcher in the Rye.'" Tallin: Eesti raamat, 1973.

1398.   Reda, Jacques. "*Franny and Zooey*." *Cahiers du Sud*,
        55 (April 1963), 151.

1399.   Reich-Raniski. "Der Fänger in DDR--Roggen." *Die
        Zeit*, 11 May 1973, p. 13.

1400.   Riihimäki, Antti. "Luettua." *Teini*, No. 3 (March
        1961), 30.

1401.   Rizawa, Yukio. *Salinger: Seijuko e no Dokei [Sal-
        inger: A Case of Arrested Development]*. Tokyo:
        Tojusha, 1978.

1402.   Röder, Rudolf. *Welt and Wort*, 9 (April 1954), 130.

1403.   Rose-Werle, Kordula. *Harlekinade--Genealogie und
        Metamorphose: Struktur und Deutung des Motive
        bei J.D. Salinger und V. Nabokov.* Frankfort,
        Germany: Lang, 1979.

1404.   Rosenthal, Jean. "J.D. Salinger." *Information et
        documents*, 1 February 1963, pp. 24-28.

1405.   Rót, Sándor. "J.D. Salinger muvei a modern stilis-
        ztika fenyeben ["Problems of Modern Stylistics
        in J.D. Salinger's Work"]." *Filológiai Közlöny*,
        24 (1978), 37-54.

1406.   Runnquist, Ake. "J.D. Salinger." *All Världens Berät-
        tare*, No. 5 (May 1954), 428.

1407.   ————. "Jerome David Salinger." *All Världens Berät-
        tare*, No. 5 (May 1966), 20.

1408.   S., E. "Around the Bookshops." *Jerusalem Post*, 17
        July 1953, p. 8.

1409.   Sadeya, Shigenobu. "The Modern Lonely Catcher: On
        J.D. Salinger's *The Catcher in the Rye*." *Studies
        in English Language and Literature*, 3 (September
        1962), 85-106.

1410.   Saheki, Shoichi. *Bungakukai*, 15 (November 1961),
        165-168.

1411.   Saitô, George, and Philip Williams, eds. *Sôseki and
        Salinger: American Students on Japanese Fiction.*
        Tokyo: Eihosha, 1971.

1412.   Sakamoto, Masayuki. "Salinger ni okeru 'Sezuku' to
        'Chozoku' ["Profane and Sacred in Salinger"]."
        Eigo Seinen [The Rising Generation], 115 (1969),
        692-693.

1413.   Salzman, Jack. "Prelude to Madness: A Look at 'Sol-
        dier's Home' and 'For Esme: With Love and Squal-
        or.'" *Rikkyo Review of Arts and Letters*, 33
        (1973), 103-112.

1414.   Santavuori, Martti. "Kuohuvaa nuoruutta." *Aamulehti*,
        2 April 1961, p. 13.

1415.   Sato, Hiroko. "The World of J.D. Salinger." *Essays
        and Studies in British and American Literature*,
        10 (Winter 1962), 42-53.

1416.   Savolainen, Erkki. "Kova, kerkkä kundi." *Savon Sano-
        mat*, 22 March 1961, p. 5.

1417.   Schnack, Elisabeth. "Jerome David Salinger." *Ameri-
        kanische Erzähler von F. Scott Fitzgerald bis*

William Boyen. Zürich: Manesse Verlag, 1957,
pp. 606-607.

1418. ———. "Nachwort." *Für Esmé.* München: Nymphenburg-
er Verlagshandlung, 1959, pp. 148-150.

1419. Schulz, Milan. "Smutné mládí." *Literárni Noviny,* 17
September 1960, p. 4.

1420. Schwark, H.G. "Der geheimnisvolle Jerome David Salinger." *Deutsche Zeitung,* 8 June 1961.

Donald Fiene (see item 341) lists this item as
including a "paraphrase in translation of Edward
Kosner's *New York Post* article, Shirley Blaney's
interview, and a reprint of the April 30 *Post* drawing."

1421. Segedin, Petar. "Jerome David Salinger." *Telegram,*
1 September 1961, p. 12.

1422. Setälä, Rauno. "Mieletön juttu." *Turun Ylioppilas-
lehti,* 24 March 1961, p. 4.

1423. Sethom, Mahamed. "La Societe dan l'oeuvre de J.D.
Salinger." *Etudes Anglaises,* 22 (July-September
1969), 270-278.

1424. ———. "L'univers verbal de J.D. Salinger." *Etudes
Anglaises,* 21 (1968), 57-64.

1425. Sharer, N.A. "Rechevaya Kharakteristika yazyka
Dzheroma Selindzhera v romane 'Nad propast'yu vo
rzhi' ["The Speech Characteristics of the Language of Jerome David Salinger in the Novel 'The
Catcher in the Rye'"]." *Nauchnye trudy Tashkents-
kogo universiteta,* 383 (1971), 270-279.

1426. Shedd, Margaret. "Salinger's *New Yorker* Series on
Glass Family Now in Book Format." *The News,* 3
September 1961, Sec. 1, p. 8A.

1427. Shigeo, Hisashi. "The Genealogical Record of the
Glasses." *Hiyoshi Ronbunshu,* No. 14 (September
1963), 14-28.

1428. ———. "Hashi gaki." *A Perfect Day for Bananafish.*
Tokyo: Shohakusha, 1961, pp. 1-7.

1429. ———. "J.D. Salinger o megutte, No. 1: 'The Catcher in the Rye' o megururonso." *Eigo Seinen [The
Rising Generation],* 1 March 1962, p. 141.

1430. ———. "J.D. Salinger no shinsaku." *Eigo Kyoiku:
The English Teachers' Magazine,* 11 (May 1962),
20-21.

238 Foreign Criticism

1431. ———. *Salinger no Bungaku* [*Salinger's Writing*].
Tokyo: Bunkenshobo, 1970.

1432. Skibniewska, Maria. "Od Redakcji." *Buszujacy w
zbozu*. Warszawa: Państwowe Wydawnictowo, 1961,
pp. 5-6.

1433. *Skizze*, 10 (November 1961), 14.

1434. Skovmand, Steffan. "I: J.D. Salinger; II. *The Catcher in the Rye*." In *Six American Novels: From New
Deal to New Frontier A Workbook*. Eds. Jens Bøgh
and Steffan Skovmand. Aarhus: Akademash Boghandel,
1972, pp. 151-182.

1435. Staub, H.U. "For Esmé--with Love and Squalor." *Neue
Zürcher Zeitung*, 11 August 1953, p. 1.

1436. Stawinski, Julian. "Na krawedzi urwiska." *Nowe
Ksiazki*, 1 October 1961, pp. 1102-1105.

1437. Steiner, Dorothea. "Zur Autor-Leser Besiehung bei
J.D. Salinger: Autonomie und Manipulation." In
Essays in Honour of Professor Tyrus Hillway. Ed.
Edwin A. Stürzl. Salzburg: Inst. für eng. Sprache
and Lit., Univer. Salzburg, 1977, pp. 191-211.

1438. Stepf, Renate. *Die Entwicklung von J.D. Salinger
Short Stories und Novelettes*. Frankfurt and
Berne: Lang, 1975.

1439. St[reza], S[ergiu]. "... bataia unei Singure palme."
Convorbiri literare, 11 (June 1973), 12.

1440. ———. "Salinger si cei doi 'A' ["Salinger the Two
'A'"]." *Cronica*, 5, No. 42 (October 1970), 9.

1441. Tabah, Mireille. "*Die neuen Leiden des jungen W.*:
Ulrich Plenzdorf entre Goethe et Salinger."
Etudes Germaniques, 30 (1975), 335-344.

1442. Takahashi, Masao. *America Sengo Shosetsu no Shoso*
[*Aspects of Post-War Novel in America*]. Tokyo:
Toyamashobo, 1979.

1443. Takenaka, Toyoko. "On Seymour's Suicide." *Kyushu
American Literature*, 12 (1970), 54-61.

See item 995.

1444. Takigawa, Motoo. *America Bungaku no Mondai Ishiki*
[*Major Themes in American Literature*]. Tokyo:
Man'undo, 1977.

1445. Tanaka, Keishi. "Seymour e no Banka: Salinger no

Chinmoku." In *Bungaku to America: Ohashi Kenza-boro Kyoju Kanreki Kinen Ronbunshu*. Tokyo: Nanundo, 1980, pp. 329-344.

1446. Tischler, Helmut. "J.D. Salinger." *Five Modern American Short Stories*. Frankfurt-am-Main: Verlag Moritz Diesterweg, 1962, pp, 5, 69-71.

1447. Toebosch, Wim. "Revelatie ot belofte: De opkomst van J.D. Salinger in de amerikaanse literatur." *De Vlaamse Gids*, 46 (1962), 725-735.

1448. Uchuyama, Miyazo. "Salinger's Religious Phases in Their Development." *Eigo Eibungako Ronso*, n.v. (January 1964), 115-126.

1449. Uitonniemi, Henrikki. "Nykysuomea." *Suomen Kuvalehti*, 25 March 1961, p. 36.

1450. Vasileva, Ekaterna. "Nie, decata, vaprosite. 'Spasi-teljat v razta' v Narodnija teatar na mladezta ["We, the Children and the Questions. 'The Catcher in the Rye' at the National Youth Theatre"]." *Teatar*, 9 (1967), 46-78.

1451. *Vsesvit: Literaturno-Mystets'kyi ta Hromade'ko-Politychnyi Zhurnal*, 7 (July 1980), 90-91.

Dan McCall's *Jack the Bear* compared to J.D. Salinger's *The Catcher*.

1452. Veza, Laurette. "L'attrape--coeur, ou Holden Resartus." *Les Langues Modernes*, 61 (January-February 1967), 56-65.

1453. Villelaur, Anne. *Les Lettres Francaises*, 28 December 1961-3 January 1962, p. 2.

1454. Vladimov, Georgi. "Tri dnya iz zhizni Holden." *Novy Mir*, No. 2 (February 1961), 254-258.

1455. Vučković, Gavrilo. "Ostroumno i duhovita." *Borba*, 9 February 1954, p. 4.

1456. Waltari, Satu. "Näkötorvi." *Me Naiset*, 29 March 1961, p. 19.

1457. Washizu, Hiroko. "The Sound of One Hand Clapping: A Note on 'A Perfect Day for Bananafish.'" In *American Literature in the 1950's*. Tokyo: Tokyo Chapter, American Literary Circle of Japan, 1976, pp. 83-89.

1458. Weaver, William. "Duo Giovani Scrittor: Americani." *Lo Spectatore Italiano*, 5 (March 1952), 161-162.

1459. Wikborg, Eleanor. *Pilot Book to J.D. Salinger, "The Catcher in the Rye."* Stockholm: Almqvist and Wiksell, 1971.

1460. Yamada, Yoshinari. "Salinger Saidoku ["Salinger Reread"]." In *America Shosetsu no Tenkai [Development of the American Novel]*. Tokyo: Shohakusha, 1977, pp. 283-296.

1461. Zapponi, Niccolò. "J.D. Salinger e l'estetica dell'innocenza." *Studi Americani*, 16 (1970), 393-405.

1462. Zavadskaya, E.V. "Chto Selindzher ishehet v 'dzen'? ["What is Salinger Looking for in 'Zen'?"]." In *Istoriko-filologicheskie issledovaniya*. Moscow: Sbornik Statei k 75-letiyu akademika N.I. Konrada, 1967, pp. 451-456.

III.   AUTHOR INDEX

241

Author Index

IV. TITLE INDEX